THE I CHING

LANDSCAPES OF THE SOUL
Revisiting an Ancient Chinese Oracle

THE I CHING

LANDSCAPES OF THE SOUL

Revisiting an Ancient Chinese Oracle

FRITS BLOK

KÖNEMANN

About the author: Frits Blok was born in Amsterdam, the Netherlands, in 1947. His long journey into mysticism has led him from the hidden layers of the Hebrew Bible to the refined beauty of the I Ching. Along the way he has raised a child, planted a tree, and built a house. He is the inventor of the *I Ching Sticks* and creator of the *I Ching Meditation Experience*.

With special thanks to my love, Andrea Dingemans, for translation and initial editing of the manuscript

Copyright © 2000 Blozo Products Amsterdam

Concept and Text: Frits Block
Artwork, Cover design, and Layout: Erik Thé
Editing and Copy-editing: Lisa Michel
Production assistance: Iwan Baan and Radha Pancham
Landscape symbols: Milo Rottinghuis
Chinese calligraphy: Tang Xu
Cover calligraphy: Shi Danqiu

Copyright © 2001 of this edition
Könemann Verlagsgesellschaft mbH
Bonner Strasse 126, D-Cologne 50968

Prodution: Ursula Schümer
Printing and Binding: Stige, Società Torinese/Industrie Grafiche Editoriali
S.p.A., San Mauro (Turin)
Printed in Italy

ISBN 3-8290-4859-9

10 9 8 7 6 5 4 3 2 1

The I Ching, Landscapes of the Soul

Introduction

The I Ching, one of the classic books of China, ranks amongst the oldest philosophical works in the world and since ancient times has been used as an oracle. The book is based on sixty-four hexagrams or configurations which are composed of six undivided ('strong') lines or divided ('weak') lines. Legend has it that the perfect symbolic and mathematical structure of the book was laid down by the Chinese scholar Fu Hsi some 5,000 years ago. Two millennia later, King Wên and his son, the Duke of Chou, added the first known commentary to the hexagrams. Since then, many famous Chinese scholars have studied and discussed the profound meaning of both the text and the hexagrams.

Each hexagram is a symbolic representation of a natural situation which has occurred over and over since creation began and will continue to do so until the end of time. A situation in life is never permanent. Life is a continuous sequence of situations, so a hexagram not only describes the situation of the moment, but also refers to its natural consequences in the future. The metaphorical nature of the ideas conveyed by the hexagrams, and of the associated Chinese characters or symbolic pictures which express the thoughts of the writer, make the situations open to more than one interpretation. Symbols speak in a language that is beyond words and provide an elasticity when it comes to answering questions. This latitude makes the I Ching, or the Book of Changes, an oracle by definition.

Introduction to The Trigrams Composing the Hexagrams

The hexagrams or ancient six-line 'bar-codes' that look so modern to us today are made up of different combinations of eight basic trigrams (three-line configurations), each of which represents a natural element. The upper and the lower trigram determine the structure of a hexagram. Thus, different combinations of these eight trigrams result in 8 x 8 = 64 hexagrams.

The natural elements represented by the trigrams are as follows: ☰ Heaven, ☷ Earth, ☴ Wind, ☳ Thunder, ☲ Fire/Sun, ☱ Marsh/Moon, ☵ Rain/River and ☶ Mountain. The different qualities of these trigrams are fully explained on pages 8-11, inclusive.

Methods of constructing a Hexagram

In ancient times, the lay person consulted scholars and diviners to interpret the I Ching for them. The most ancient method used, as far as we know, involved the division and subdivision of fifty yarrow stalks (*Millefolium Siberica*). This process eventually yielded a particular number which indicated whether a line was divided or undivided, changing or unchanging.

Later, as people became more emancipated and felt they were capable of consulting the I Ching on their own, the coin method became popular. With this method, a person constructs a hexagram by successive throws of a coin, and then interprets the answers received. Because the questioner is now also the diviner, it is important to keep one's question clearly in mind and not allow oneself to be distracted during the process of composing the hexagram.

The six lines of the hexagram are derived by throwing six times, with three coins at once. For example, if you throw three heads, you read this as a divided/weak changing line which is written down as -x-. Three tails mean an undivided/strong changing line which is written as -o-. Two heads and one tail give an undivided/strong stable line which is written as —, and two tails and one head give a divided/weak stable line which is written as --. The first line (or baseline) of the hexagram is derived from the first throw, and successive throws build progressively upwards to the top of the hexagram, or the sixth line.

A new and much easier way to compose a hexagram is to use a set of six I Ching Sticks. You take these sticks in your hand and formulate a question. When your question is clear, you roll the sticks between your hands as if you were washing them. While rolling the sticks you empty your mind so that the only thought that remains is your question. The moment you feel ready, you transfer the sticks to the palm of one hand and turn them over with a flat hand onto the table. Your complete hexagram now lies before you, ready for interpretation.

How to look up the hexagram you have constructed

The hexagram that you have either built up using the coin method or composed with the I Ching Sticks can be looked up at either the beginning or the end of this book. A line with an **o** represents an undivided (changing) line and a line with an **x**, a divided (changing) line. If, for example, the three top lines in the hexagram are ☷ and the bottom lines ☳, you have thrown hexagram 28, Vigorous Mind. The meaning of the hexagram can be found in this book. Read the text and the description of the changing lines, if present. Changing lines denote further developments and point to a future situation, described in a new hexagram. (For more information about the changing lines, see below).

If the coin method is used, you derive your final hexagram from an initial hexagram that includes changing lines by drawing a new hexagram beside the one you first constructed. Do this by replacing any divided/weak changing lines (-**x**-) with undivided/strong stable lines (—), and any undivided/strong changing lines (-**o**-) with divided/weak stable lines (- -).

When you use the I Ching Sticks, all you have to do is turn over any sticks showing changing lines (-**o**- or -**x**-) to the face on the opposite side of the stick and you will have the final hexagram. Note that you should consider a line to be 'changing' only when a changing line shows on both the side facing upwards and the vertical side facing towards you. This will ensure that the chance of a changing line when using the I Ching Sticks is the same as when using the coin method.

Once you have a picture of the final hexagram, you can look this up in the book, just as you did for the initial hexagram that contained changing lines.

The text of the initial hexagram describes the situation relating to your question. The changing lines offer suggestions as to how you can improve your situation. The final hexagram describes the situation after you have followed this advice and change has taken place, and gives clues as to what subsequently lies in store for you.

The Changing Lines

The undivided and divided lines represent yang (—) and yin (- -). Yang indicates the masculine, creative, active, causal, heavenly or expanding force of creation. The yin principle is related to the feminine, receptive, material, restricting or decreasing aspect of the universe. According to Chinese philosophy, both cosmic primal opposites are bound by an indissoluble tie and function optimally when they are in balance. Their interaction and harmony is responsible for all spiritual and material processes in life.

The sixty-four hexagrams of the I Ching are images of all possible relationships that can occur between yang and yin in life. They not only depict our physical and spiritual condition, but also show which psychological and social perspectives are opened by the yang/yin balance. The interaction between yin and yang is always a search for the right balance in life, which generally comes down to strengthening the one and weakening the other. The practical advice given by the I Ching is based on this principle. Too much yang, for example, leads to recklessness, arrogance, fanaticism, aggressive behavior, and a rigid or intolerant attitude to life. Someone with an overdose of yin runs the risk of becoming prey to passivity, exaggerated docility, oversensitivity, or fear of failure.

According to the I Ching, nothing in life is immobile; everything in the universe is in constant motion and liable to the laws of change. If the dance of yang and yin comes to an end, change comes to an end. This standstill implies non-existence or death. As long as you can be aware that when the sun is at its zenith it starts to set, and as soon as the moon is full it starts to wane, you can also be sure that zest for life will grow out of grief. Every situation, even one that looks like a blind-alley, opens a door to self-knowledge through change. Every time we do not take such a chance for change we are committing a sin against life itself.

The changing lines point out the direction in which you need to shift. Undivided/strong changing lines (-**o**-) mean that you should try to temper your action so that a specific situation does not get out of hand. By contrast, the divided/weak changing lines (-**x**-) urge you to put more effort into satisfying your needs, so that you do not remain a victim of your circumstances.

The I Ching in the Western World

Today's version of the I Ching includes the Chinese characters as they were represented in about 650 A.D. It is probable that the original characters were modified between 1200 B.C. and 650 A.D as a result of changes to the system of writing during that period. Therefore, the I Ching we know today is not precisely the same as it was when King Wên and the Duke of Chou or other ancient Chinese scholars devised it.

The first translations of the I Ching into Western languages were carried out in the nineteenth century by the Roman Catholic missionary P. Regis and by the Reverend Canon McClatchie of Shanghai. The most interesting translation of that century, published in 1882, was the work of the British Sinologist, James Legge.

It was the translation by German theologian, Richard Wilhelm, however, that really introduced the Book of Changes into the Western world and made it so popular that hundreds of interpretations and translations have appeared since. All these versions, prior to this edition, were more or less founded on the work of Legge and Wilhelm and take the same approach of first trying to pin down the literal meaning of the Chinese characters and then using this information to bestow meaning on the interaction between the upper and lower trigram of each hexagram.

What is New in this Edition: Deconstructing The I Ching

The Deconstruction of the Hexagrams and their Associated Characters.

This method takes you by the hand and leads you on an adventure, into the Landscapes of the Soul.

Although a basic hexagram is formed by its upper and lower trigrams, each hexagram contains two more 'hidden' trigrams. Unlike all the I Ching interpretations before it, this ground-breaking version of the I Ching is based on the action of all four trigrams, or natural elements, that are at play in each hexagram. This is the approach that must have been used by King Wên, the first commentator on the I Ching. Whether he was indeed the first scholar to shed light on the hexagrams, or whether he based his written commentary on oral tradition, the only way he could have proceeded was to first study the symbolic meaning of the hexagrams and then put his interpretation into words.

In this book, you will find each hexagram has been broken down into its four component trigrams, next to which the natural elements they represent are shown. The trigrams are discussed in detail on pages 8-11.

Original illustrations created especially for this edition portray each hexagram as a landscape composed of natural elements. The elements represented in a particular landscape and their position relative to each other reflect the composition of a particular hexagram and the order in which its component trigrams appear. In this way, the illustrations visualize the metaphorical idea behind each hexagram and therefore make it more accessible.

When going deeper into a hexagram and deconstructing it to its very bones, one should not overlook the significance of the so-called inner hexagrams.

These inner hexagrams can be found by putting together the upper trigram with the second trigram, the upper trigram with the third trigram, the second trigram with the third trigram, the second trigram with the fourth trigram, and the third trigram with the fourth trigram. Thus, each hexagram contains five inner hexagrams.

These hexagrams give an additional and deeper insight into the situation evoked by the basic hexagram. By reading the summaries for each of these inner hexagrams in the order specified in the text, those using this book can learn how to deal with the situation in which they find themselves.

The upper line of each hexagram is part of only one trigram, and the same is true of the bottom line. However, the second and fifth lines are each part of two different trigrams, and the third and fourth lines each belong to three different trigrams.

Deconstruction of the hexagrams into trigrams, or natural elements, shows how each individual line is influenced by the play of forces between the elements. Such a glimpse behind the scenes helps to lift the veil created by King Wên's often cryptic commentaries on the lines. Using this approach, one can see that the king has tried to find the Chinese characters that best symbolized the natural situation he saw played out in each individual line.

Hexagrams evoke natural, macrocosmic situations. Because humans are conscious beings and united to the very depth of their souls with the macrocosmos, they can sense any of these situations in themselves and take action according to what they see and feel is happening around them.

For this reason, the analysis of each hexagram in this book includes an illustration in which the hexagram's individual lines are superimposed on the figure of a person. This approach points out how each layer of the natural elements at play in the hexagram is associated with a particular part of the body, and thereby affects human behavior.

Chinese characters are essentially pictures. In this book, the Chinese characters King Wên attributed to each hexagram are deconstructed into their components.

Chinese characters are more the symbolic representations of the thoughts and ideas of the writer than they are his exact words. Each character serves as a bridge between the realm of thought and spoken language. Words cannot convey the wisdom of profound insights. When reading poetry, we try to read the mind of the poet by 'tasting' the meaning of the words in the poem, but when we look at a symbol we try to read the mind of the creator directly.

By taking a closer look at the individual parts making up a character and reading what each represents, we find clues to what the writer perceived in each specific hexagram.

The deconstruction of the hexagrams and their associated characters provides a fresh perspective on the situations portrayed. By pausing to analyze the separate components making up each 'landscape of the soul', diviners can both grasp the details of the situation they are in and, at the same time, achieve a better overview. This book provides a unique opportunity to do so.

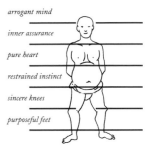

arrogant mind

inner assurance

pure heart

restrained instinct

sincere knees

purposeful feet

Original illustrations created especially for this edition portray each hexagram as a landscape composed of natural elements.

Sheepskin 革

Two hands

The raw hide of a skinned sheep lies spread out and is being worked on by two hands.

Heaven

The infinite depth of the heavens, which encircle the earth and in one way or another ensure a balance that keeps this pearl in her orbit, lends itself to being filled by every conceivable illusion. The heavens are the unfaltering source of creative energy and symbolize the unknown, in which the secret of life is hidden.

The heavens can be compared with the innate, inner emptiness of human beings, which in the course of a lifetime is filled in with ideas and ideals that are experienced as Truth. The most honest way to deal with the heavens is to face their infinite depth without making up all kinds of stories that lull your fears to sleep. Some hexagrams contain more than one heaven. Since there can only be one true heaven, the others are products of the human mind. So heaven can also mean the idea of a glorious, mythical heaven, an imperfect heaven (that is, a hell), or a heaven on earth created by making a god of material things. In the trigram depicting heaven, the center line represents the core of the heavens, and, depending on the way they are connected with other elements in the hexagram, the outer lines can mean either the outermost limits of the heavens or the heavens closest to the earth.

Earth

The earth is the receptive principle which is impregnated, as it were, by the creative energy of the heavens, so that all the potential in the universe comes to fruition on earth. By looking for the essence of all things that the earth brings forth, you may come to discover the secret of life. If you want to unite with the earth, you should follow her rhythm. Then you will know intuitively when it is time to be active and when it is time to rest. It is unwise to become too attached to this fertile, female power. Those who have a mature relationship with the earth keep in touch with the infinite depth of the heavens and regard earthly matter as the wet nurse from whose breast they will, sooner or later, be torn. The earth can be seen as a metaphor for the human body, with the surface of the earth (the upper line of the earth trigram) symbolizing your behavior, which is an outward display of the state of your inner being (the lower lines or underground levels). The lower lines of the earth trigram may indicate a growth process but may also suggest that you are hanging on to the roots of your past, which will have to be removed before a fresh crop can grow and thrive at the earth's surface.

Some hexagrams contain two or three earth trigrams mingled together. In this case, the upper line of each earth trigram represents a different bodily function which is sensed by your inner self and aroused by your environment.

Wind

The strong upper lines of the wind indicate that it blows from the heavens, or the unknown, over the earth (the weak lower line). The wind symbolizes breathing, thinking, and speaking.
The process of breathing, which regulates inner tension and therefore one's attitude, is for every being the essence of life.
Breathing is characterized by an eternal connection to the here and now. More than any other organism, human beings are conscious of past and future, which exert a constant hold over them and cause psychological problems that affect their breathing and, therefore, their physical condition.
While breathing out, one speaks and thinks; breathing in creates a natural pause in these processes. If your breathing is as calm as the infinite depth of the heavens and flows with the constant rhythm of the rotating earth, you are in balance with the macrocosmos. If your thoughts are agitated by feelings, illusions or imagined future events, your breathing becomes unstable. The upper line of the wind trigram indicates the beginning of the wind and symbolizes an unconscious mind or natural breathing. The middle line stands for consciousness, and breathing in and out. The lower open line can mean spoken words (which are always dualistic), being out of breath, or the moment for inhalation.

Fire/Sun

Fire feeds on fuel. The fuel is represented by the weak middle line of the trigram. The strong lines symbolize heat and flames which rise upwards to the infinite depth of the heavens — from where the energy released out of the fuel originally came. The fire trigram is a symbol of your inner light, or insight, which, like the sun, has an overview of earthly matters and which uses your body as fuel.
This inner fire is kindled by the wind, or your breathing, and is fanned or smothered whenever emotions, anger, or exhausting impotence get a hold on you. When the earth turns away from the sun, it seems to someone on earth that the sun has stopped shining. Even a clouded sky can give the impression that the sun no longer exists. In reality, the sun is always shining. If you do not hide your insight behind dark thoughts, which veil this inner assurance like clouds masking the sun, and if you do not think in moments when you see no light that there is no light at all, you are attuned to the macrocosmic idea of what the sun represents. The upper line of the trigram indicates the setting sun but, depending on its place in the hexagram, it can also suggest an overview of life. The middle line usually represents the fiery heart of the sun and the core of your inner fire, or insight. The lower line indicates the rising sun or the dawning of insight.

Rain/River

Water symbolizes the cycle of life: it falls from the heavens and then streams to the sea, where it evaporates and returns as rain again. The strong line in the center of the rain/river trigram represents the heavenly force of the sun which frees the sweet and nutritious water from the salty seas. Life is founded on the seas and sustained by its streams. Rain represents fertility and growth, while the river — which springs forth so passionately and flows into the sea so calmly — symbolizes life's path. This trigram can also stand for dark rainclouds blocking one's view, like dark thoughts that prevent one from grasping the essence of a situation and acting wisely. In general, the upper line of the trigram represents the beginning of the rain, the surface of the river, or the last wisps of a raincloud. In the event that the trigram is situated on the top of the mountain, it indicates a lake of fertile knowledge which has the potency to bring growth on earth. The middle line can mean the core of the raincloud, the middle of the running river, or water seeping out of the lake at the top of the mountain. The lower line can signify the last wisps of a raincloud, the bottom of the lake of fertile knowledge, or water flowing away freely.

Marsh/Moon

The two strong lower lines of the trigram suggest the heavens, or the unknown, which are veiled by the weak upper line representing the earthly, dualistic world. The weak line is like a mirror or the reflecting surface of the marsh/moon in which you see only the outward appearance of things and behind which the true, inner being is hidden. The moon receives its light from the sun and reflects this light to the earth. This suggests a process of giving and taking in a balanced way. The marsh also conveys the idea of such a balance. If it dries up, it becomes a stinking, muddy place and when it overflows, the vegetation drowns. The moon affects the water balance on earth and thereby the flow of bodily fluids. The subtle energy of the moon has an almost intangible influence on earthly activities. It awakens sexual desires, which conquer reason and elevate the value of the physical above that of the spiritual. You learn from this energy by intuition, and if you dare to trust these feelings, they develop into an inner conviction. The upper line of this trigram represents the full moon or the reflecting surface of the marsh. The middle line is the waxing moon or the turbid, murky water under the reflecting surface of the marsh. The lower line indicates the dark moon or the new moon and the muddy bottom of the marsh.

Mountain

The lower lines of this trigram rising up from the earth to the heavenly strong line, clearly suggest the outline of a mountain. The mountain symbolizes a place for solitary retreat, where one has an overview of earthly matters and is in touch with the infinite depth of the heavens. The mountain is an indomitable presence which evokes a sense of trustworthiness, wisdom, impassiveness, challenge, and awareness. The combination of a rain/river trigram above a mountain suggests that the rainwater collecting on the top of the mountain forms a lake of fertile knowledge. By adopting the qualities of the mountain, as described above, a person can distribute this productive knowledge on earth. In hexagrams where the thunder is below the mountain, one can see a gap of open lines between the strong lines, which suggests an open mouth. In this case, the top line of the mountain trigram represents the idea of the impassive upper jaw, which has to control the eager lower jaw (symbolized by the bottom line of the thunder trigram) so that one does not bite unthinkingly into everything that comes one's way. Obviously, the upper line of the mountain trigram usually represents the top of the mountain, while the lower line is its foot. It follows that the middle line represents the mountain slope and, therefore, the way up and down the mountain.

Thunder

The upper weak lines of this trigram represent the movement of the thunder, and the strong lower or heavenly line is its invisible, and often unknown, source. All terrestrial and celestial bodies are in continuous motion. This motion is determined by the volume of the body and the energy it contains. One cannot always understand what the idea behind an action is. The thunder may represent the continuous beating of the human heart, or the force that is driving the moon and the earth on their unfaltering orbital paths. The upward movement of the thunder may also indicate the inner energy that powers the development of a being's ideas and ideals. This process can be symbolized by the struggle of a germinating seed which sprouts in the soil (or the inner being), breaks through the earth's surface (or into the outside world), and grows upwards in the direction of the sun so that it can thrive and bloom. The sun represents clear insight and having an overview, so the upward direction of the thunder can imply an attempt to develop these qualities in the inner being, which naturally has this drive for completion. The lower line of this trigram indicates the beginning of the thunder, the middle line is its core, and the force of the thunder comes to an end at the upper line.

1. The Chinese Character

The characters shown here were created by King Wên around 1200 BC and convey his idea of the meaning of the hexagrams, which stem from about 3000 BC. A Chinese character is a picture. Each component expresses a separate thought. It is impossible to put exactly into words what King Wên was thinking when he wrote them down. The language of the I Ching is beyond words. However, by taking a close look at the individual components making up each character and studying their verbal description, we find clues as to what the writer might have had in mind.

2. The Hexagram

Each hexagram (six line model) portrays a situation which is determined by the interplay of forces contained in four trigrams (three line models). Each of the four trigrams hidden in the hexagram symbolizes a natural element. These trigrams are highlighted in the miniature hexagrams to the right of the large hexagram, alongside an icon of the corresponding natural element. In the situation shown on this page, the upper trigram is the earth. The second trigram is also the earth. The third trigram is the thunder and the lower trigram is the marsh/moon.

3. Description of the Situation

The hexagrams and their corresponding Chinese characters are symbols of thoughts and ideas. As such, they serve as bridges between the realm of thought and spoken language. Words cannot convey the wisdom of profound insights. When reading poetry, we try to read the mind of the poet by 'tasting' the meaning of the words in the poem, but when we look at a symbol, we try to read the mind of the creator directly.

Beneath each Chinese character is a section describing a situation. This situation reflects the emotional or spiritual circumstances in which the person using the I Ching (the diviner) finds himself or herself. The description sheds light on the symbolic meaning of the Chinese character and connects this insight with the dynamics of the hexagram. In this way, the description aims to heighten the diviner's perception of the ancient symbols and open a door to the ideas behind them. It is advisable, therefore, to read this section before moving on to study the inner hexagrams and individual lines.

4. The Contents of the Hexagram

The general meaning of a hexagram is derived from the upper and lower trigrams. By confining yourself to this method, however, you will overlook significant clues for understanding your situation which are imparted by the so-called inner hexagrams. To see these inner hexagrams, put the upper trigram with the second trigram, the upper trigram with the third trigram, the second trigram with the third trigram, the second trigram with the fourth trigram, and the third trigram with the fourth trigram.

Thus, each hexagram contains five inner hexagrams. These hexagrams give an additional and deeper insight into the situation evoked by the basic hexagram. For guidance on how to deal with the situation you are in, read the summaries given here, in the order indicated in the text. (Sometimes you should read from top to bottom, at other times from bottom to top.) If you require more detail about an inner hexagram, turn to the spread with the number shown to the right of the summary that interests you.

How to read the hexagram

1 *The Chinese Character*

2 *The Hexagram*

3 *Description of the Situation*

The Contents of the Hexagram **4**

10. *The Composition of the Hexagram*
The basic hexagram is formed by the upper trigram and the lower trigram. The inner hexagrams are formed as follows: 1. The upper trigram with the second trigram; 2. The upper trigram with the third trigram; 3. The second trigram with the third trigram; 4. The second trigram with the fourth trigram; 5. The third trigram with the fourth trigram.

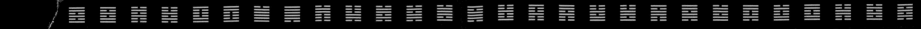

Illustration

*...original illustrations created for this edition of the I Ching portray
...igrams in terms of the natural elements they represent. Look at the
...tion of these natural elements in relation to each other in order
to understand the play of forces in the hexagram as a whole.
Seen together, these interactive natural elements form a landscape.
This conveys the metaphorical significance of the hexagram in a form that
many readers may find more direct and accessible than the line combinations.*

11

5 *The Individual lines
and the Human Body*

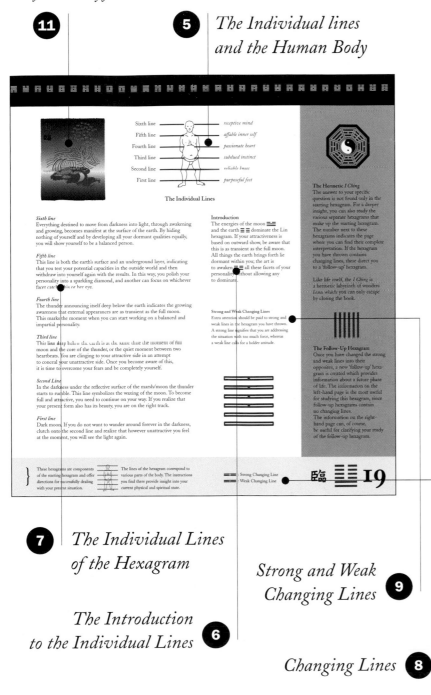

7 *The Individual Lines
of the Hexagram*

*Strong and Weak
Changing Lines* **9**

*The Introduction
to the Individual Lines* **6**

Changing Lines **8**

5. The Individual lines and the Human Body

The hexagrams portray situations relating to the natural macrocosmos. Because humans are conscious beings who are united at the deepest spiritual level with the macrocosmos, they can sense any of these situations within themselves and take action according to what they see and feel is happening around them.

6. The Introduction to the Individual Lines

This section provides an overview of the dominant forces at work in the hexagram. It points out where the bottlenecks in your situation are and how to avoid or overcome them.

7. The Individual Lines of the Hexagram

In general, people using the I Ching only consult the individual lines when they are marked as changing lines in the hexagram they have composed. These changing lines are particularly important because they indicate what you need to do in order to move on to a new phase. Nevertheless, you will find that reading about all the individual lines will bring you to a deeper understanding of the various phases in the evolution of the situation portrayed in the hexagram. You will gain a better understanding of where you are heading.

Each line corresponds to a specific state of being which is connected not only with a particular part of the body but also with the circumstances in which you now find yourself. For example, in the hexagram shown here, the first line is the bottom line of the marsh/moon trigram, indicating that you are down at the bottom of the marsh. The first line also represents your feet. Put together, these images evoke a sense of hopelessness (there is no glimmer of light) and show that you are not yet capable of taking action to improve things (your feet are stuck in the muddy bed of the marsh).

8. Changing Lines

Changing lines in a hexagram demand your special attention. A changing line points to a particular attitude or circumstance which is hindering you from achieving the inner change that would enable you to handle your present situation, so that a new situation can dawn.

To see what you can expect once the specific problem represented by the changing line has been overcome, change this line to its opposite. A new hexagram, portraying a new situation, now presents itself. You may choose to read only the left-hand page, which describes the new situation. However it is advisable to read the right-hand page as well, so that you will understand the further bottlenecks that lie in wait.

9. Strong and Weak Changing Lines

A strong changing line is marked by a circle and a weak changing line is marked by a cross. A strong changing line means that you need to temper your action to prevent a specific situation from getting out of hand. By contrast, a weak changing line urges you to put more effort into achieving what you need, so that you do not remain a victim of your circumstances.

The Hermetic *I Ching*

Hexagrams are symbols or abstractions of situations that occur in real life. When consulting the I Ching, you are initially directed to one of 64 possible hexagrams that shed light on your particular situation. Changing lines in the hexagram you have composed open the door to one of the 63 other hexagrams. Given that you can also consult the inner hexagrams for more information, the Book of Changes is a complex labyrinth, just as surprising and hermetic as real life can be. One can roll from one situation into another. Those who consult the I Ching are not only the interpreters of their current situation but also the diviners of their own future.

Each hexagram described in this book can be regarded as a chapter in a cyclic and ever-repeating story. You can read the book from cover to cover, or you can consult the I Ching with a specific question in mind. When you use the I Ching as an oracle, there are some hexagrams (5, 6, 9, 10, 11, 12, 15, 16, 17, 18, 21, 22, 25, 26, 35, 36, 45, 46, 47, 48, 51, 52) you will only encounter if you happen to compose that particular hexagram or if you are referred to it by the changing lines in the hexagram you have composed. You will not be directed towards them by the inner hexagrams. This, too, is a reflection of real life, in which you have far less chance of encountering some situations than others. Nevertheless, once you have, by chance, stumbled across these hexagrams (or situations), their inner hexagrams will invite you to wander further into the labyrinth of self discovery. Whatever paths you may take, have a wonderful journey.

The 64 I Ching Symbols

The Hermetic *I Ching*
The answer to your specific question is not found only in the starting hexagram. For a deeper insight, you can also study the various separate hexagrams that make up the starting hexagram. The number next to these hexagrams indicates the page where you can find their complete interpretation. If the hexagram you have thrown contains changing lines, these direct you to a 'follow-up' hexagram.

Like life itself, the *I Ching* is a hermetic labyrinth of wonders from which you can only escape by closing the book.

The Follow-Up Hexagram
Once you have changed the strong and weak lines into their opposites, a new 'follow-up' hexagram is created which provides information about a future phase of life. The information on the left-hand page is the most useful for studying this hexagram, since follow-up hexagrams contain no changing lines.
The information on the right-hand page can, of course, be useful for clarifying your study of the follow-up hexagram.

Heaven

Heaven

Heaven

Heaven

landscape

sun

乾

mist

*The sun beams in the heavens. The mist impeding
the view lifts, and reveals the landscape.*

KHIEN (Creative Energy)

The character Khien signifies the creative energy of the heavens, which
makes life on earth possible. The interaction between water and fire,
or body and spirit, is the basis of this incomprehensible phenomenon.
The sun makes all things visible, so you do not have to grope in the
dark and can tell by looking at a shape what more there is behind it.
This demystifies appearances. If you carefully study the situations you
come across, you will be inspired with insights with which you can
enlighten others.

The hexagram is made up of closed lines, which suggests that in
this phase of your life you are observing your surroundings and offering
others advice — impersonally and unasked, as the heavens do —
without exceeding the bounds of courtesy. Given that the hexagram
is built up of four heavens, of which the uppermost is the inexplicable
depth of the visible universe, you cannot claim to speak Truth, but you
can shed some light on matters by pointing out to others that the
confrontation with this true heaven offers the most certainty. In this
way you reject the heavens that lie below which represent a glorious
mythical heaven, an imperfect heaven (that is, hell), and a heaven on
earth—an idea that elevates matter to godliness.

Creative Energy

(1)

The infinite depth of the heavens that encircle the
earth and in one way or another ensure a balance that
keeps this pearl in her orbit, lends itself to being filled
by every illusion imaginable.

If you strive for spiritual development and steadfastly reject all illusion, you translate the universal
power play into an inner balance of offering and
receiving. By being as neutral and free as the heavens,
you give others the opportunity to behave like the
earth, turning away from you when they have
received what they need. They are free to think you
crazy when they don't understand you, to abuse you
for your perceived cruelty, but also to adore you
if they wish. Keep in mind that Truth is open to
interpretation, but do not dream up any stories that
give your innate emptiness an arbitrary mythical
significance. Enjoy the beauty and perfection of
earthly life and encourage others to enjoy it, without
giving it a godly status or trying to change it to fit
your norms and values.

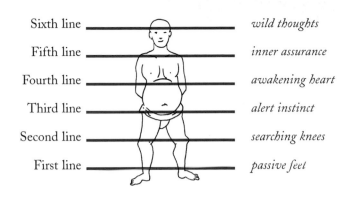

Sixth line — *wild thoughts*

Fifth line — *inner assurance*

Fourth line — *awakening heart*

Third line — *alert instinct*

Second line — *searching knees*

First line — *passive feet*

The Individual Lines

Sixth line
The infinite depth of the heavens cannot be rationally understood, so the honest person refrains from spreading all sorts of speculations and illusions that will confuse others and instead recommends that they allow their thoughts to dissolve into these heavenly depths through meditation.

Fifth line
With inner assurance based on earthly experiences that have given you spiritual insight, you can form a tentative and intuitive idea of the creative energy of the heavens. This is possible because you come close to knowing how this potential is expressed in your own body.

Fourth line
Your heart is a guide for living, for it beats faster at those unpredictable moments when your thoughts stumble upon something that you instantly recognize as Truth. It impresses on you that you know, and that you are, more than you think. Do not attribute this moment of revelation, which is gone as fast as it came, with any more significance than it deserves.

Third line
Your survival instinct warns you when danger is near. By day, be on the alert and observe the energy that drives all forms of life; by night, turn your watchful attention to the universe. Do not lull your survival instinct to sleep with the idea of a glorious mythical heaven where you would be received as a hero for having sacrificed your life to a 'sacred purpose'.

Second line
The sign of an honest attitude is that you are shamelessly who you are. Do not live weighed down by borrowed ideas. If you want to get on top of Truth, seek someone who reaches out as impersonally and unasked as the heavens, and who will allow you to turn away without criticizing you.

First line
Your body is made up of creative energy, and you do not understand how this energy is temporarily anchored in you. Look at what you are in relation to the universal play of forces before you bother others with your ideas. For the time being, you have as much insight as your feet.

Introduction
If all the lines in the Khien hexagram are changing lines, the hexagram changes into *Restrained Energy (2)*. This is an extraordinarily favorable sign, for it indicates that you can put your creative energy into practice and learn to understand the significance of all that the earth brings forth.

Strong and Weak Changing Lines
Extra attention should be paid to strong and weak lines in the hexagram you have thrown. A strong line signifies that you are addressing the situation with too much force, whereas a weak line calls for a bolder attitude.

The Hermetic *I Ching*
The answer to your specific question is not found only in the starting hexagram. For a deeper insight, you can also study the various separate hexagrams that make up the starting hexagram. The number next to these hexagrams indicates the page where you can find their complete interpretation. If the hexagram you have thrown contains changing lines, these direct you to a 'follow-up' hexagram.

Like life itself, the *I Ching* is a hermetic labyrinth of wonders from which you can only escape by closing the book.

The Follow-Up Hexagram
Once you have changed the strong and weak lines into their opposites, a new 'follow-up' hexagram is created which provides information about a future phase of life. The information on the left-hand page is the most useful for studying this hexagram, since follow-up hexagrams contain no changing lines.
The information on the right-hand page can, of course, be useful for clarifying your study of the follow-up hexagram.

}

These hexagrams are components of the starting hexagram and offer directions for successfully dealing with your present situation.

The lines of the hexagram correspond to various parts of the body. The instructions you find there provide insight into your current physical and spiritual state.

: Strong Changing Line

: Weak Changing Line

A loose cord is pulled taut by two hands. This character came to signify a man girding himself. Meaning: extend, develop, open and increase.

hand cord hand

坤

The earth which brings forth all things.

K'UN (Restrained Energy)

The character K'un stands for the earth, or the receptive principle which is impregnated, as it were, by the creative energy of the heavens, so that all the potential in the universe comes to fruition on earth. If you look for the essence of all things that the earth brings forth, you may come to discover the secret of life.

The hexagram is made up entirely of open lines and indicates that all you can do in this phase of your life is open yourself to the outside world, weigh up these experiences, and digest them. You are like the earth which constantly looks outwards, while internally concerned with the developing seed she has taken in. The earth is inseparably linked to the sun and the moon, which light her way and supply her life force. The sun provides insight and transformative energy, while the reflective moon regulates the movement of the seas and running waters. It is wise, therefore, to study these forces which are the earth's most obvious influences, and see how they influence you.

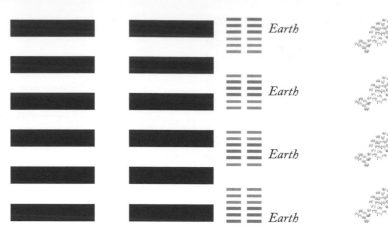

Earth

Earth

Earth

Earth

Restrained Energy

The loose cord that is drawn tight in the character K'un symbolizes the elasticity of earthly life. **(2)**

When something peaks it will decline, and when it reaches rock bottom it will rise again.
This indicates that growth exists due to decay, and that effort is made possible by relaxation. The reverse is also true. The process of breathing, which regulates inner tension and therefore one's attitude, is for every being the essence of the earthly play of forces.
By matching your degree of effort and relaxation to the natural, rotating rhythm of the earth (which leads to day and night), you are attuned to the right dose of the cosmic forces poured over her.

Your breathing should be based purely on your degree of physical exertion. Breathing is characterized by an eternal connection to the here and now. More than any other organism, human beings are conscious of past and future, which exert a constant hold over them and cause psychological problems that affect breathing, and therefore physical condition. It is wise, therefore, to take the time every evening to emotionally process the impressions you have absorbed during the day. Your body then remains connected to the energy of which it is composed.

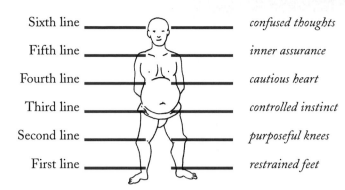

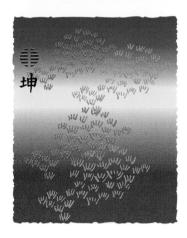

Sixth line ———————— *confused thoughts*

Fifth line ———————— *inner assurance*

Fourth line ———————— *cautious heart*

Third line ———————— *controlled instinct*

Second line ———————— *purposeful knees*

First line ———————— *restrained feet*

The Individual Lines

Sixth line
The earth's surface, which brings forth all things and even offers a view of the heavens, will overwhelm your rational self unless you are selective in registering impressions. Stay with the here and now and look no further ahead than is strictly necessary so that you can more clearly read the situation in which you find yourself.

Fifth line
Inner assurance is based on earthly experiences that have led you to spiritual insight. If you can truly read a situation, you understand the forces driving it, so that the next time you come across this kind of situation you can deal with it. In this way, you will slowly but surely come to be at peace with life.

Fourth line
Your heart, which quickens at those unpredictable moments when an uncontrollable desire is aroused in you, is a guide for cautiously investigating life's situations. Whenever you encounter something that moves you, there is something to be learned.

Third line
Your survival instinct warns you whenever you are fearful or in danger by contracting your stomach and activating your neck, which is the site of your inner assurance. The more you can overcome your fears, the more easily you can move through life. Don't avoid them, therefore, but push on calmly to the heart of the matter.

Second line
The sign of an honest attitude to life is that you are shamelessly who you are. Do not pretend to be a lion when you feel like a lamb. If you present yourself as something other than what you really are, your needs will never be fulfilled.

First line
You move forward hesitantly, not because there is something wrong with your feet but because of inner uncertainty. As long as this is the case, you would be better off avoiding situations that make you feel insecure. Wait to see which way the wind blows, and study the behavior of others.

Introduction
If all the lines in the K'un hexagram are changing lines, the hexagram changes into *Creative Energy (1)*. This is an extraordinarily favorable sign, for it shows that you fully understand earthly existence. This in turn gives you insight into the heavenly play of forces, which manifests its infinite potency on earth.

Strong and Weak Changing Lines
Extra attention should be paid to strong and weak lines in the hexagram you have thrown. A strong line signifies that you are addressing the situation with too much force, whereas a weak line calls for a bolder attitude.

The Hermetic *I Ching*
The answer to your specific question is not found only in the starting hexagram. For a deeper insight, you can also study the various separate hexagrams that make up the starting hexagram. The number next to these hexagrams indicates the page where you can find their complete interpretation. If the hexagram you have thrown contains changing lines, these direct you to a 'follow-up' hexagram.

Like life itself, the *I Ching* is a hermetic labyrinth of wonders from which you can only escape by closing the book.

The Follow-Up Hexagram
Once you have changed the strong and weak lines into their opposites, a new 'follow-up' hexagram is created which provides information about a future phase of life. The information on the left-hand page is the most useful for studying this hexagram, since follow-up hexagrams contain no changing lines. The information on the right-hand page can, of course, be useful for clarifying your study of the follow-up hexagram.

} These hexagrams are components of the starting hexagram and offer directions for successfully dealing with your present situation.

The lines of the hexagram correspond to various parts of the body. The instructions you find there provide insight into your current physical and spiritual state.

——○—— : Strong Changing Line
——×—— : Weak Changing Line

坤 **2**

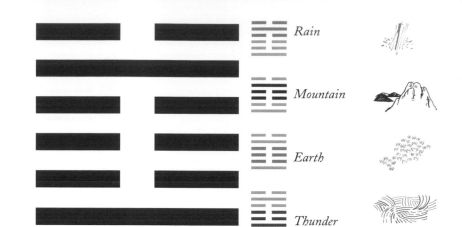

The tender shoot of a plant ——————
The earth's surface ——
Two seed lobes ——
The root system ——————

TUN (Confusion)

The character Tun represents the struggle of a germinating plant to grow through the earth's surface and come to full bloom. Whatever form this process takes — the birth of new life, new love, a project, an idea or some other entity — it always moves from darkness (the inner self) to light (the exterior world).

In the hexagram, the upward movement of the thunder symbolizes a beating heart which powers the development of a being's ideas and ideals. The downward movement of the rain, which is both nourishing and destructive, evokes resistance or opposition. Therefore, you experience the growth process as a mountain looming over you. Keep in mind that without such opposition there can be no victory, and therefore no growth. The confusion this opposition generates can always be mastered by turning to the forces operating in this hexagram.

Rain

Mountain

Earth

Thunder

Confusion
Growth and confusion go hand in hand, but if you study the directions shown below *(reading from bottom to top)* and know that you can always fall back on them in times of need, you can plant something whose fruits will be to your taste. (3)

Initial Difficulty
During a growth process, you will continually be faced with situations that demand solutions. On the one hand this creates confusion, but on the other it is an extra incentive to bring your efforts to fruition. 39

Union
Although you remain responsible for your own growth process, it can do no harm to seek a good example and/or the right companions. A good example is a useful guide, and many hands make light work. 8

The Destruction of the Past
If you are fixated on things that are long gone, you will not be aware of the opportunities presenting themselves in the here and now. Let go, and focus on the future — unencumbered by the past. 23

Nourishment
Without the right physical and spiritual nourishment any growth process is doomed to failure. 27

Winter Solstice, Awakening
The first logical step towards creating something is to start. 24

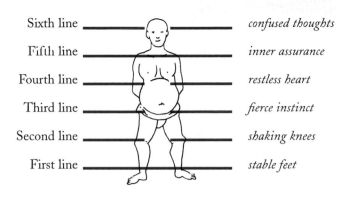

Sixth line	*confused thoughts*
Fifth line	*inner assurance*
Fourth line	*restless heart*
Third line	*fierce instinct*
Second line	*shaking knees*
First line	*stable feet*

The Individual Lines

Sixth line
The rainwater that collects on the top of the mountain and cannot flow away is like a head full of confused and obsessive thoughts. Impotence and anger are bad counsellors. The best option is to let go, and wait for liberating insight.

Fifth line
You radiate lofty calm, like the top of the mountain or the firm upper jaw that cannot be pried open, and others look to you for instruction. Because of the turbulence around you, this is not the time for far-reaching decisions. You would be wise to exert your healing influence sparingly.

Fourth line
You are struggling to free yourself from your past, but you cannot find your footing. You are in danger of slipping away, like water draining into the earth. The knowledge that you can count on companions and that clarity is within your grasp encourages you to stand firm.

Third line
Beneath the earth, where the thunder beats at the foot of the mountain, you are like a hunter following the tracks of a deer without a ranger to guide you. You are lost in the woods, and wisdom dictates that you call off the hunt and think more carefully about what you are doing.

Second line
The thunder deep below the surface of the earth is like a beating heart that quickens with expectation. You may be tempted to bask in dreams on the safe bed of the first line, but the right approach is to get up and actually face the future. Only the plant that grows will blossom.

First line
Full of energy, like the rolling thunder or the lower jaw that is eager to get its teeth into things, you face a confusing situation. Do not try to force a resolution. Proceed quietly but resolutely, and look for like-minded companions.

Introduction
The movement in the Tun hexagram is determined by *Nourishment (27)*. The lower jaw (first line) strives to meet the upper jaw (fifth line). The blockage is in *Initial Difficulty (39)*. The rainwater forms a lake on the top of the mountain rather than flowing freely.

Strong and Weak Changing Lines
Extra attention should be paid to strong and weak lines in the hexagram you have thrown. A strong line signifies that you are addressing the situation with too much force, whereas a weak line calls for a bolder attitude.

The Hermetic *I Ching*
The answer to your specific question is not found only in the starting hexagram. For a deeper insight, you can also study the various separate hexagrams that make up the starting hexagram. The number next to these hexagrams indicates the page where you can find their complete interpretation. If the hexagram you have thrown contains changing lines, these direct you to a 'follow-up' hexagram.

Like life itself, the *I Ching* is a hermetic labyrinth of wonders from which you can only escape by closing the book.

The Follow-Up Hexagram
Once you have changed the strong and weak lines into their opposites, a new 'follow-up' hexagram is created which provides information about a future phase of life. The information on the left-hand page is the most useful for studying this hexagram, since follow-up hexagrams contain no changing lines.
The information on the right-hand page can, of course, be useful for clarifying your study of the follow-up hexagram.

} These hexagrams are components of the starting hexagram and offer directions for successfully dealing with your present situation.

The lines of the hexagram correspond to various parts of the body. The instructions you find there provide insight into your current physical and spiritual state.

⊜ : Strong Changing Line
⊟ : Weak Changing Line

3

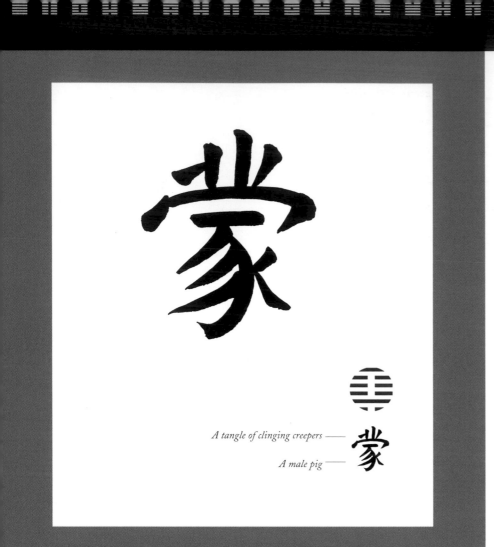

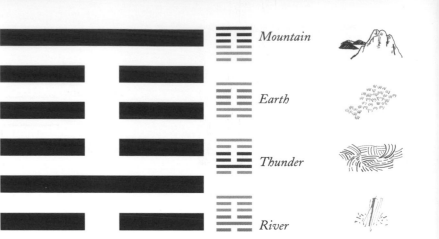

Mountain

Earth

Thunder

River

A tangle of clinging creepers ———

A male pig ———

蒙

MENG (Youthful Innocence)

A male pig (the boar), the symbol of unbridled energy, tries to free himself from a tangle of clinging creepers. The character Meng represents the first audacious strides to realize yourself, your ideas or ideals. This clearly has to do with youthful and innocent fanaticism and the fact that you are not yet familiar with the norms and values of a civilized society.

This is symbolized in the hexagram by the turbulent river that plunges down the mountain and by the upwards movement of the thunder which tries to stem the flow. The wild water that always finds its way down — no matter what — is the symbol of a child, who inevitably becomes an adult. Only a wise teacher (the thunder) using solid arguments, patience and love can offer an upbringing that changes a child from a wild, flooding mountain stream into a peaceful, babbling brook that irrigates fields and is a joy to itself and others. The play of forces at work in the hexagram indicates how youthful innocence can develop into adult behavior.

 Youthful Innocence
You are like water plunging freely down a mountain, or a wild, unchained boar bursting through the shrubbery. Try to absorb the following directions, so that you can put on the brakes in time. (4)

 The Destruction of the Past
Do not let go of the past before you have plucked its fruits. 23

 Nourishment
Strengthen yourself with the food of experience, which is offered to you by wise people who have preceded you on this path. 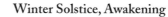 27

 Winter Solstice, Awakening
Take off your blinkers and look around. Try to see that life can offer you more than the limited vision with which you justify your impetuous action. It is better to turn back halfway than push on until you are completely lost. 24

 The Army
An army without leadership turns into a plundering mass which, like a turbulent river, destroys everything in its path. When each soldier, or each cell of your body, is fully aware that destruction of his surroundings will also mean his own demise, the point where youthful innocence turns towards maturity has been reached. 7

 Cutting the Knot
Anyone who at this stage still persists in following the blind course set by inexperience is asking to be pulled firmly into line. 40

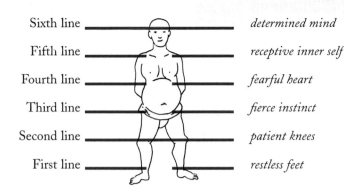

Sixth line ——————— *determined mind*

Fifth line ——————— *receptive inner self*

Fourth line ——————— *fearful heart*

Third line ——————— *fierce instinct*

Second line ——————— *patient knees*

First line ——————— *restless feet*

The Individual Lines

Sixth line
If you perceive that youthful innocence instinctively seeks limits, you will realize that punishment is pointless. The most you can do for others is steer them away from unnecessary suffering. For the rest, be a beacon of sublime tranquility, like the top of the mountain or the immovable upper jaw.

Fifth line
At the upper line of the earth, which nestles snugly against the top of the stalwart mountain, you are like a field ready to receive the seeds of wisdom.

Fourth line
Hidden beneath the surface of the earth, where the thunder beats against the foot of the mountain, you behave like a frightened prisoner rattling the chains that keep him in the dungeon of his own ignorance.

Third line
Deep below the surface of the earth, the thunder attempts to calm the wild water. You are advised not to let yourself be led along the path of least resistance. Put your trust in wise advice from companions who can lead you to a safe haven.

Second line
In this position, you are like the approaching thunder or the lower jaw rising to meet the upper jaw. You are expected to behave like a wise general who keeps an overview at all times and brings his mutinous troops into line with tact and patience.

First line
One way of dealing with the reckless who flout the bounds of acceptability is to take a hard line with them. If this does not solve the problem, resign yourself to the fact that you can lead a horse to water, but you cannot make it drink.

Introduction
The movement in the Meng hexagram is determined by *Nourishment (27)* and the river ☵. The upper jaw (sixth line) is immovable, but a flood of senseless chatter forces down the lower jaw (second line/the beginning of the thunder). Try to unite your lower jaw with your upper jaw, in order to create a breathing space that gives you time to think.

Strong and Weak Changing Lines
Extra attention should be paid to strong and weak lines in the hexagram you have thrown. A strong line signifies that you are addressing the situation with too much force, whereas a weak line calls for a bolder attitude.

The Hermetic *I Ching*
The answer to your specific question is not found only in the starting hexagram. For a deeper insight, you can also study the various separate hexagrams that make up the starting hexagram. The number next to these hexagrams indicates the page where you can find their complete interpretation. If the hexagram you have thrown contains changing lines, these direct you to a 'follow-up' hexagram.

Like life itself, the *I Ching* is a hermetic labyrinth of wonders from which you can only escape by closing the book.

The Follow-Up Hexagram
Once you have changed the strong and weak lines into their opposites, a new 'follow-up' hexagram is created which provides information about a future phase of life. The information on the left-hand page is the most useful for studying this hexagram, since follow-up hexagrams contain no changing lines.
The information on the right-hand page can, of course, be useful for clarifying your study of the follow-up hexagram.

} These hexagrams are components of the starting hexagram and offer directions for successfully dealing with your present situation.

The lines of the hexagram correspond to various parts of the body. The instructions you find there provide insight into your current physical and spiritual state.

—○— : Strong Changing Line
—x— : Weak Changing Line

蒙 ䷃ **4**

Rain

Fire/Sun

Marsh/Moon

Heaven

HSÜ (Biding One's Time)

Heavenly order —————
Rain —————
A plant that is firmly rooted in the earth —————

Heaven knows when the rain will fall. The firmly rooted plant can do nothing but wait in readiness for the floodgates of heaven to open. The character Hsü, which is generally translated as 'waiting', illustrates that the future should not be filled in at random. In the knowledge that life consists of a string of moments, a wise person enjoys each moment. Therefore he or she can wait and welcome the fertile rain, which comes in its own good time like a new, challenging phase of development.

In the hexagram, the heavens symbolize the source of all unexpected things that may present themselves. For the moment, the sun wards off the rain and illuminates the beautiful reflection of the full moon or the marsh's surface. The wise person enjoys this moment because he or she knows that the moon wanes again, that the enticing marsh evaporates and turns into a muddy pool, and that the inevitable rain eventually washes away the moment as if it has never existed. Understanding this play of forces gives you a solid base for facing the future.

Biding One's Time
 (5)
The rain clouds in the heavens symbolize future developments. It is certain that something will present itself, but what and when is a mystery. You can do nothing but wait. The following steps tell you how to do so.

Successful Movement
 63
The raincloud that descends from the heavens like the unpredictable future is warded off by the sun. Enjoy the moment, and if you can maintain this attitude, every moment that follows will be equally pleasurable.

Regular and Orderly
 60
When there is too much rain the marsh floods, and when there is too little it dries up. Do not try to hang on to a beautiful moment forever. On the other hand, do not let it pass without enjoying it.

Duality
 38
The moon waxes and wanes. Joy is followed by grief and rain by sunshine. The sun always shines. Do not think that there is no more light just because you cannot see it for the moment.

Profound Insight, Great Possession
 14
If you understand the preceding directions, you are like the sun which has an overview of heavenly developments that will come to fruition on earth, and you see with complete clarity what the future signifies.

Fulfilment
 43
The only thought that remains is that you can enjoy the earthly game without losing yourself in illusions.

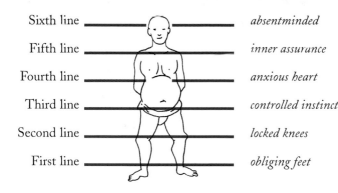

Sixth line ——— absentminded

Fifth line ——— inner assurance

Fourth line ——— anxious heart

Third line ——— controlled instinct

Second line ——— locked knees

First line ——— obliging feet

The Individual Lines

Sixth line
Shrouded in thick mist, you move blindly forward on the stream of life. If you keep in mind that the sun always shines in the heavens and will sooner or later dip the world in a beautiful play of colors, you can face the future with pleasure.

Fifth line
The brilliant sun laughs at every threatening rain-cloud. If you have this insight, nothing can get you down. You can celebrate and enjoy whatever is served up to you, knowing that pain and grief are merely ingredients of the sauce that makes a meal spicy and appetizing.

Fourth line
The rose-red full moon, which is illuminated by the sun, bathes in the reflective surface of the marsh. The climax of the moment has been reached. The moon wanes and the marsh evaporates and turns into a muddy pool. You have no alternative but to open yourself courageously to future events.

Third line
Under the reflective surface of the marsh is a layer of sludge. You are in the mire. You think you can get out of this situation by looking with fiery hope to the future, but this is the sort of thinking that keeps you in the mire. Deal with today before you begin on tomorrow.

Second line
The bottom of the enticing marsh rests like shifting sand at the core of the heavens. Heaven knows that in the future no grain of sand will stay put. You are advised to thoroughly investigate your current situation. Do not run ahead of events, even though others will call you a stick in the mud.

First line
At the outer limits of the heavens there is no question of a future, so this is not the moment to immerse yourself in it. Just handle today's concerns calmly and with dignity.

Introduction
The Hsü hexagram derives its potency from *Profound Insight, Great Possession (14)*. Armed with this insight ≡≡, you do not see the future ≡ as threatening clouds ≡≡ on the horizon, so you can enjoy each moment ≡≡.
Hsü/waiting indicates that life is a train of events and every single one of them has its own beauty.

Strong and Weak Changing Lines
Extra attention should be paid to strong and weak lines in the hexagram you have thrown. A strong line signifies that you are addressing the situation with too much force, whereas a weak line calls for a bolder attitude.

The Hermetic *I Ching*
The answer to your specific question is not found only in the starting hexagram. For a deeper insight, you can also study the various separate hexagrams that make up the starting hexagram. The number next to these hexagrams indicates the page where you can find their complete interpretation. If the hexagram you have thrown contains changing lines, these direct you to a 'follow-up' hexagram.

Like life itself, the *I Ching* is a hermetic labyrinth of wonders from which you can only escape by closing the book.

The Follow-Up Hexagram
Once you have changed the strong and weak lines into their opposites, a new 'follow-up' hexagram is created which provides information about a future phase of life. The information on the left-hand page is the most useful for studying this hexagram, since follow-up hexagrams contain no changing lines.
The information on the right-hand page can, of course, be useful for clarifying your study of the follow-up hexagram.

} These hexagrams are components of the starting hexagram and offer directions for successfully dealing with your present situation.  The lines of the hexagram correspond to various parts of the body. The instructions you find there provide insight into your current physical and spiritual state.

—⊙— : Strong Changing Line
—×— : Weak Changing Line

需 ䷄ **5**

Words flow unreservedly from the mouth. — 訟

Treating everyone equally

SUNG (Tension)

The character Sung represents frankly speaking your mind without taking into account rank or status, friend or enemy.

The structure of the hexagram confirms how natural this release is. The infinite depth of the heavens shows that no subject is out of bounds and that sincerity underlies your conclusions. The wind stands for your intellectual capacity and the sun for the passionate intensity of your thoughts. The downpour of rain represents your stream of words; when the storm breaks, it affects everyone within its sphere of influence. It is clear that once the rain falls, the process cannot be reversed. Be aware of the danger that a bottled-up thought will fan the fire like a whirlwind and discharge in a cracking thunderclap that will inevitably cause great damage. You are the one who determines what you extend to others: a miserable drizzle, lashing rain, or a refreshing spring shower that is conducive to growth. Insight into this play of forces ensures that you do not call forth more problems than you set out to solve.

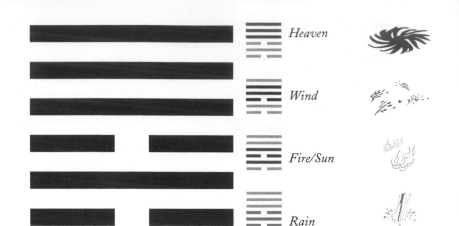

Heaven

Wind

Fire/Sun

Rain

Tension

The will of the heavens manifests itself in fruitful rain which brings growth. The heavens are not troubled by fears and emotions and therefore freely distribute their blessings. If you also want to express your hidden thoughts in peace and sincerity, be guided by the following directions. (6)

A Mature Relationship
Do not be too attached to earthly possessions, otherwise you run the risk of making a mountain out of a molehill. 44

Unanimous Purpose
First shine your inner light over your motives, to feel whether you are free of fears and emotions that might influence your words. 13

The Management of the Inner Being
Breathe calmly, so you can order your thoughts. Let your inner fire burn evenly like a pure flame that will not be fanned or dimmed by consuming anger or exhausting impotence. 37

Redemption
You have yourself completely under control. You are free from fears and emotions. Thought and word have become one. Speak! 59

Restricted Movement
Now that you have said what you wanted to say, the subject is closed. To keep pushing will bring trouble. You are like the sun that no longer has any power over the rain. The only thing you can do is wait and see how your words will be received. 64

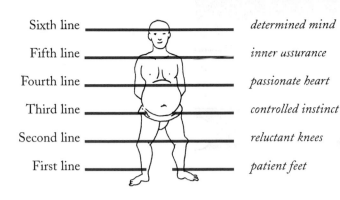

Sixth line	——————	*determined mind*
Fifth line	——————	*inner assurance*
Fourth line	——————	*passionate heart*
Third line	——————	*controlled instinct*
Second line	——————	*reluctant knees*
First line	——————	*patient feet*

The Individual Lines

Sixth line
At the outer limits of the heavens, deep silence reigns. Even so, it is not wise to remain silent as the grave if others make an urgent appeal for your opinion. Speak the words you feel will cause the least damage.

Fifth line
You look into the heart of the heavens or the depths of your soul and a sincere thought flashes into your mind. Do not weigh your words any longer, but express what you have seen so clearly before you.

Fourth line
Fiery arguments well up in you. You do not have the peace you need to speak sincerely. You would be well advised to try once again to clarify your inner motives.

Third line
Your thoughts are well considered and sincere. Nevertheless, the fire of doubt has been awakened in you because you do not know exactly what effect your words will have. Do not hesitate; speak out your initial, pure thoughts. If you want to demonstrate that you are straightforward, it is nonsense to think about the consequences.

Second line
Fire rises up and water always finds its way down. Let your words die on your lips. Your arguments are too ill-considered and forced to be sincere. Swallow what you were going to say and let sleeping dogs lie.

First line
The truth, as you see it, is out. You can count on opposition. Do not try to defend yourself and do not attack. Stick to the standpoint that you expressed frankly, from the depths of your soul.

Introduction
The essence of Sung/to speak frankly, is in the hexagram underlined by *Unanimous Purpose (13)*. Try to get a clear view ☲ of the bone of contention ☰ that caused your aggrieved thoughts ☲ before the words gush from your mouth ☱.

Strong and Weak Changing Lines
Extra attention should be paid to strong and weak lines in the hexagram you have thrown. A strong line signifies that you are addressing the situation with too much force, whereas a weak line calls for a bolder attitude.

The Hermetic *I Ching*
The answer to your specific question is not found only in the starting hexagram. For a deeper insight, you can also study the various separate hexagrams that make up the starting hexagram. The number next to these hexagrams indicates the page where you can find their complete interpretation. If the hexagram you have thrown contains changing lines, these direct you to a 'follow-up' hexagram.

Like life itself, the *I Ching* is a hermetic labyrinth of wonders from which you can only escape by closing the book.

The Follow-Up Hexagram
Once you have changed the strong and weak lines into their opposites, a new 'follow-up' hexagram is created which provides information about a future phase of life. The information on the left-hand page is the most useful for studying this hexagram, since follow-up hexagrams contain no changing lines.
The information on the right-hand page can, of course, be useful for clarifying your study of the follow-up hexagram.

} These hexagrams are components of the starting hexagram and offer directions for successfully dealing with your present situation.

The lines of the hexagram correspond to various parts of the body. The instructions you find there provide insight into your current physical and spiritual state.

⚊ⵔ : Strong Changing Line
⚊ⵝ : Weak Changing Line

訟  **6**

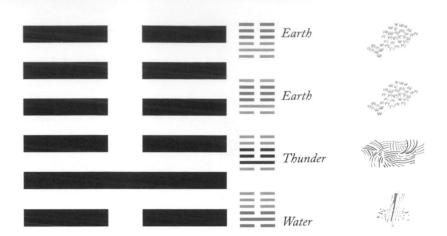

Sloping or raised terrain
A military bastion or a city —— 師

Turning on an axis

SZE (The Army)

Above a city flaps the standard of the commander-in-chief — a sign that everything is running smoothly, like a wheel turning on its axis. The character Sze, generally translated as 'the army', indicates a community that is well-organized and therefore thriving and able to defend itself. In peaceful times the military power takes a back seat. When threatend, the people will undoubtedly defend their well-being and fall in behind the general's banner. This sort of collaboration may refer to a state, a city, a company, a family or your own body.

In the hexagram, the fruitful earth that brings forth all things stands for prosperity. The water which plunges, fearless and free, from high mountains into deep ravines is found here beneath the earth and symbolizes the people's army. The thunder which pulsates under the earth and pushes the water upwards indicates a wise general who does not interfere with the economic affairs on the earth's surface, but will take action in times of danger. His standard serves to rally the army in times of need, just as an Archimedean screw draws water to the surface when required.

Earth

Earth

Thunder

Water

The Army
Self-assurance, strategic acumen and an indomitable attitude that does not exclude brute force: these are the characteristics of a defense force worthy of being called an army. Check the following pointers to find out whether you fill these criteria. (7)

Restrained Energy
The fruitful earth not only brings prosperity, but also offers the means by which one can continue to thrive. The earth hexagram is bottomless and this points to modesty, generosity and understanding for all that she (the earth) brings about. Do not think that you have to show such profound altruism, patience and love, but if you are graced with these characteristics you will not make many enemies. 2

Winter Solstice, Awakening
To emphasize the importance of continuous watch-fulness, this sign appears twice. The strong bottom line in this hexagram suggests a state of alertness, and underlines the fact that opportunity makes the thief. 24

The Army
In this hexagram the strong line has moved up one place. Red Alert! You stand, adopting an indomitable defensive stance to keep the enemy at a distance. Behave like a seasoned general. Keep an overview, basc your strategy on the common good, and do not allow yourself to be carried away by egotism, anger or other emotions. (7)

Cutting the Knot
If your intimidatory stance proves futile and confrontation is unavoidable, remember the words of the brilliant stategist Sun Tzu: 'The battlefield prescribes the strategy to follow. Most battles are won by deception.' 40

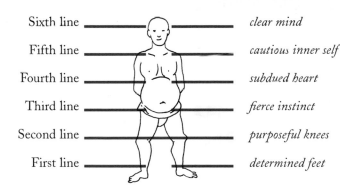

Sixth line ———————————— *clear mind*

Fifth line ———————————— *cautious inner self*

Fourth line ———————————— *subdued heart*

Third line ———————————— *fierce instinct*

Second line ———————————— *purposeful knees*

First line ———————————— *determined feet*

The Individual Lines

Sixth line

At the surface of the earth, only the external appearance of situations are discernible. The roots, or the underlying motives, are hidden. Do not go into battle on the basis of rational evaluations alone. If you first think and then strike, you will always be too late.

Fifth line

This line, just under the earth's surface, symbolizes your inner assurance, or intuition. It is that small voice which has so often proved to be perfectly right, but to which your heart and head do not always dare to listen. If you switch off these two for the moment and let your intuitive impulse flow directly to your knees (second line), you will always stand firmly, in even the most threatening situations.

Fourth line

Beneath the earth, the thunder loses force. If you are facing a superior force and are threatened with destruction, it is not shameful to take in sail. In your heart, stay true to the voice of your inner assurance and do not allow yourself to be carried away by your emotions.

Third line

Deep beneath the earth, the thunder whips the surface of the water into white-caps. Your emotions threaten to gain the upper hand which will disturb the power relationship between your inner assurance and the purposeful position of your knee joints, which determine your physical stance. Fear and rage are poor counselors in matters of survival.

Second line

The thunder drives the water upwards. Your knees take the impetus over from your inner assurance, or intuition (fifth line). Every cell of your body (which, after all, is about eighty percent water) aligns with your indomitable posture, which is determined by the position of your knee joints.

First line

Water always seeks the lowest point. There is some danger of running away. In a physical battle, footwork is of crucial importance. But without the knee joints, there can be no footwork. It is the foot that follows the knee, and not the other way around. Take care, therefore, not to let your feet run away with you.

Introduction

The strong second line, or knee joint, is the axis of the Sze hexagram. The knee is the hinge that gives a person flexibility and determines his or her physical combativeness. If you can put even one of your opponent's knees out of action, the battle is won. Like a general called up for battle by his sovereign, your knee follows the intuitive reflex of your inner surety (fifth line).

Strong and Weak Changing Lines

Extra attention should be paid to strong and weak lines in the hexagram you have thrown. A strong line signifies that you are addressing the situation with too much force, whereas a weak line calls for a bolder attitude.

The Hermetic *I Ching*

The answer to your specific question is not found only in the starting hexagram. For a deeper insight, you can also study the various separate hexagrams that make up the starting hexagram. The number next to these hexagrams indicates the page where you can find their complete interpretation. If the hexagram you have thrown contains changing lines, these direct you to a 'follow-up' hexagram.

Like life itself, the *I Ching* is a hermetic labyrinth of wonders from which you can only escape by closing the book.

The Follow-Up Hexagram

Once you have changed the strong and weak lines into their opposites, a new 'follow-up' hexagram is created which provides information about a future phase of life. The information on the left-hand page is the most useful for studying this hexagram, since follow-up hexagrams contain no changing lines. The information on the right-hand page can, of course, be useful for clarifying your study of the follow-up hexagram.

These hexagrams are components of the starting hexagram and offer directions for successfully dealing with your present situation.

The lines of the hexagram correspond to various parts of the body. The instructions you find there provide insight into your current physical and spiritual state.

═⊙═ : Strong Changing Line
═x═ : Weak Changing Line

師

7

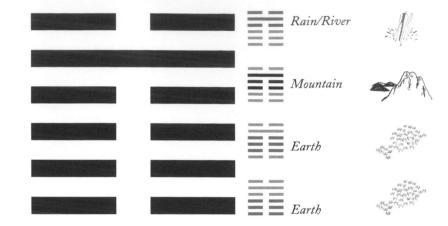

比

Two men walk on together.

PÎ (Union)

In the character Pî, which indicates both cooperation and following, the one who walks ahead is a master showing the way to a follower. Example is better than precept. The wise master knows when a disciple is ready to assimilate knowledge, and so never casts pearls before swine.

In the hexagram, the lake on the top of the mountain symbolizes a master in possession of a rich source of fertile knowledge. At the foot of the mountain, his followers thirst for knowledge like fallow fields asking to be sown. Before it can be planted, a field must be cleared of weeds, ploughed and harrowed. In the same way, a disciple has to be ready to absorb knowledge. If a master offers his wisdom too soon, his words will not fall on fertile ground. If he waits too long, the earth will be dry and hard. Moreover, his pool of knowledge will have become a water reservoir straining at its banks; the danger is that he will finally burst out in an uncontrollable flood of words that the pupil will not be able to follow. An awareness of measure and time gives this interplay of forces the subtlety of a crystal-clear mountain brook that sometimes brims and swirls excitingly but never overflows its banks or dries up.

Rain/River

Mountain

Earth

Earth

Union

In the relationship between a teacher who offers knowledge and a student who is open to it, both parties have their own responsibilities. The steps that follow explain how this interplay can lead to a fruitful union. (8)

Initial Difficulty
The rainwater forms a lake on the top of the mountain. The teacher has to decide when to release the fertile information he can offer, and in what dose, before he opens the floodgates of his mind. It is clear that he must hand out his insights eventually, because gravity forces water to find its way downwards. 39

Union
Self-control, a sense of responsibility, and insight into the growth process are the qualities that determine whether the knowledge bestowed by the teacher will fall on fertile or stony ground. (8)

The Destruction of the Past
The fact that this sign appears twice in the hexagram underlines its importance. The teacher has to convince his students that they need to work through their past experiences before a new stimulus can cause any breakthrough in their way of thinking. The students' task is to weed their fields so they are ready for the new planting. 23

Restrained Energy
Once the student presents himself as virgin ground that is ready for any crop, the teacher is able to plant his insights in the knowledge that this seed can grow into the fruits of his wisdom. Given that a tree is recognized by its fruits, the success or otherwise of this union will become obvious in time. 2

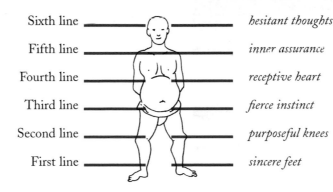

The Individual Lines

Sixth line ——— *hesitant thoughts*

Fifth line ——— *inner assurance*

Fourth line ——— *receptive heart*

Third line ——— *fierce instinct*

Second line ——— *purposeful knees*

First line ——— *sincere feet*

Sixth line
The rainwater has formed a lake on the top of the mountain. You should speak out. It would be a bad thing to bottle up your knowledge until it almost chokes you. The flood of words you would then expel would not fall on fertile ground.

Fifth line
This strong line is the top of the mountain. Like a wise teacher who has an overview of the situation and therefore knows when the time is ripe for giving, you can distribute your insights — asked or unasked — with the subtlety of a crystal-clear mountain brook.

Fourth line
The fertile surface of the earth nestles snugly against the top of the mountain and drinks in the wholesome water. If you thirst for knowledge, take a good look around you to find someone you can trust and to whom you can safely lend an ear.

Third line
The foot of the mountain is hidden under the earth. In this position, you cannot figure out the nature of the person with whom you are seeking union. It is quite conceivable that you will make the wrong choice.

Second line
The roots of the harvested crop can still be found below ground level. Crop rotation prevents depletion of the soil. You are ready to wipe the slate clean, so that you can absorb new insights which can lead to a breakthrough in your consciousness.

First line
Deep under the field's surface is virgin ground, where no root has ever taken hold. You are as sincere and innocent as your feet. Like a blank page, you are open to the wisdom that others can offer you.

Introduction
The rainwater ⚏ in the Pi hexagram will eventually unite with the earth ☷, no matter what.
In the meantime, the water forms a lake on the top of the mountain until *The Destruction of the Past (23)* has been accomplished. This is the way that true sages convey their wisdom to willing students.

Strong and Weak Changing Lines
Extra attention should be paid to strong and weak lines in the hexagram you have thrown. A strong line signifies that you are addressing the situation with too much force, whereas a weak line calls for a bolder attitude.

The Hermetic *I Ching*
The answer to your specific question is not found only in the starting hexagram. For a deeper insight, you can also study the various separate hexagrams that make up the starting hexagram. The number next to these hexagrams indicates the page where you can find their complete interpretation. If the hexagram you have thrown contains changing lines, these direct you to a 'follow-up' hexagram.

Like life itself, the *I Ching* is a hermetic labyrinth of wonders from which you can only escape by closing the book.

The Follow-Up Hexagram
Once you have changed the strong and weak lines into their opposites, a new 'follow-up' hexagram is created which provides information about a future phase of life. The information on the left-hand page is the most useful for studying this hexagram, since follow-up hexagrams contain no changing lines.
The information on the right-hand page can, of course, be useful for clarifying your study of the follow-up hexagram.

} These hexagrams are components of the starting hexagram and offer directions for successfully dealing with your present situation.

The lines of the hexagram correspond to various parts of the body. The instructions you find there provide insight into your current physical and spiritual state.

—o— : Strong Changing Line
—x— : Weak Changing Line

比 **8**

To divide something that is already small.
A flash, or a moment.

Female, yin, instinctive. Also profound, mysterious,
to nurture, to feed, docility. Cattle in a field, earthly life.

小畜

HSIÂO KHÛ (A Moment of Insight)

The characters Hsiâo and Khû indicate a flash of insight.
For an instant, you realize that there is more to life than the daily grind
in which you are apparently caught up.

The third line of the hexagram represents an aperture in the
heavens. It is as if the fire/sun grants you a glimpse of the secret of life.
The full moon which will wane and the reflecting surface of the marsh
which will evaporate point to the temporary nature of this beatific
perception. The wind is the symbol of the flashing thought that you
try, in vain, to hold. You rack your brains to find the right words to
describe the moment. There is no chance of rain and therefore no
immediate possibility of internalizing this insight as fertile knowledge.
What remains is both a profound conviction that there is a hidden
reason for your existence, and the knowledge that it must be possible
to evoke such insights of your own volition.

Wind

Fire/Sun

Marsh/Moon

Heaven

A Moment of Insight
In a moment of insight the heavens seem to open
themselves to you and in a flash you take in the truth,
which had been shrouded by semblance.
The following directions may help to demystify this
seemingly uncontrollable process. (9)

The Management of the Inner Being
Those who can control their breathing can direct their
thoughts and emotions. Meditation shows the way. 37

Sincerity
If you are sincere, you will perceive and accept the fact
that the secret of life cannot be captured in words. 61

Duality
As long as you live, you will be vulnerable to the
effects of duality. Do not think that losing touch
with your insight means that it is lost forever. 38

Profound Insight, Great Possession
If you can understand the preceding directions you
are like the sun which overlooks the game of
semblance and reality and you know from experience
that meditation widens your horizons. 14

Fulfilment
You are left with just one thought, which is that you
can enjoy the earthly game without giving yourself
over to illusions. 43

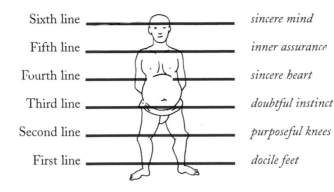

Sixth line —— *sincere mind*

Fifth line —— *inner assurance*

Fourth line —— *sincere heart*

Third line —— *doubtful instinct*

Second line —— *purposeful knees*

First line —— *docile feet*

The Individual Lines

Sixth line
This line is the mysterious source of the wind and here symbolizes the back of your mind, where the flash of insight is tucked away.
It is not sensible to rack your brains over how you can bring that insight back to consciousness. Proceed with everyday things. As soon as you really need this knowledge, it will come back to you.

Fifth line
The middle line of the wind and the top line of the fire/sun signify your forehead. Thanks to your inner assurance, the insight wells up in you so clearly that you can capture its essence in words.

Fourth line
The aperture in the heavens. If a flash of insight moves you deeply, do not try to hang on to it for dear life. In your complete sincerity, you know that this moment is as temporary as a full moon caught in the stillness of a sultry summer evening as it bathes in the mirroring surface of a marsh bordered with sweet-smelling flowers.

Third line
A hazy light penetrates the waters below the surface of the marsh. Any insights that are gathered here will create confusion. You seem to feel this in the depths of your being. It would be wise to abandon this muddled brainwave.

Second line
From the bottom of the marsh, which rests at the core of the heavens, the water's luminous surface is vaguely visible. You may have the sensation that there is something in your life whose significance you are missing. Being stronger than a moth, which cannot resist the candlelight, you continue with what you had been doing.

First line
Darkness reigns at the outer limit of the heavens. Do not let yourself be distracted by idle speculations which are not at all relevant now.

Introduction
In the Hsiâo Khû hexagram the fourth line represents the moment of insight. This line is:
1. the reflecting surface of the marsh which evaporates or the full moon which wanes ☱;
2. the center of the fire or the setting sun ☲;
3. the underside of the wind ☴ that passes by or dies down.

Strong and Weak Changing Lines
Extra attention should be paid to strong and weak lines in the hexagram you have thrown. A strong line signifies that you are addressing the situation with too much force, whereas a weak line calls for a bolder attitude.

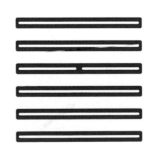

The Hermetic *I Ching*
The answer to your specific question is not found only in the starting hexagram. For a deeper insight, you can also study the various separate hexagrams that make up the starting hexagram. The number next to these hexagrams indicates the page where you can find their complete interpretation. If the hexagram you have thrown contains changing lines, these direct you to a 'follow-up' hexagram.

Like life itself, the *I Ching* is a hermetic labyrinth of wonders from which you can only escape by closing the book.

The Follow-Up Hexagram
Once you have changed the strong and weak lines into their opposites, a new 'follow-up' hexagram is created which provides information about a future phase of life. The information on the left-hand page is the most useful for studying this hexagram, since follow-up hexagrams contain no changing lines.
The information on the right-hand page can, of course, be useful for clarifying your study of the follow-up hexagram.

These hexagrams are components of the starting hexagram and offer directions for successfully dealing with your present situation. —— The lines of the hexagram correspond to various parts of the body. The instructions you find there provide insight into your current physical and spiritual state.

⚊○⚊ : Strong Changing Line
⚋✕⚋ : Weak Changing Line

小畜   **9**

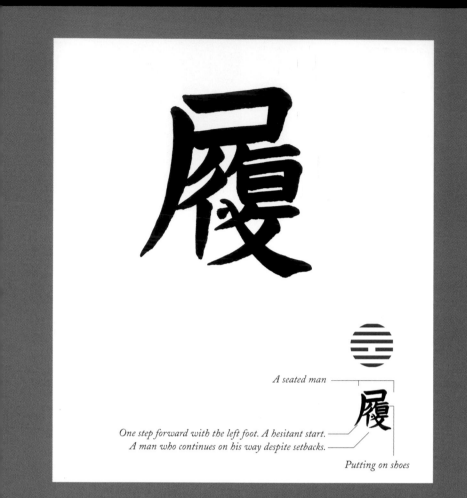

A seated man

One step forward with the left foot. A hesitant start.
A man who continues on his way despite setbacks.

Putting on shoes

LÎ (On the Road with Cheerful Courage)

The composition of the character Lî suggests plucking up one's courage and, after some hesitation, taking action in a sincere and uninhibited way.

In the hexagram, the infinite depth of the heavens indicates that your goal is to embark upon a situation that is, for you, terra incognita. The play of the other three forces shows how you can overcome your hesitance. The wind blowing from the heavens stands for sincere thoughts and the sun represents radiant openness. In an environment where you understand nothing of the etiquette, your mistakes will be forgiven if you are sincere and honest. Your presence will be joyful and exuberant, as conveyed by the reflecting surface of the marsh or the full moon. Because the marsh will evaporate and the moon will wane, it is obvious that this situation is temporary. Enjoy the moment. Do not attract misfortune by tip-toeing through life or being too big for your britches. If you do, your environment will leap on you like a tiger and not rest until sharp claws have ripped your facade apart.

Heaven

Wind

Fire/Sun

Marsh/Moon

On the Road with Cheerful Courage
The frail beauty of the marsh or the moment of full moon, set against the overwhelming depth of the heavens, symbolizes an unflinching person striking out on unknown paths, without hiding anything. How you, too, can stride out boldly is explained here step by step.

(10)

A Mature Relationship
Do not be too focused on whether or not your mission will succeed. Informality and spontaneity often yield unexpected contacts.

44

Unanimous Purpose
Shine your inner light over your motives to feel whether you are free from fears and emotions that may influence your behavior.

13

The Management of the Inner Being
Concentrate on your breathing so that your heart beats calmly, and neither fear nor reckless thoughts can take hold.

37

Sincerity
If you are sincere, you will know that language is an inadequate tool for expressing your feelings. Use it carefully.

61

Duality
No situation is everlasting. With this in mind, you can freely determine your own time of coming and going.

38

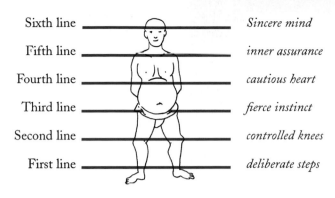

Sixth line ——— *Sincere mind*

Fifth line ——— *inner assurance*

Fourth line ——— *cautious heart*

Third line ——— *fierce instinct*

Second line ——— *controlled knees*

First line ——— *deliberate steps*

The Individual Lines

Sixth line
From the outer limits of the heavens you can review the experiences you have been through recently. If they have not left you with negative feelings or fears, you have been completely successful. On the other hand, if you have been left with a bad taste in your mouth, you know exactly what to do next time.

Fifth line
The heart of the heavens and the beginning of the wind indicate that you have put your head in the lion's mouth. You have not yet had time to process your first impressions, so you do not know exactly what to say or how to behave. Be spontaneous and open. Then there is no need to fear the consequences of your actions.

Fourth line
This line represents: the beginning of the heavens, or the threshold of the unknown; the core of the wind, or your consciousness; and the sun at its zenith, or the inner sincerity that radiates from your outer appearance. If you are consciously sincere, you will enter into new situations successfully. You will act with such subtlety that you will not wake a sleeping tiger even if you step on its tail.

Third line
Outward appearances prevail. You do not realize that the light reflected by the full moon derives from the sun. You proclaim your lies as Truth and pretend to understand the unknown before you have even experienced it. If you go on in this way your facade will be in tatters before you have even crossed the threshold.

Second line
Beneath the reflecting surface of the marsh, where the sunlight is vaguely visible, you are like the waxing moon. Deep meditation reveals that the road you will inevitably take is flat and easy. The only thing you have to do is follow the source of the light that appears.

First line
Deep beneath the surface of the marsh, or when the moon is dark, there is no question of you being called on to step into the unknown. Just stick to your daily routine and do not be tempted to embark prematurely on something that is quite unclear to you.

Introduction
The Lî hexagram suggests a stairway with a dangerous step (third line) which leads to the unknown (fifth line/the core of the heavens ☰). If you elevate external appearances ☰ to truths and deny your inner beauty ☱ along with the sincere thoughts ☲ associated with it, a deep fall is inevitable.

Strong and Weak Changing Lines
Extra attention should be paid to strong and weak lines in the hexagram you have thrown. A strong line signifies that you are addressing the situation with too much force, whereas a weak line calls for a bolder attitude.

The Hermetic *I Ching*
The answer to your specific question is not found only in the starting hexagram. For a deeper insight, you can also study the various separate hexagrams that make up the starting hexagram. The number next to these hexagrams indicates the page where you can find their complete interpretation. If the hexagram you have thrown contains changing lines, these direct you to a 'follow-up' hexagram.

Like life itself, the *I Ching* is a hermetic labyrinth of wonders from which you can only escape by closing the book.

The Follow-Up Hexagram
Once you have changed the strong and weak lines into their opposites, a new 'follow-up' hexagram is created which provides information about a future phase of life. The information on the left-hand page is the most useful for studying this hexagram, since follow-up hexagrams contain no changing lines.
The information on the right-hand page can, of course, be useful for clarifying your study of the follow-up hexagram.

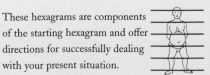
These hexagrams are components of the starting hexagram and offer directions for successfully dealing with your present situation.

The lines of the hexagram correspond to various parts of the body. The instructions you find there provide insight into your current physical and spiritual state.

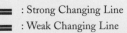 : Strong Changing Line

: Weak Changing Line

履 **10**

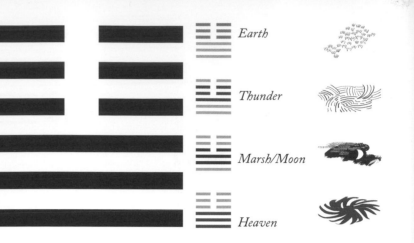

A man struggles to keep his head above water. —
His hands search desperately for something to hang on to. —

Running water. A river.

THÂI (Preparation)

The running water symbolizes time. The person desperately seeking to gain a hold over the flow of time represents the vain attempt to cling on to something that will disappear forever. The character Thâi shows that the unpredictable future will open for you if you are prepared to give up temporary things.

In the hexagram, the infinite depth of the heavens symbolizes the unfathomable future. The full moon, or the reflective surface of the marsh embedded in the heavens, symbolizes the fleeting beauty of a moment. The thunder rolling out of the heavens is like a heart whose every beat marks the passage of time. It is obvious that if you cling on to the moment, the natural rhythm of life will falter. The earth, which brings forth all things, bears the evidence of a productive attitude in the past. If nothing grows, this is a sign that you have wrestled with time in the past. The quality of the crop that does surface is a measure of how well-prepared you were for your task.

 Earth

 Thunder

 Marsh/Moon

 Heaven

Preparation
The number of strong lines in each hexagram progressively increases, from bottom to top. This construction points out the preparatory steps that can give you the strength and insight to face up to the mysterious future. (11)

Winter Solstice, Awakening
In order to realize a plan you first have to be sure of your ground (first line). 24

Attraction
Your knees (second line) give you the elasticity you need in order to adopt the right stance for a given situation. 19

Fertility
The most fruitful time for action is initially sensed intuitively (fourth line). As you dare to trust these feelings, they develop into an inner conviction. 54

Vital Energy
If you have to force yourself to achieve something, you are on the wrong track. True vital energy (third line), which is grafted onto the heavens, is characterized by a minimal waste of energy. 34

Fulfilment
The only thought that remains reflects the knowledge (fifth line) that you can enjoy the earthly game of past, present and future without losing yourself in transient illusions. 43

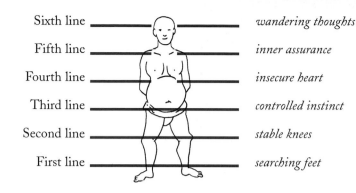

Sixth line ———————————— *wandering thoughts*

Fifth line ———————————— *inner assurance*

Fourth line ———————————— *insecure heart*

Third line ———————————— *controlled instinct*

Second line ———————————— *stable knees*

First line ———————————— *searching feet*

The Individual Lines

Sixth line

There is no sign of growth on the earth's surface. It would appear that you are trying to turn past illusions into reality. Rather than denying with all your might that you have failed, put your affairs in order, otherwise you will later regret having wasted even more time.

Fifth line

Beneath the surface of the earth, the thunder rumbles like an excitedly beating heart. You take the future in your own hands once you realize that the present continuously changes into the past and that a new moment dawns with each heartbeat.

Fourth line

Deep beneath the earth the thunder pounds like a heart excited by the full moon. You may become depressed if you linger in a situation that once moved you deeply. Find your vitality again and trust in your inner assurance, knowing that each moment is as transient as the meal you have just consumed.

Third line

Beneath the marsh or during the waxing of the moon, when life seems to proceed peacefully, the heavens relentlessly announce the future with the ominous sound of approaching thunder. You can enjoy life without worrying as long as you are aware that there is no serene moment that is not threatened by disturbance.

Second line

The dark moon, or the obscure bed of the marsh, which rests on the heart of the heavens, represents a moment when past, present, and future play no role. You are advised to float along on life's current and not to make any intractable decisions.

First line

At the outer limits of the heavens you are in a position to see the future. It is as if you pull out a blade of couch grass that turns out to be connected to an endless network of roots. No lovelier voyage of discovery is imaginable for the spirited person who does not shun adventure.

Introduction

The Thâi hexagram offers insight into the concepts past, present and future. With each heartbeat ☷, the future ☰ changes into the past. By anxiously clinging to the moment ☷ you linger in illusions and your potential capacities will never come to light ☷.

Strong and Weak Changing Lines

Extra attention should be paid to strong and weak lines in the hexagram you have thrown. A strong line signifies that you are addressing the situation with too much force, whereas a weak line calls for a bolder attitude.

The Hermetic *I Ching*

The answer to your specific question is not found only in the starting hexagram. For a deeper insight, you can also study the various separate hexagrams that make up the starting hexagram. The number next to these hexagrams indicates the page where you can find their complete interpretation. If the hexagram you have thrown contains changing lines, these direct you to a 'follow-up' hexagram.

Like life itself, the *I Ching* is a hermetic labyrinth of wonders from which you can only escape by closing the book.

The Follow-Up Hexagram

Once you have changed the strong and weak lines into their opposites, a new 'follow-up' hexagram is created which provides information about a future phase of life. The information on the left-hand page is the most useful for studying this hexagram, since follow-up hexagrams contain no changing lines.
The information on the right-hand page can, of course, be useful for clarifying your study of the follow-up hexagram.

} These hexagrams are components of the starting hexagram and offer directions for successfully dealing with your present situation.

The lines of the hexagram correspond to various parts of the body. The instructions you find there provide insight into your current physical and spiritual state.

━●━ : Strong Changing Line
━x━ : Weak Changing Line

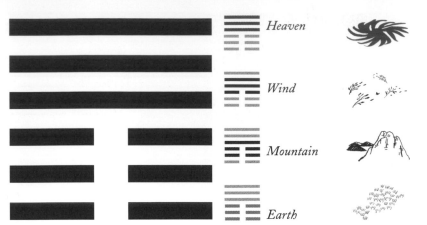

Heaven

Wind

Mountain

Earth

A bird flies straight to heaven. ——
A mouth —— 否

PHÎ (Inner Calm)

The character Phi represents a mouth saying no. This is not a matter of denial or blunt refusal, but of mental abstraction. The bird flying to the heavens is your consciousness that withdraws during sleep.

In this hexagram the earth looks deserted. There is no activity at all: no sun, no moon, no rain, no thunder. The mountain reaching up into the heavens radiates a profound sense of peace. The only sign of life is the wind, or your breathing, which blows from the unfathomable depths of the heavens where the secret of life is hidden. As long as you are conscious of your breathing, your thoughts are restless. Before sleep overcomes you, you are assailed by a whole range of questions and possible answers about your adventures. You would be wise to process them, so that in the next phase you can open yourself as much as possible to the future, unrestricted by experiences that would fix your mind on the past.

Inner Calm
The number of strong lines progressively decreases in each hexagram, from bottom to top. The gradual transition to weak lines points to the progressive development of an attitude that enables you to sleep such a refreshing sleep that you wake as if reborn.

(12)

A Mature Relationship
As long as you are not too attached to earthly things, you can nimbly disentangle yourself (first line) from them.

44

Withdrawal
Your knees (second line) provide you with the agility to turn away from any tense situation.

33

The Blessed Marriage
If you live light-heartedly (fourth line) you only take action when you have the inner assurance that it is time to act, and you withdraw on the same condition.

53

Observation, Contemplation
Your fierce instinct (third line) comes to rest if you can focus your attention completely on your breathing. Once your horizons are no longer obscured by the veils of emotion and sentiment, you will see that the naked truth is less complicated then you ever could have thought.

20

The Destruction of the Past
Now that all your bodily functions are relaxed, you lose the conscious hold over your inner surety (fifth line) and so slip into a deep sleep. Freed from intrusive thoughts, your body can now recuperate in a natural way.

23

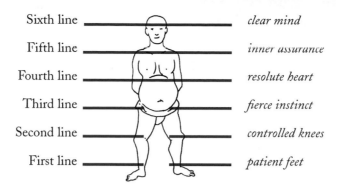

The Individual Lines

Sixth line — *clear mind*
Fifth line — *inner assurance*
Fourth line — *resolute heart*
Third line — *fierce instinct*
Second line — *controlled knees*
First line — *patient feet*

Sixth line
The outer limit of the heavens indicates a profound sleep. If you have followed and understood the play of forces in the hexagram, you will rise completely refreshed.

Fifth line
This line is the heart of the heavens, from which all creativity arises, and also the beginning of the wind or the back of your mind where an endless network of existential questions is lurking. If you enter this labyrinth you will lose your way. You are advised to concentrate purely on your breathing and not admit a single thought, so that you can fall into a profound sleep.

Fourth line
The core of the wind, or the rhythm of breathing in and out, and the mountain top reaching up into the heavens, suggest the twilight state between consciousness and sleep. You can enter this state of being by deliberately reducing your breathing to its natural rhythm during sleep. No superficial thought can disturb you if you concentrate completely.

Third line
The earth stretching before you below the top of the mountain, and the end of the wind or the moment of breathing in, evoke the idea that you are staring into the grave of your past and recalling unprocessed emotions. Realize that what is done cannot be undone. Only striving for inner peace offers a way out.

Second line
At the foot of the mountain which is hidden beneath the earth, you face a choice: you can either examine your past or withdraw to the peace of the mountain top. Decide what will be best for you on the basis of your physical condition.

First line
Deep beneath the earth, you can summon the past by imagining that the first thought that crosses your mind is a blade of couch grass which, if followed, will turn out to be connected to an endless network of roots. If you strive for inner peace, this is the moment for a thorough spring-cleaning of your inner self.

Introduction
In the Phi hexagram, the past is represented by the deserted earth ☷. The mountain ☶ indicates that it is time to withdraw into a period of profound rest. The wind ☴ embedded in the infinite depths of the heavens ☰, symbolizes the endless flow of pointless thoughts about past, present and future that confront you before you fall asleep.

Strong and Weak Changing Lines
Extra attention should be paid to strong and weak lines in the hexagram you have thrown. A strong line signifies that you are addressing the situation with too much force, whereas a weak line calls for a bolder attitude.

The Hermetic *I Ching*
The answer to your specific question is not found only in the starting hexagram. For a deeper insight, you can also study the various separate hexagrams that make up the starting hexagram. The number next to these hexagrams indicates the page where you can find their complete interpretation. If the hexagram you have thrown contains changing lines, these direct you to a 'follow-up' hexagram.

Like life itself, the *I Ching* is a hermetic labyrinth of wonders from which you can only escape by closing the book.

The Follow-Up Hexagram
Once you have changed the strong and weak lines into their opposites, a new 'follow-up' hexagram is created which provides information about a future phase of life. The information on the left-hand page is the most useful for studying this hexagram, since follow-up hexagrams contain no changing lines.
The information on the right-hand page can, of course, be useful for clarifying your study of the follow-up hexagram.

} These hexagrams are components of the starting hexagram and offer directions for successfully dealing with your present situation.

The lines of the hexagram correspond to various parts of the body. The instructions you find there provide insight into your current physical and spiritual state.

‑‑‑ : Strong Changing Line
‑‑x‑‑ : Weak Changing Line

A lid that perfectly fits the mouth of a pot ——

A person's legs. Standing erect or with a straight back ——

同人

THUNG ZÂN (Unanimous Purpose)

The characters Thung and Zân point to a human being's innate need to search for spiritual guidance in order to find the answers to existential questions. These answers provide a spiritual shelter that enables one to energetically get on with life.

The lid symbolizes the heavens. The hexagram contains two heavens. The upper heaven is the infinite, true heaven which harbors the secret of life. The lower one represents a limited, mythical universe created by human imaginings. The wind, or realm of thought, which is grafted onto the true heaven and blows through the lower heaven, evokes the idea of covering up your innate, inner emptiness by adopting a faith that bestows meaning to your existence. If you recognize that the lower heaven is a product of the human mind and turn your attention to the true heavens, the prevailing belief system will see you as an apostate. Your inner fire was initially fanned by the wind representing the stream of mythical thoughts, but is now fueled by the wind descending from the true heavens in the form of pure awareness. This provides you with the sort of flexible life rhythm that was always meant to be.

Heaven

Heaven

Wind

Fire

Unanimous Purpose
If you follow the instructions *(reading from bottom to top)*, you will be aware of the possibility of losing yourself momentarily in the all-embracing potential of the cosmos. If you have come this far on your lonely path which requires you to shake off the mythical universe, you will see that you are not alone at all. This purpose is ultimately shared by all humans.

(13)

Creative Energy
There are no words sufficient for describing the universe, but you might experience something of this immense ocean of creative energy by allowing your consciousness to dissolve into it completely.

1

A Mature Relationship
This sign appears twice, which underlines that you should not adhere too strongly to any theories concerning material forms. Once you can easily let go of material things, you are open to the unknown.

44

Unanimous Purpose
Who am I, where do I come from, where am I going? For millennia, human beings have turned to the infinite depths of the heavens with such questions, and thought up answers that ease their fears and give meaning to their lives. Since no answer has ever been shown to be the Truth, every individual is free to look for a way of filling in his or her own existence.

(13)

The Management of the Inner Being
Attune your breathing to the intense peace radiated by the heavens. Do not let your inner fire be fanned or damped down by fear of the unknown, the promise of a paradise, or the dire vision of a hell.

37

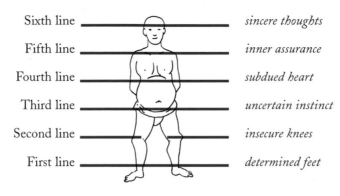

Sixth line ———— *sincere thoughts*

Fifth line ———— *inner assurance*

Fourth line ———— *subdued heart*

Third line ———— *uncertain instinct*

Second line ———— *insecure knees*

First line ———— *determined feet*

The Individual Lines

Sixth line

This uppermost line of the true heavens is not influenced by the mythical universe. Liberated from all belief systems, you stand on the shore of an infinite ocean of creative energy and feel free to reunite your consciousness with it.

Fifth line

The heart of the true heavens is overshadowed by the uppermost line of the mythical universe. Trust in your profound inner conviction that you need have no fear of danger. This calls for courage and will cause you pain, but it will enable you to let go of the myth that has obscured your vision. You can confront the unknown with a smile.

Fourth line

The beginning of the true heavens lies deeply hidden beneath the heart of the mythical universe. The wind that rises here is like the dim notion of a concealed truth. This shakes your belief in the myth to which you have adhered. It is not yet time to free yourself from it completely. First try to bring that dim awareness to consciousness.

Third line

Your stream of thoughts, or the core of the wind, which is grafted onto the true heavens or your subconscious, has lost its initial purity under the influence of the mythical universe. In uncertainty, your inner fire dims and flares alternately. Adopt the steady breathing that is based on the deep composure of the true heavens.

Second line

Your inner fire is kept alight by the wind, or your stream of thoughts which fill you with faith in a mythical universe. You think yourself safe amongst fellow believers, while deep in your heart you know that you are actually bowed down by fear of the unknown.

First line

The fire rises up. If this truth has penetrated to the depths of your soul, you are sure enough of your ground to penetrate the veils of the mythical universe and confront the unfathomable depths of the true heavens.

Introduction

The second line is the crux of the Thung Zân hexagram. It represents your knees, which literally and figuratively enable you to bow to the pantheon of the mythical universe or to get up and stand erect so that you can look into the overwhelming depths of the true heavens.

Strong and Weak Changing Lines

Extra attention should be paid to strong and weak lines in the hexagram you have thrown. A strong line signifies that you are addressing the situation with too much force, whereas a weak line calls for a bolder attitude.

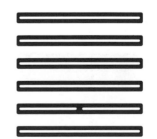

The Hermetic *I Ching*

The answer to your specific question is not found only in the starting hexagram. For a deeper insight, you can also study the various separate hexagrams that make up the starting hexagram. The number next to these hexagrams indicates the page where you can find their complete interpretation. If the hexagram you have thrown contains changing lines, these direct you to a 'follow-up' hexagram.

Like life itself, the *I Ching* is a hermetic labyrinth of wonders from which you can only escape by closing the book.

The Follow-Up Hexagram

Once you have changed the strong and weak lines into their opposites, a new 'follow-up' hexagram is created which provides information about a future phase of life. The information on the left-hand page is the most useful for studying this hexagram, since follow-up hexagrams contain no changing lines.
The information on the right-hand page can, of course, be useful for clarifying your study of the follow-up hexagram.

} These hexagrams are components of the starting hexagram and offer directions for successfully dealing with your present situation.

The lines of the hexagram correspond to various parts of the body. The instructions you find there provide insight into your current physical and spiritual state.

—o— : Strong Changing Line
—x— : Weak Changing Line

同人 13

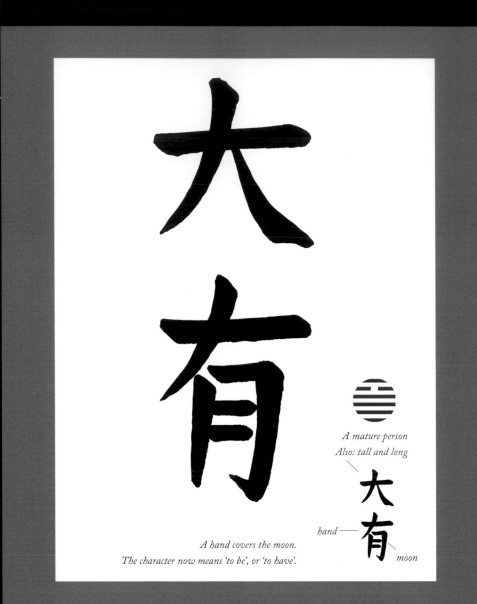

A mature person
Also: tall and long

hand — 大有 — moon

A hand covers the moon.
The character now means 'to be', or 'to have'.

TÂ YÛ (Profound Insight, Great Possession)

The characters Tâ and Yû portray a mature person who rightly estimates the value of earthly enticements. The hand covering the moon indicates that one's vision is no longer troubled by deceptive appearances and that the essence of life has been discovered.

In the hexagram, the ever-shining sun is comparable with a mature way of thinking. The sun is high above the marsh/moon and the two heavens. The upper heaven, with which the illusory moonlight is mostly associated, represents the clear blue dome of the sky, or the earth's atmosphere which encircles material reality. Frightened by the thought of confronting the infinite depths of the lower, true heaven, the immature person clings on desperately to material things. Thus, earthly semblance is elevated to heavenly reality, and material goods and pleasures are given an almost divine value. If you are a mature person, you can enjoy the earthly game in a natural and unforced way because you need no smoke screen to hide you from the infinite depths of the universe.

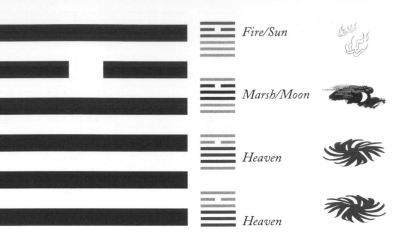

Fire/Sun

Marsh/Moon

Heaven

Heaven

 Profound Insight, Great Possession
The construction of the hexagram indicates that semblance and reality merge. Profound insight into the workings of this duality is required if you are to unite opposites and stop yourself being blinded by one side or the other. The following steps can bring this great possession within reach. (14)

 Duality
As long as you live, you are subject to the workings of duality. Somewhere, deep inside, you know you are connected with the unity from which every opposite arises. Hold on to that awareness and do not think your inner assurance is lost forever if you do not feel it for the moment. 38

 Profound Insight, Great Possession
Love demonstrates that opposites can be united, whereas fear and grief pushes them further apart. Deep insight grows out of the knowledge that while duality presents itself to you through your external environment, it in fact lies hidden within your internal experience. (14)

 Fulfilment
This direction appears twice, warning you to be on the alert constantly for the seductiveness of material gain. Then there is little chance of you becoming entangled in the game of illusions that is played on earth. 43

 Creative Energy
Once you see duality for what it is, you can experience something of the indescribable ocean of creative energy by allowing your consciousness to dissolve into this energy completely. Then, having reclaimed your conscious hold over yourself, you will know how to enjoy the creation of which you are part. 1

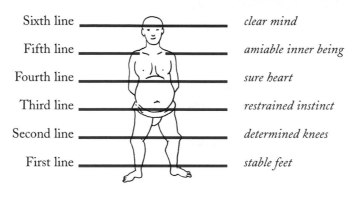

Sixth line _____ *clear mind*

Fifth line _____ *amiable inner being*

Fourth line _____ *sure heart*

Third line _____ *restrained instinct*

Second line _____ *determined knees*

First line _____ *stable feet*

The Individual Lines

Sixth line
The uppermost line of the sun which floats above the hexagram like a loose lid, implies that you are ready to allow your consciousness to become one with the heavenly ocean of creative energy. The insights you will acquire in this way will enable you to freely and happily enjoy the creation of which you are part.

Fifth line
The core of the sun and the reflective surface of the full moon suggest a period in which you can give and take with complete sincerity. Make sure that you can count on the qualities represented by the strong lines. You will then radiate a majestic power that will ensure you are treated respectfully.

Fourth line
The sun is high in the heavenly dome, or the earth's atmosphere encircling material reality, and its influence on the reflective surface of the moon declines. This symbolic representation of the waning moon points out that you are not in a position, at this time, to share your rich store of insights.

Third line
In the centre of the heavenly dome is the earthly reality, from where you turn your attention to the heavens. Be as open as the black moon, which wants to receive and bestow everlasting sunlight. Once you perceive the duality of earthly life you can establish within yourself the unity you crave.

Second line
From the heart of the true heavens, you can see the heavenly dome that encircles material reality, and see the earth moving in her orbit like a heavily laden wagon. Now that the influences of sun and moon are laid out before you, you realize how you can enjoy earthly matter without becoming caught up in it.

First line
Meditation and sleep can temporarily take you to the shore of the endless ocean of creative energy, and so give the illusion that you have escaped material reality. Keep in mind that you cannot escape duality as long as you live, so you had better investigate and understand its workings.

Introduction
In the Tâ Yû hexagram, the sun ☲ indicates unity or the principle of pure giving. The reflection of the marsh/moon ☱ symbolizes a duality of giving and receiving.
You also possess these qualities.
Do not rank one higher than the other if you want to live in harmony with the heavenly will ☰.

Strong and Weak Changing Lines
Extra attention should be paid to strong and weak lines in the hexagram you have thrown. A strong line signifies that you are addressing the situation with too much force, whereas a weak line calls for a bolder attitude.

The Hermetic *I Ching*
The answer to your specific question is not found only in the starting hexagram. For a deeper insight, you can also study the various separate hexagrams that make up the starting hexagram. The number next to these hexagrams indicates the page where you can find their complete interpretation. If the hexagram you have thrown contains changing lines, these direct you to a 'follow-up' hexagram.

Like life itself, the *I Ching* is a hermetic labyrinth of wonders from which you can only escape by closing the book.

The Follow-Up Hexagram
Once you have changed the strong and weak lines into their opposites, a new 'follow-up' hexagram is created which provides information about a future phase of life. The information on the left-hand page is the most useful for studying this hexagram, since follow-up hexagrams contain no changing lines.
The information on the right-hand page can, of course, be useful for clarifying your study of the follow-up hexagram.

} These hexagrams are components of the starting hexagram and offer directions for successfully dealing with your present situation.

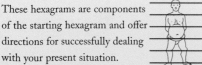

The lines of the hexagram correspond to various parts of the body. The instructions you find there provide insight into your current physical and spiritual state.

━●━ : Strong Changing Line
━x━ : Weak Changing Line

大有 **I4**

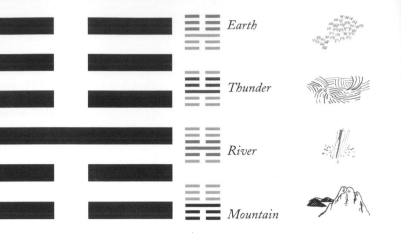

		Earth
		Thunder
		River
		Mountain

grain

A hand binds the grain in sheaves.

To form a unity

hand

Words flow unreservedly from the mouth.

KHIEN (Modesty)

The structure of the character Khien suggests a sincere person whose unassuming behaviour leads to victory. To achieve his goal, he hides amongst the common people like a cornstalk in a sheaf. By speaking the language of the heart, he forges sympathizers into an invincible army.

The position of the mountain beneath the earth in the hexagram underlines the value of this approach. This underground rock symbolizes a person you can bank on. He is wise, as attested to by the freshwater stored on top of the mountain like a subterranean lake of fertile knowledge, but he does not show off this wisdom. The thunder rolling upwards from the peak symbolizes his voice expressing sincere insights. Out of survival instinct, the speaker keeps his voice low, but it is nonetheless stirring. His wisdom wells up like crystal-clear, refreshing water from an underground spring. By contrast, the earth looks desolate: there is no wind, no heaven, no sun and no moon. The core hexagrams indicate the ousting of a repressive regime through a secretly prepared uprising.

Modesty
You, too, are part of a whole and must therefore contribute to the well-being of those around you, even if this means hiding your true character for a time. The following directions *(reading from bottom to top)* lead you out of darkness into light. **(15)**

Winter Solstice, Awakening
The turning point is in sight: light will conquer darkness. But there is still much work to be done before the situation is normalized. Do not be carried away by the first flush of victory. Behave as humanely as you did when you started out on this endeavour. **24**

The Army
A good general stays amidst his troops and sets an example for them. Keep an overview, base your strategy on the common good, and do not allow yourself to be carried away by pride, anger, or other emotions. **7**

Cutting the Knot
The time for action has dawned. Any hesitation now means losing the advantage of a surprise attack. No one comes out of a fight unscathed — but this is something you should think about before you strike. **40**

Repression
If you are under the influence of a totalitarian regime, the best strategy is to lie low. Trim your sails to the wind, stay on the alert, and wait calmly for the right moment to strike. **62**

Initial Difficulty
The rainwater forms a lake on the top of the mountain. Just as water is forced by gravity to find its way downwards, you will inevitably have to impart your knowledge to others. It is up to you to carefully determine the best moment and the right pace for doing so. **39**

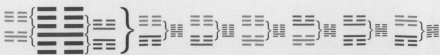

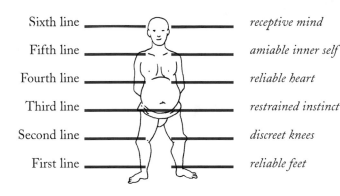

Sixth line ———————— *receptive mind*

Fifth line ———————— *amiable inner self*

Fourth line ———————— *reliable heart*

Third line ———————— *restrained instinct*

Second line ———————— *discreet knees*

First line ———————— *reliable feet*

The Individual Lines

Sixth line
This line is the surface of the earth, where the battle will be fought. If you have followed the path of discretion so far, you can now go on the attack. Realize that you only need to restore the peace in your environment. Do not pursue the enemy into his own territory.

Fifth line
Hidden beneath the earth, you express your insights frankly but as discreetly as the rippling thunder. Do not boast about possessions or status. Only through modesty and wisdom will you win the support of others. After that, you can decide when it is time to take up your weapons.

Fourth line
Hidden deep beneath the earth, you realize that victory is only possible if you keep your fears and feelings under control. If your heart is inundated with emotions and makes a thunderous din as it pounds in your chest, your clear insights will degenerate into muddled yells that scare people away.

Third line
Here is the point of equilibrium, where your survival instinct radiates all the calm of a steadfast rock and your heart beats steadily with the restrained power of the thunder rumbling in the distance. You can now offer your insights in a way that is both modest and convincing, and your battle will become a true victory march.

Second line
Under the top of the mountain, you are so deeply sunk in thought that it is as if you are trying to force your way to the very bottom of your swirling lake of knowledge. Gradually, it begins to dawn on you that the only way to fight this battle is with inner peace and discretion.

First line
At the foot of the mountain you are aware that only great discretion can lift you out of this abyss. With this knowledge engraved on your soul, you can look forward to a great victory.

Introduction
In the Khien hexagram, the third line — or your survival instinct — is the axis on which everything turns in a perilous situation. Like the rock ⚏ hidden under the earth ☷, lie low and be inconspicuous. You can win supporters by carefully distributing your insights ☵, tempered by the honest power of the thunder ☳.

Strong and Weak Changing Lines
Extra attention should be paid to strong and weak lines in the hexagram you have thrown. A strong line signifies that you are addressing the situation with too much force, whereas a weak line calls for a bolder attitude.

The Hermetic *I Ching*
The answer to your specific question is not found only in the starting hexagram. For a deeper insight, you can also study the various separate hexagrams that make up the starting hexagram. The number next to these hexagrams indicates the page where you can find their complete interpretation. If the hexagram you have thrown contains changing lines, these direct you to a 'follow-up' hexagram.

Like life itself, the *I Ching* is a hermetic labyrinth of wonders from which you can only escape by closing the book.

The Follow-Up Hexagram
Once you have changed the strong and weak lines into their opposites, a new 'follow-up' hexagram is created which provides information about a future phase of life. The information on the left-hand page is the most useful for studying this hexagram, since follow-up hexagrams contain no changing lines.
The information on the right-hand page can, of course, be useful for clarifying your study of the follow-up hexagram.

} These hexagrams are components of the starting hexagram and offer directions for successfully dealing with your present situation.

The lines of the hexagram correspond to various parts of the body. The instructions you find there provide insight into your current physical and spiritual state.

⚊⊙⚊ : Strong Changing Line
⚋⚋ : Weak Changing Line

謙  **15**

A palm receiving and a palm giving;
Thus, to hand on, or to pass something from hand to hand.
Also; to give and to take, and I or we

 豫

The elephant, symbol of equilibrium and power

YÛ (Balanced Motion)

The components of the character Yû indicate a cogent and level-headed leader who invests others with authority.

In the hexagram, the mountain rising up out of the earth is a focus of power and stability. It symbolizes the leader. The thunder suggests his/her voice, which speaks from a sincere heart and distributes the wisdom that is stored on the top of the mountain as a lake of fertile knowledge. Despite the presence of the enduring mountain, there is a desolate look to the earth because of the absence of wind, heaven, sun and moon. Coming after hexagram 15, Yû suggests a period of reconstruction after a successful revolt against a repressive regime. The core hexagrams reinforce this. Clearly, after the intoxication of victory, you will need much diplomacy and insight to carry out the work of restoration. Before you know it, you could be seen as a dictator as well. History demonstrates that everything is subject to change, so even your good intentions can fall apart. Nevertheless you must get to work. After all: nothing ventured, nothing gained.

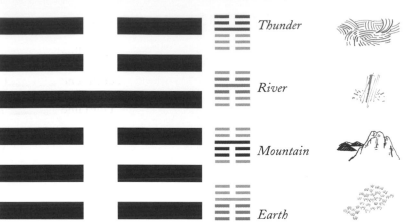

Thunder
River
Mountain
Earth

Balanced Motion
Balanced motion is characteristic of the rhythm of the universe. Everything stays in balance through a play of attraction and rejection, or giving and taking. A force that rigidly keeps to itself sooner or later collapses. This truth is laid out *from bottom to top* for your contemplation.

 (16)

Cutting the Knot
Once you realize that fate will catch up with you whether or not you try to keep everything in hand, you will take the plunge and appoint assistants who disseminate your policy far and wide. Of course, there is a risk that this will lead to misinterpretations, which may have repercussions in the future.

 40

Repression
If you appoint assistants, you run the risk that one or more of them will turn against you sooner or later, and start a sordid battle for power. History confirms this.

 62

Initial Difficulty
Those close to the lake of fertile knowledge drink in its insights directly. The farther away the message flows, the more confused it becomes. It would seem sensible to appoint trustworthy assistants who will convey your insights literally.

 39

Union
Now that all have turned expectantly to the future and are buckling down together to the task of reconstruction, new policy plans should be drawn up.

8

The Destruction of the Past
After a victory, it is advisable to remove all traces of the former regime so that reconstruction can be started with new zest.

 23

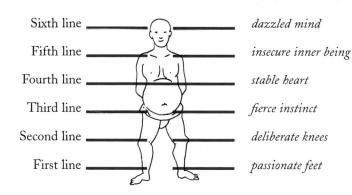

Sixth line — *dazzled mind*

Fifth line — *insecure inner being*

Fourth line — *stable heart*

Third line — *fierce instinct*

Second line — *deliberate knees*

First line — *passionate feet*

The Individual Lines

Sixth line
The uppermost line of the thunder evokes the idea of letting your heart speak and your mind trust that your words will be balm to others' souls forever. Keep in mind that those who are content with you now can later turn against you, for dozens of reasons.

Fifth line
The core of the thunder and the surface of the lake of fertile knowledge indicate that you want to give, but you cannot find any adequate words to express what you want to say from the bottom of your heart. The knowledge that others will project their own thoughts onto you if you keep silent may help you to overcome this eternal obstacle.

Fourth line
Here is the center of equilibrium, where your vital force evokes the calm of the enduring mountain and your heart beats steadily with the restrained power of the thunder rumbling in the distance. You are ready to entrust others with your insights in order to spread them further afield.

Third line
From the earth's surface, you have one ear cocked to the wise words issuing from the depths of the lake on the mountain top and calling for reconstruction. But you are still so caught up in the flush of victory that you grasp only half of the knowledge received. As a result, there is a real chance of misunderstandings.

Second line
Beneath the earth, at the foot of the mountain, you are already looking expectantly towards the future even though all around you the victory celebrations are in full swing. With the mountain as your guide, you are as stable as a rock. You avoid the intoxication of victory and shrug off the burden of the past.

First line
Deep beneath the earth, you are so caught up in the intoxication of victory that you fail to see you are still wrestling with the roots of the past. You would be better off sobering up, freeing yourself from the past, and turning your attention to the future.

Introduction
The fourth line, or your vital force, is the heart of the Yû hexagram. The calm of the mountain ☶ ensures you of inner power, so that you bestow your gifts of knowledge with a steadily beating heart ☳. You spread your insights over the earth ☷ via the river ☵, hoping that they will still be as clear at the river's mouth as they were at the source.

Strong and Weak Changing Lines
Extra attention should be paid to strong and weak lines in the hexagram you have thrown. A strong line signifies that you are addressing the situation with too much force, whereas a weak line calls for a bolder attitude.

The Hermetic *I Ching*
The answer to your specific question is not found only in the starting hexagram. For a deeper insight, you can also study the various separate hexagrams that make up the starting hexagram. The number next to these hexagrams indicates the page where you can find their complete interpretation. If the hexagram you have thrown contains changing lines, these direct you to a 'follow-up' hexagram.

Like life itself, the *I Ching* is a hermetic labyrinth of wonders from which you can only escape by closing the book.

The Follow-Up Hexagram
Once you have changed the strong and weak lines into their opposites, a new 'follow-up' hexagram is created which provides information about a future phase of life. The information on the left-hand page is the most useful for studying this hexagram, since follow-up hexagrams contain no changing lines.
The information on the right-hand page can, of course, be useful for clarifying your study of the follow-up hexagram.

}

These hexagrams are components of the starting hexagram and offer directions for successfully dealing with your present situation.

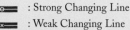

The lines of the hexagram correspond to various parts of the body. The instructions you find there provide insight into your current physical and spiritual state.

──o── : Strong Changing Line
──x── : Weak Changing Line

豫 **16**

The left hand offers assistance to the
skilful right (and righteous) hand
Sloping terrain that is easily accessible

隨

Walking step by step
Strips of dried meat hanging in a bundle

SUI (Cheerful and Willing)

The common translation of the character Sui is 'to follow'. The composition of the character points to another, deeper meaning: a skillful and approachable person who calmly reaches out a helping hand and thus wins the hearts of followers.

In the hexagram, the mountain is the symbol of a stable person. The marsh/moon on the top of the mountain indicates the quality of affectionate and timely giving and receiving. The wind blowing down the mountain from the marsh represents breathing in and breathing out—opposites that are fundamental to the duality of earthly life. While breathing in, the wise person looks at and listens to the needs of others. While breathing out, he or she speaks friendly words that remove uncertainties and bring prosperity. The thunder rolling up towards the top of the mountain suggests followers who open their hearts to this accessible source of affectionate helpfulness.

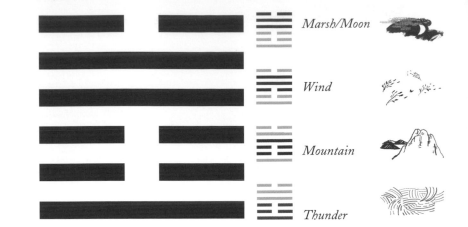

Marsh/Moon

Wind

Mountain

Thunder

Cheerful and Willing

If you radiate stable calm and friendliness, others will listen to your ideas with pleasure, and cheerfully and willingly put them into practice. The following pointers can show you the way to develop these qualities.

(17)

Vigorous Mind

Willpower and inner assurance are necessary for giving and taking in a bold but affectionate way.

28

The Game of Love

The dignified demeanor of the stable mountain is your reference point. If you are in doubt, or do not know the correct answer, admit that openly.
Any lie will breach the rock-solid trust that others place in you.

31

The Blessed Marriage

Keep listening and looking carefully. Then, on the basis of your observations, determine when it is time to speak and when it is time to be silent.

53

Increase

If you see goodness you stimulate it, and if you see deviancy you withdraw. Remain calm and dignified, because only friendliness can promote joy in the hearts of others and the stability of a fertile union.

42

Nourishment

The right spiritual nourishment is the basis for ensuring physical nourishment.

27

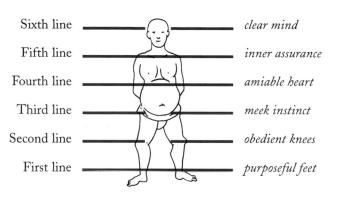

Sixth line ——————— *clear mind*

Fifth line ——————— *inner assurance*

Fourth line ——————— *amiable heart*

Third line ——————— *meek instinct*

Second line ——————— *obedient knees*

First line ——————— *purposeful feet*

The Individual Lines

Sixth line

The reflective surface of the marsh or the full moon evokes the idea of sincere and affectionate giving and receiving. The marsh will evaporate and the moon will wane. Therefore, lock this sincere attitude into your heart so that you are not dependent on the moment to supply the nourishment that is needed.

Fifth line

The wind rises beneath the reflective surface of the marsh/moon. You are able to see past the outward display of the moon. Once you have learned her secret, you can give and receive with a breath that is as regular and joyful as her unfaltering cycle.

Fourth line

The stable mountain is crowned with the bottom of the marsh or the dark moon, and the middle of the wind or the moment between breathing in and breathing out. Followers look up to you, but you have nothing to say. Do not pretend otherwise.

Third line

Below the top of the mountain, wind and thunder meet. You have the wisdom and love of life required to give and to receive with the ease and regularity of calm breathing, which makes for a satisfied heart.

Second line

The core of the thunder rumbles at the foot of the mountain. You are opening your heart to someone who does not have the right qualities. To find one who does, you will have to learn to see further than the end of your nose.

First line

The beginning of the thunder, or the lower jaw absentmindedly meeting the upper jaw (fourth line) which has nothing to report, are signs that you are not being fed. It is time to take the initiative and turn to someone who listens to your needs and offers nourishing food.

Introduction

The Sui hexagram is dominated by the interaction between *Vigorous Mind (28)* and *Nourishment (27)*.

This nourishment may refer to followers or to your own body; either way, it is always the purity with which you receive and give that determines the productivity of the whole.

Strong and Weak Changing Lines

Extra attention should be paid to strong and weak lines in the hexagram you have thrown. A strong line signifies that you are addressing the situation with too much force, whereas a weak line calls for a bolder attitude.

The Hermetic *I Ching*

The answer to your specific question is not found only in the starting hexagram. For a deeper insight, you can also study the various separate hexagrams that make up the starting hexagram. The number next to these hexagrams indicates the page where you can find their complete interpretation. If the hexagram you have thrown contains changing lines, these direct you to a 'follow-up' hexagram.

Like life itself, the *I Ching* is a hermetic labyrinth of wonders from which you can only escape by closing the book.

The Follow-Up Hexagram

Once you have changed the strong and weak lines into their opposites, a new 'follow-up' hexagram is created which provides information about a future phase of life. The information on the left-hand page is the most useful for studying this hexagram, since follow-up hexagrams contain no changing lines.

The information on the right-hand page can, of course, be useful for clarifying your study of the follow-up hexagram.

} These hexagrams are components of the starting hexagram and offer directions for successfully dealing with your present situation.

 The lines of the hexagram correspond to various parts of the body. The instructions you find there provide insight into your current physical and spiritual state.

 : Strong Changing Line

: Weak Changing Line

隨 **17**

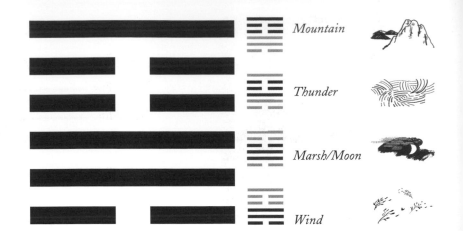

	Mountain
	Thunder
	Marsh/Moon
	Wind

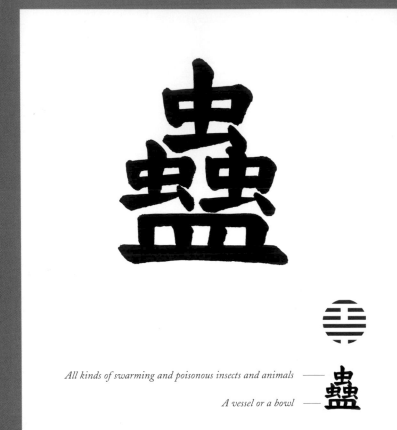

All kinds of swarming and poisonous insects and animals — 蠱

A vessel or a bowl — 蠱

KÛ

(Putting an End to Compulsive Behavior)

The character Kû refers to a vessel filled with rainwater which is collected from a loam or straw roof swarming with vermin. Hence the meaning: insidious poisoning caused by using unpurified water.

In the hexagram, the top of the mountain symbolizes a wise person who, standing on the roof of the world, turns his eyes to heaven and feels free from everyday, material worries. The marsh/moon at the foot of the mountain is like the vessel with stagnant water or knowledge that is corrupted, either deliberately or not, in the telling. The thunder rolling out of the marsh towards the mountain top suggests the desperately pounding heart of someone who is being sucked down by the mud and is open to wise advice that would free him. The wind, or breathing, lies under the marsh and causes an irregular heartbeat. This arrhythmia is inevitable, for the person is struggling to breathe in the foul air beneath the marsh, or under the roof of his house. The rotting ideas and ideals propagated in this house are compulsively absorbed on breathing in and pronounced on breathing out.

 Putting an End to Compulsive Behavior
Generally, compulsive behaviour creeps into your innocent soul as a child as a result of the way you are brought up, and can only be broken down again later in life. The following directions *(reading from bottom to top)* may help you to counteract this poison. (18)

Nourishment
Do not let your lower jaw hang slackly; swallow your past or spit it out, and take in the new spiritual food that your clear mind is offering. 27

 Relaxation
What is new about your situation now is that you can relax your inner being in the knowledge that you are guarded by the stable mountain, or your clear mind which calls you to order as soon as the past starts gnawing at you. 41

Fertility
Observe the movement of the moon, which waxes and wanes, and realize that letting go of the old and grasping the new is typical of earthly life. 54

Continuity, Balanced Movement
Do not allow your thoughts to dwell on affairs that tear you apart inside. Counteract the poison by breathing evenly, which will make your heart beat regularly and clear your mind. 32

 Vigorous Mind
By trusting your survival instinct and adopting an uncompromising stance, you can avoid giving way to pity for those you are leaving behind in order to be free. 28

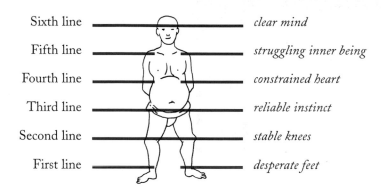

The Individual Lines

Sixth line — clear mind
Fifth line — struggling inner being
Fourth line — constrained heart
Third line — reliable instinct
Second line — stable knees
First line — desperate feet

Sixth line

The top of the mountain suggests that you have an overview of the petty worries that became part of you in your youth. If your only truth is the infinite depth of the heavens, from which all creative energy derives, you will no longer bow down to distorted 'truths'.

Fifth line

The thunder turns to the mountain top for assistance, like your heart that is open to the wise advice of someone who has gone before you on this path. This is a commendable way of putting an end to the compulsive behavior that served as your example in your parental home.

Fourth line

At the foot of the mountain, the thunder disturbs the surface of the marsh by swirling up all sorts of debris. Your heart is still filled with accusations against your paternal home. If you do not let go of them, you will not be open to wise advice.

Third line

Beneath the surface of the marsh, you rediscover the memory of your first heartbeat (the start of the thunder) and your first breath (the beginning of the wind) and once again become aware of your survival instinct. By breathing as peacefully as a baby, you can slowly but surely regain the feeling that you are virgin soil in which anything you desire can grow.

Second line

At the bottom of the marsh and in the middle of the wind (or at the point of either swallowing or suffocating), the thought that flashes through your mind is that you cannot sink any deeper. Straighten your back and throw off the obsequious attitude you adopted when attached to the yoke of your parental home.

First line

The end of the wind symbolizes breathing out. This is the moment to say what you think of your upbringing. By revealing your dissatisfaction you may open the eyes of those who raised you. And even if this does not happen, you will at least dispel forever your own idea that you are a docile lamb they can burden with their inadequacies.

Introduction

The Kû hexagram is determined by *Nourishment (27)* and *Vigorous Mind (28)*. Only by letting your survival instinct (third line) prevail and adopting an uncompromising stance (second line) can you escape the compulsions that have come with your upbringing and take in spiritual food that is truly nourishing.

Strong and Weak Changing Lines

Extra attention should be paid to strong and weak lines in the hexagram you have thrown. A strong line signifies that you are addressing the situation with too much force, whereas a weak line calls for a bolder attitude.

The Hermetic *I Ching*

The answer to your specific question is not found only in the starting hexagram. For a deeper insight, you can also study the various separate hexagrams that make up the starting hexagram. The number next to these hexagrams indicates the page where you can find their complete interpretation. If the hexagram you have thrown contains changing lines, these direct you to a 'follow-up' hexagram.

Like life itself, the *I Ching* is a hermetic labyrinth of wonders from which you can only escape by closing the book.

The Follow-Up Hexagram

Once you have changed the strong and weak lines into their opposites, a new 'follow-up' hexagram is created which provides information about a future phase of life. The information on the left-hand page is the most useful for studying this hexagram, since follow-up hexagrams contain no changing lines. The information on the right-hand page can, of course, be useful for clarifying your study of the follow-up hexagram.

} These hexagrams are components of the starting hexagram and offer directions for successfully dealing with your present situation.

The lines of the hexagram correspond to various parts of the body. The instructions you find there provide insight into your current physical and spiritual state.

▬▬o▬▬ : Strong Changing Line
▬▬x▬▬ : Weak Changing Line

蠱  18

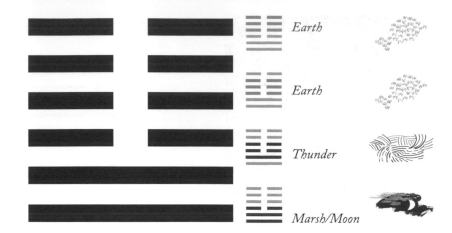

Earth

Earth

Thunder

Marsh/Moon

LIN (Attraction)

Taken together, the components of the character Lin signify a delegate who treats everyone with equal friendliness, irrespective of their birth or rank.

In the hexagram, the moon is the delegate of the sun, her ruler. The thunder symbolizes the moon's beating heart, whose rhythm keeps her in her orbit so that she can lovingly receive the light of the sun and reflect it, just as lovingly and fairly, to everyone on earth. You have the potential to become as impartial a force as the moon. But first, you have to appreciate that people are attracted to each other because of their perceived differences and because they want to enrich themselves with these attractively different qualities. What people forget is that they do not want to see the dark side; they reject the other as soon as this unattractive aspect emerges. The distinction between yourself and anyone else is only removed once you have united all the attractive and unattractive qualities within yourself. You are then like the moon: able to show others your light and dark sides, lovingly and impartially. And everyone can feel attracted to you or rejected by you, as they choose.

Attraction

If you are impartial and treat everyone, regardless of rank or birth, in a friendly way, you will be both honored and maligned. In either case, your capacity for drawing others to you is indisputable; the problem lies with the ones who choose to make a distinction between themselves and another. The rules of this game are explained to you *from bottom to top*.

(19)

Restrained Energy

By uniting in yourself all the essential differences that the earth generates, you realize that each component you have initially designated as being 'better' or 'worse' has an equal right to exist.

2

Winter Solstice, Awakening

This rule of play, which appears twice, emphasizes that you have to be aware of your dark side, as well as your light side. Of course, you will not necessarily experience your 'light' side as light and your 'dark' side as dark; these distinctions are drawn by others, who according to their own bent determine what is attractive in you and what is not. Since you cannot please everybody, at least be pleased with yourself.

24

Attraction

You can try to show to another only the side of yourself that you think he or she finds attractive. But sooner or later, the other will find out that you have not revealed your whole personality and you will be rejected again.

(19)

Fertility

The moon moves around the earth in many guises. When she is full, she looks more attractive than when she is dark. This duality also applies to you. As long as you rate one thing above another you are only grasping half of the whole picture.

54

 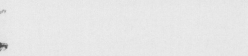
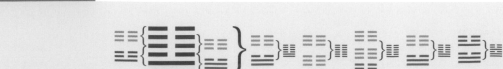

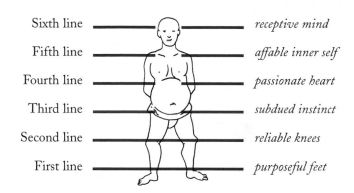

Sixth line —— receptive mind

Fifth line —— affable inner self

Fourth line —— passionate heart

Third line —— subdued instinct

Second line —— reliable knees

First line —— purposeful feet

The Individual Lines

Sixth line
Everything destined to move from darkness into light, through awakening and growing, becomes manifest at the surface of the earth. By hiding nothing of yourself and by developing all your dormant qualities equally, you will show yourself to be a balanced person.

Fifth line
This line is both the earth's surface and an underground layer, indicating that you test your potential capacities in the outside world and then withdraw into yourself again with the results. In this way, you polish your personality into a sparkling diamond, and another can focus on whichever facet catches his or her eye.

Fourth line
The thunder announcing itself deep below the earth indicates the growing awareness that external appearances are as transient as the full moon. This marks the moment when you can start working on a balanced and impartial personality.

Third line
This line deep below the earth is at the same time the moment of full moon and the core of the thunder, or the quiet moment between two heartbeats. You are clinging to your attractive side in an attempt to conceal your unattractive side. Once you become aware of this, it is time to overcome your fears and be completely yourself.

Second Line
In the darkness under the reflective surface of the marsh/moon the thunder starts to rumble. This line symbolizes the waxing of the moon. To become full and attractive, you need to continue on your way. If you realize that your present form also has its beauty, you are on the right track.

First line
Dark moon. If you do not want to wander around forever in the darkness, clutch onto the second line and realize that however unattractive you feel at the moment, you will see the light again.

Introduction
The energies of the moon ☷ and the earth ☷ dominate the Lin hexagram. If your attractiveness is based on outward show, be aware that this is as transient as the full moon. All things the earth brings forth lie dormant within you; the art is to awaken ☷ all these facets of your personality without allowing any to dominate.

Strong and Weak Changing Lines
Extra attention should be paid to strong and weak lines in the hexagram you have thrown. A strong line signifies that you are addressing the situation with too much force, whereas a weak line calls for a bolder attitude.

The Hermetic *I Ching*
The answer to your specific question is not found only in the starting hexagram. For a deeper insight, you can also study the various separate hexagrams that make up the starting hexagram. The number next to these hexagrams indicates the page where you can find their complete interpretation. If the hexagram you have thrown contains changing lines, these direct you to a 'follow-up' hexagram.

Like life itself, the *I Ching* is a hermetic labyrinth of wonders from which you can only escape by closing the book.

The Follow-Up Hexagram
Once you have changed the strong and weak lines into their opposites, a new 'follow-up' hexagram is created which provides information about a future phase of life. The information on the left-hand page is the most useful for studying this hexagram, since follow-up hexagrams contain no changing lines.
The information on the right-hand page can, of course, be useful for clarifying your study of the follow-up hexagram.

} These hexagrams are components of the starting hexagram and offer directions for successfully dealing with your present situation.

 The lines of the hexagram correspond to various parts of the body. The instructions you find there provide insight into your current physical and spiritual state.

══○══ : Strong Changing Line
══✕══ : Weak Changing Line

 19

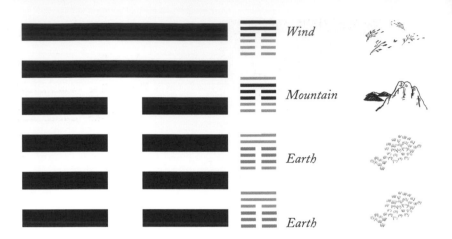

The heron, the paragon of balanced observation

An eye on the lower half of a human body.
To look or to see

KWÂN (Observation, Contemplation)

The eye on the lower half of the human body gives the character Kwân the meaning of looking around and/or scrutinizing your spiritual condition. This significance is confirmed by the behavior of the heron, which always maintains an overview of its hunting ground. Standing absolutely still on one leg, the acme of balance, the heron creates the impression of having cut itself off from the outside world — and yet nothing escapes its attention.

In the hexagram, the wind blowing from the stable mountain represents steady breathing and a calm, contemplative view of the earthly bustle. This suggests that, on the one hand, you are looking back over the way you have come and taking stock of what you have achieved. On the other hand, the world is your oyster and you can choose your own target from amongst the abundant possibilities she has to offer. Before you make this shift, it would be wise to work through your past. If you face the future burdened with unprocessed emotions, your new impressions will always be tarnished.

 Wind

 Mountain

 Earth

 Earth

Observation, Contemplation

 In general, you only see what you want to see. Your prejudices filter out the information useful to you and you fail to notice the rest, so you are continuously being confirmed in your way of thinking. If you alter your points of view, new things will attract your attention. The following directions may help you. (20)

The Blessed Marriage

 Frequently step back from the earthly bustle and quietly contemplate the things you have experienced. 53

Observation, Contemplation

 Steady breathing enables you to investigate the impressions you have acquired. If your breath falters or quickens when you come to a particular image, you know that you have run up against an unprocessed emotion, which you will have to digest before you go any further. Discuss with yourself why certain images disturb you and others satisfy you. (20)

The Destruction of the Past

 In the process of looking back and looking forward, it is important that you do not let go of the past before you have plucked its sweet and sour fruits. Work through your experiences to the point where you are in balance and they can have no distorting effect on a new stimulus that could trigger a break-through in your way of thinking. 23

Restrained Energy

 The earth, which brings forth all things, is strewn with an abundance of ideas and ideals. You can set yourself a particular goal, but if you look back over your life you will see that all sorts of 'accidental' circumstances have shown you the way. Therefore, you can always trust your environment to provide for your spiritual and physical needs in the future. 2

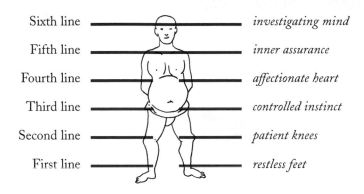

Sixth line — *investigating mind*

Fifth line — *inner assurance*

Fourth line — *affectionate heart*

Third line — *controlled instinct*

Second line — *patient knees*

First line — *restless feet*

The Individual Lines

Sixth line

The beginning of the wind represents breathing in, or a period in which your attention is directed inwards. You are faced with the task of investigating your spiritual condition in order to see whether you are free of undigested emotions.

Fifth line

The top of the mountain and the core of the wind, or the moment between breathing in and breathing out, symbolize the cool contemplation of your path through life. If the images you call to mind do not cvokc any emotions, you have inner assurance and can proceed on your way.

Fourth line

The location of the lowest line of the wind, or the end of your breath, below the top of the mountain suggests that you have taken in enough information from the earth's surface. It would benefit you to withdraw to the top of the mountain and digest your experiences in complete peace and quiet.

Third line

This line symbolizes the foot of the mountain, which lies both under the earth's surface and level with it. This indicates that you have not yet acquired much information from your surroundings. You can either continue on your way through life, or reflect on it, as you please.

Second line

From this subterranean position, you spy on your surroundings. This is no way to acquire experience. If you have not experienced something first hand, and all your impressions of it are based on observation from a distance, you are fooling yourself with half-truths.

First line

Deep beneath the earth, you are like a child moving between the legs of adults. There is nothing wrong with this, of course, if you are a child. But if you count yourself as an adult, it is time you dared to face life at your own level.

Introduction

In the Kwân hexagram, your investigating mind (sixth line) considers the fruits you have plucked on your path through life, and you process these into inner assurance (fifth line). So balanced, you can grab with clean hands the abundant fare of earthly experiences that are constantly laid out before you.

Strong and Weak Changing Lines

Extra attention should be paid to strong and weak lines in the hexagram you have thrown. A strong line signifies that you are addressing the situation with too much force, whereas a weak line calls for a bolder attitude.

The Hermetic *I Ching*

The answer to your specific question is not found only in the starting hexagram. For a deeper insight, you can also study the various separate hexagrams that make up the starting hexagram. The number next to these hexagrams indicates the page where you can find their complete interpretation. If the hexagram you have thrown contains changing lines, these direct you to a 'follow-up' hexagram.

Like life itself, the *I Ching* is a hermetic labyrinth of wonders from which you can only escape by closing the book.

The Follow-Up Hexagram

Once you have changed the strong and weak lines into their opposites, a new 'follow-up' hexagram is created which provides information about a future phase of life. The information on the left-hand page is the most useful for studying this hexagram, since follow-up hexagrams contain no changing lines.
The information on the right-hand page can, of course, be useful for clarifying your study of the follow-up hexagram.

} These hexagrams are components of the starting hexagram and offer directions for successfully dealing with your present situation.

The lines of the hexagram correspond to various parts of the body. The instructions you find there provide insight into your current physical and spiritual state.

▆▬▬ ∘ : Strong Changing Line
▆▬▬ × : Weak Changing Line

觀  **20**

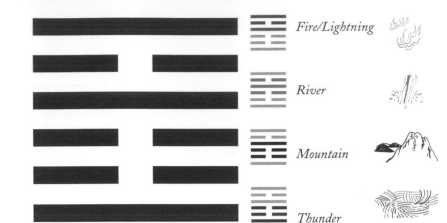

嗤嗑

The yarrow stalks (millefolia siberica)
used by diviners to consult the oracle.
The mouth chews over the answer that is received

Mouth
Yarrow
Diviner — 嗤
嗑 — Lid
Dish — Contents

A covered dish filled with offerings. The mouth suggests the
sound of invisible voices speaking from the dish

SHIH HO (Biting Through Till Union)

The characters Shih and Ho indicate a moment in your life when you do not know what to think and you seek wise advice. If you endlessly chew over the impartial advice you receive, you will immobilize yourself to the point where you are a prisoner of your own indecision.

In the hexagram, the water on the top of the mountain indicates that you are not able to let your fertile knowledge flow freely. It would seem that a particular situation is so important to you that you feel incapable of making a decision. Even though you know better, you block your natural rhythm of life. The fire/lightning evokes impartial, wise advice offered to you from beyond yourself; this makes you realize, deep in your heart, that you have to remove the blockade. The thunder rolling up from below represents agitation in the lower part of your body, which is an urgent signal of the need for a breakthrough.

 Fire/Lightning

 River

 Mountain

Thunder

Biting Through Till Union
You feel impotent because you cannot reconcile yourself to a decision you have to make.
The following directions may help you to avoid becoming a victim of this situation. (21)

Restricted Movement
You are like a young fox that has wet its tail. If you want to know how to prevent this in future, you had better ask an old fox for advice. 64

The Wise Man
The wise man is like the sun that crowns the top of the mountain. Inner peace equips him to give you impartial and illuminating advice. If you do not know where to find him, you can consult the I Ching — which, it is said, was developed by him. Since you have done so, you already know his advice: push on! 56

Initial Difficulty
Gravity forces the water on the mountain top to find a way down. At this stage, you still have everything in hand and you are equipped with wise advice, so it would be unwise to postpone your decision. 39

Confusion
Now that you have bitten the bullet, be aware that growth and confusion go hand in hand. Every decision provokes new resistance. 3

Nourishment
The way is open. The obstacle that was separating your lower jaw from your upper jaw has been swallowed. Having bitten through on this occasion, you will know exactly what to do next time. 27

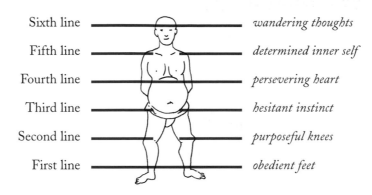

Sixth line ——————— *wandering thoughts*

Fifth line ——————— *determined inner self*

Fourth line ——————— *persevering heart*

Third line ——————— *hesitant instinct*

Second line ——————— *purposeful knees*

First line ——————— *obedient feet*

The Individual Lines

Sixth line

The uppermost line of the fire/lightning indicates that you hear the illuminating advice, but you do not act on it. If you remain deaf to this advice and allow your mind to keep playing with other solutions you have already considered hundreds of times, you will become the prisoner of your own impotence.

Fifth line

The heart of the fire/lightning, or the illuminating advice, radiates out over the surface of the lake which symbolizes your fertile knowledge. Somewhere in the back of your mind, you see the light. If you bite the bullet and follow the wise advice that is slowly becoming clear to you, your internal struggle will be resolved.

Fourth line

The fire/lightning has penetrated below the surface of the lake on the mountain top. You have fully absorbed the illuminating advice and, knowing that it is better to bend than break, you make the bold decision to lift the blockade.

Third line

Below the top of the mountain, the thunder batters the bed of the lake. You produce all sorts of arguments for postponing the decisive moment. Your survival instinct grows sick of your indecisiveness and urges you to take the plunge.

Second line

The thunder shakes the mountain to its foundations. You are so determined to solve your problem that you get bogged down. The right procedure is to conduct a thorough self-examination before you ask someone else for advice.

First line

The beginning of the thunder, or the lower jaw which cannot unite with the upper jaw, indicate that you are imprisoned by your problem. You want to make your presence felt by rattling your chains.

Introduction

The Shih Ho hexagram is determined by *Nourishment (27)*. Between the lower and upper jaws, something near to your heart (fourth line) prevents you from taking in fresh 'food' and growing. Your inalienable sense of self–preservation will make you realize that biting through is the only appropriate action.

Strong and Weak Changing Lines

Extra attention should be paid to strong and weak lines in the hexagram you have thrown. A strong line signifies that you are addressing the situation with too much force, whereas a weak line calls for a bolder attitude.

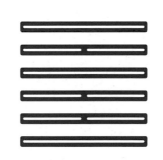

The Hermetic *I Ching*

The answer to your specific question is not found only in the starting hexagram. For a deeper insight, you can also study the various separate hexagrams that make up the starting hexagram. The number next to these hexagrams indicates the page where you can find their complete interpretation. If the hexagram you have thrown contains changing lines, these direct you to a 'follow-up' hexagram.

Like life itself, the *I Ching* is a hermetic labyrinth of wonders from which you can only escape by closing the book.

The Follow-Up Hexagram

Once you have changed the strong and weak lines into their opposites, a new 'follow-up' hexagram is created which provides information about a future phase of life. The information on the left-hand page is the most useful for studying this hexagram, since follow-up hexagrams contain no changing lines.

The information on the right-hand page can, of course, be useful for clarifying your study of the follow-up hexagram.

} These hexagrams are components of the starting hexagram and offer directions for successfully dealing with your present situation.

The lines of the hexagram correspond to various parts of the body. The instructions you find there provide insight into your current physical and spiritual state.

▬▬⊙▬▬ : Strong Changing Line
▬▬✕▬▬ : Weak Changing Line

噬嗑      21

Decorations made from plants, flowers, vegetables and shells

PÎ (Natural Radiance)

The character Pî denotes adornments that make life pleasant but are not strictly necessary. By contrast, the appealing colors and forms found in nature primarily have to do with the survival of the species.

The hexagram conveys the same message: that inner beauty is more radiant than the ornaments and finery people use as embellishments. Thus, the stable mountain in the light of the fire/sun symbolizes a balanced person who allows himself to be seen as nature intended. The natural beauty of the glistening, sunlit mist, which for the moment envelops the mountain, represents an outward appearance that is adapted to the circumstances. The sparkling brook springing forth at the foot of the mountain denotes a movement through life that is wise, fluid, and full of zest. The thunder rolling over the mountain in the haze is your hidden survival instinct, which is always alert and impulsively lets you know which external form will offer you the best chance of survival in a given situation.

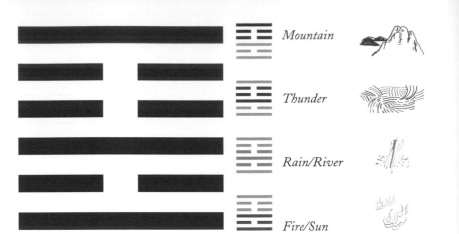

		Mountain
		Thunder
		Rain/River
		Fire/Sun

Natural Radiance
Do not be afraid to let others see you as you are. Outward show may temporarily conceal your inner impotence but sooner or later your true nature will come to light. The following steps lead to the development of inner beauty. (22)

Nourishment
Through healthy spiritual and physical nourishment, your inner self and your outward appearance can be geared to each other, so that they become complementary, rather than conflicting. 27

Youthful Innocence
The most common reasons why people are anything but themselves include: immaturity, a desire either to appear tough, to rebel against the Establishment — or, by contrast, to imitate those who have had material success. 4

Cutting the Knot
If your aim is to appear adult, you would be advised to give up the behavior described above. Otherwise your unmasking, which will come sooner or later, will be even more embarrassing. 40

Completion
When the sun reaches its zenith it starts to descend. Once you are aware that the sun keeps on shining you will realize that you can always look radiant as long as you do not admit darkness into your inner self. 55

Successful Movement
The sun may be blanketed by clouds, but it will always break through again. If you are aware of this, you will be able to adopt whatever attitude is necessary for surviving a particular situation, knowing that a pure inner self is waiting behind the scenes. 63

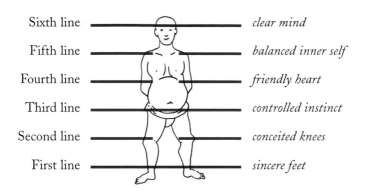

Sixth line	*clear mind*
Fifth line	*balanced inner self*
Fourth line	*friendly heart*
Third line	*controlled instinct*
Second line	*conceited knees*
First line	*sincere feet*

The Individual Lines

Sixth line
The bare mountain peak indicates that you are in possession of inner peace, surety, self-respect and a clear mind. You do not have to hide behind all sorts of fancy talk. Just be who you are.

Fifth line
The uppermost line of the thunder rolling towards the top of the mountain suggests you have left a valley of abundance bringing just one roll of precious silk. People will think you are stingy, but actually you could not care less about outward appearances. For you, what counts is the preservation of your life and climbing the mountain nimbly and safely.

Fourth line
The river begins at the foot of the mountain, amidst the thunder. The booming of the thunder sends up a spray of water from the river, creating a sparkling curtain of mist which drapes the mountain. If your heart is satisfied by the natural simplicity of this charming drapery, which has been conjured up by the circumstances, hold on to that feeling.

Third line
The river covers the initial rumblings of the thunder and the waking heat of the fire/sun. These generate mist which hangs over the river, symbolizing an outward appearance founded on survival instinct. If this instinct determines your attitude to life in unfamiliar situations, you will radiate self-esteem.

Second line
The heart of the fire/sun shines vaguely through thick clouds of mist, suggesting a countenance masked by a beard. The knees, too, convey an attitude that you think is flattering to you. Your vanity is forgiven as long as this outward appearance reflects your survival instinct.

First line
The lowest line of the fire/sun represents being who you are. This theme is evoked by your feet, which do what they are told to do. If, out of survival instinct, you regularly make use of these willing 'subjects', you will be rewarded with an attractive, lithe body.

Introduction
The Pî hexagram is determined by *Nourishment (27)*. In an emergency, the survival instinct (third line) emerges like the eager lower jaw unerringly uniting with the upper jaw (sixth line), which is controlled by a clear mind. The feet (first line) and the knees (second line) represent a sincere and graceful attitude towards life.

Strong and Weak Changing Lines
Extra attention should be paid to strong and weak lines in the hexagram you have thrown. A strong line signifies that you are addressing the situation with too much force, whereas a weak line calls for a bolder attitude.

The Hermetic *I Ching*
The answer to your specific question is not found only in the starting hexagram. For a deeper insight, you can also study the various separate hexagrams that make up the starting hexagram. The number next to these hexagrams indicates the page where you can find their complete interpretation. If the hexagram you have thrown contains changing lines, these direct you to a 'follow-up' hexagram.

Like life itself, the *I Ching* is a hermetic labyrinth of wonders from which you can only escape by closing the book.

The Follow-Up Hexagram
Once you have changed the strong and weak lines into their opposites, a new 'follow-up' hexagram is created which provides information about a future phase of life. The information on the left-hand page is the most useful for studying this hexagram, since follow-up hexagrams contain no changing lines. The information on the right-hand page can, of course, be useful for clarifying your study of the follow-up hexagram.

} These hexagrams are components of the starting hexagram and offer directions for successfully dealing with your present situation.

 The lines of the hexagram correspond to various parts of the body. The instructions you find there provide insight into your current physical and spiritual state.

▬⊙▬ : Strong Changing Line
▬✕▬ : Weak Changing Line

賁  **22**

Lopping or pruning a tree with an axe

Sharp tools. A knife or a sword

PO (The Destruction of the Past)

The character Po indicates the symmetrical pruning of a tree. Without damaging the stump, you remove dead branches, undergrowth, and any runaway offshoots. What is left is a beautiful, balanced form that is viable again and will bear much fruit. This major clean-up — usually carried out in late autumn or early spring — can also, of course, be applied to yourself.

In the hexagram, the stable mountain enthroned above the earth symbolises a person who has withdrawn in order to carry out a thorough investigation of the self. The landscape looks frozen because of the absence of other elements. This imposing silence suggests profound meditation. The branches and roots of the personality are examined to their farthest reaches deep under the earth (or within the inner being) and evenly pruned, removed or retained depending on their integral importance and condition. Bear in mind that you should not cut too deeply, otherwise you may grow back lopsided.

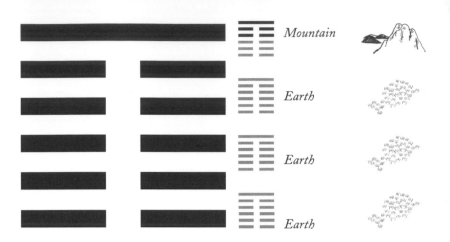

Mountain

Earth

Earth

Earth

The Destruction of the Past

(23)

The balanced processing of your past experiences demands profound insight. The fruits you have plucked in the past, both bitter and sweet, have long since withered to one heap of uniformly tasteless dust. If you can see this, you will be aware that everything that has happened to you has been significant for you becoming what you are. If you are dissatisfied at the moment, the root of this dissatisfaction must be the fact that you are so attached to the bitter or sweet aftertaste of your experiences that your tongue senses nothing else, and the menu of the day always tastes the same. By giving the here and now priority over the past, you will be able to enjoy every moment in its own right. Reviewing the day's events each evening and pruning yourself into shape once a year will keep you lighthearted.

Restrained Energy

2

The earth brings forth all things. Essentially, nature is always in balance. People upset this balance by extolling nature's sweet fruits and hiding the bitter ones. If both kinds were digested with the same degree of insight, there would be no problem. As soon as bitterness is repressed and hidden away, the natural balance is disturbed and the core of life, which is based on duality, becomes diseased. It is impossible to excise one half of a duality without damaging the unity, or medulla, from which this duality originates. For this reason the 'good and bad' that the earth brings forth must be fostered and pruned equally. Once you know the value of sweetness and bitterness, you will also understand the difference between true wisdom and the insight of a one-eyed person in the country of the blind.

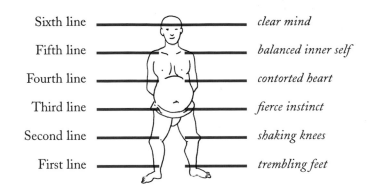

Sixth line —————————— *clear mind*

Fifth line —————————— *balanced inner self*

Fourth line —————————— *contorted heart*

Third line —————————— *fierce instinct*

Second line —————————— *shaking knees*

First line —————————— *trembling feet*

The Individual Lines

Sixth line

The top of the mountain denotes your head, with which you mentally investigate whether you have 'pruned' yourself into a balanced form. If your past is well-digested, your head will feel like a fruit that is sound to the core and borne on a healthy tree (or a perfectly balanced body). If this is not the case, you need some trimming, at the very least.

Fifth line

This line below the top of the mountain and on the surface of the earth suggests the here and now. If you look back over your path in life from your present standpoint, you will be able to see every disturbing thought in the light of your past, and realize that everything you have experienced was necessary for bringing you to the here and now.

Fourth line

The foot of the mountain, which lies both beneath and on the earth's surface, suggests that you have sold your heart to unnerving past experiences, which continue to surface in the present. They need to be lopped off, like the runaway offshoots of a tree.

Third line

Deep below the earth, and on its surface, your survival instinct stands guard and warns you if you endanger yourself by too rapidly carving down to the depths of your soul. It also comes to the fore whenever you too easily dismiss undigested experiences. Do not ignore these signals.

Second line

Deep beneath the earth, shaking knees push apart the frame of the bed; this symbolizes the restlessness and fear that take control of you while you are looking back over your past. Once you have relaxed physically, you can make a new attempt to restore your inner peace.

First line

Deep beneath the earth, trembling feet make the bed shake so hard you cannot relax; this indicates the restlessness and fear that take control of you as you prepare to review your past. Physical exercise will help restore your inner peace.

Introduction

The Po hexagram symbolizes a bed. The first line is the foot of the bed; the head lies at the closed, sixth line. Each open line of the hexagram represents a bodily function that has an influence on the thinking of the master resting on the bed.

Strong and Weak Changing Lines

Extra attention should be paid to strong and weak lines in the hexagram you have thrown. A strong line signifies that you are addressing the situation with too much force, whereas a weak line calls for a bolder attitude.

The Hermetic *I Ching*

The answer to your specific question is not found only in the starting hexagram. For a deeper insight, you can also study the various separate hexagrams that make up the starting hexagram. The number next to these hexagrams indicates the page where you can find their complete interpretation. If the hexagram you have thrown contains changing lines, these direct you to a 'follow-up' hexagram.

Like life itself, the *I Ching* is a hermetic labyrinth of wonders from which you can only escape by closing the book.

The Follow-Up Hexagram

Once you have changed the strong and weak lines into their opposites, a new 'follow-up' hexagram is created which provides information about a future phase of life. The information on the left-hand page is the most useful for studying this hexagram, since follow-up hexagrams contain no changing lines. The information on the right-hand page can, of course, be useful for clarifying your study of the follow-up hexagram.

These hexagrams are components of the starting hexagram and offer directions for successfully dealing with your present situation.

The lines of the hexagram correspond to various parts of the body. The instructions you find there provide insight into your current physical and spiritual state.

━━○━━ : Strong Changing Line
━━✕━━ : Weak Changing Line

剥  **23**

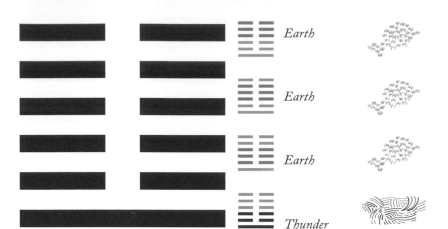

A citywall with an observation tower —

A step forwards with the left foot. A hesitant start —

To go to town or to market.

Hence, returning to a place where you have been before

FÛ (Winter Solstice, Awakening)

The composition of the character Fû points to a gradual return after a period of absence. In the light of hexagram 23, what is meant here is the return of someone who withdrew to process the past, and who is now ready for a new cycle of life.

In the hexagram, this return is symbolized by the thunder which reawakens the earth from its winter sleep. Slowly, the trees will bud; if they were not pruned into a regular shape in the autumn, you can still do something about this before the sap really starts to flow. If you apply this imagery to yourself, it suggests the moment of making a new entry into the community from which you had withdrawn. By physically confronting your past again you can find out whether you have successfully worked through all your physical and spiritual impressions. If your experiences have, indeed, been neutralized, you will be able to greet everyone as a friend, and your period of retreat will have been worth the effort. In the unlikely event that you still feel exaggerated affection or enmity, there is some refining left to be done.

Earth

Earth

Earth

Thunder

Winter Solstice, Awakening

This hexagram is generally associated with the winter solstice or the reappearance of the sun, when the days gradually start to lengthen, and the sun's energy becomes noticeable again. If you can return from a retreat like the sun, you have obviously processed the past with complete success. If you doubt that this is the case, the following two directions *(reading from bottom to top)* may be helpful. (24)

Restrained Energy

The earth brings forth all things, and it follows that all things you have experienced as good or bad in the past also persist, in one form or another, in the present. It is unnecessary and irresponsible to eliminate everything in your environment that awakens your exaggerated affection or aversion. Profound wisdom is characterized by the ability to conquer prejudice. Ensure that your spiritual and physical being seeks 'food' suited to that approach. 2

Winter Solstice, Awakening

On returning from your retreat, you should not throw yourself straight back into the fray as before. First watch and wait, seeing what comes your way and feeling how this affects you, both spiritually and physically. (24)

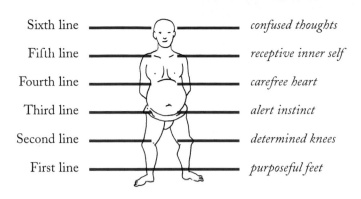

Sixth line	*confused thoughts*
Fifth line	*receptive inner self*
Fourth line	*carefree heart*
Third line	*alert instinct*
Second line	*determined knees*
First line	*purposeful feet*

The Individual Lines

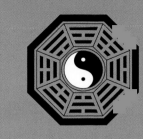

Sixth line
On the surface of the earth, all life's possible experiences are spread out for the taking. You are assailed with impatient thoughts of getting to work, but unless you want to slip back into old mistakes, just calmly wait to see what presents itself and feel how you respond, both spiritually and physically.

Fifth line
This line below the earth and on its surface represents the here and now, which in the blink of an eye becomes the past. You have the capacity to test all things that come your way against your inner surety, and calmly determine whether you feel openly neutral towards them.

Fourth line
The pulsating heart is located deep below the earth, symbolizing a satisfied, unnoticeable heartbeat, but it is also on the earth's surface, where it makes its presence felt by thumping harder and harder. This indicates that you are being troubled by matters that disturb your inner self. Do not ignore this signal.

Third line
The pulsating thunder makes you aware of your survival instinct, which initially lay hidden deep below the earth, but now starts to surface. If you have just woken up and your mind (sixth line) is not yet clear, trust your instinct which surfaces to protect you from making rash decisions.

Second line
The turbulence in the middle of the thunder deep below the earth indicates that your knees are waking up, thus restoring your physical mobility. If you are determined not to repeat the mistakes you made in the past, do not behave aggressively or defensively; adopt a tolerant, open-minded attitude.

First line
The beginning of the thunder indicates that you are awakening from a period of rest and finding that your feet are ready to hit the road again. If you can be as impersonal and subservient as your feet, which carry you purposefully and lovingly through life wherever you want to go and for as long as you want, you will not make mistakes that you will have to work through in the future.

Introduction
The Fù hexagram suggests waking up and resolutely getting to your feet (first line) in order to face life with a sense of purpose and love. The other lines indicate that you would be wise to open yourself, like virgin soil, to all impressions that come your way.

Strong and Weak Changing Lines
Extra attention should be paid to strong and weak lines in the hexagram you have thrown. A strong line signifies that you are addressing the situation with too much force, whereas a weak line calls for a bolder attitude.

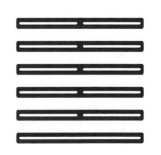

The Hermetic *I Ching*
The answer to your specific question is not found only in the starting hexagram. For a deeper insight, you can also study the various separate hexagrams that make up the starting hexagram. The number next to these hexagrams indicates the page where you can find their complete interpretation. If the hexagram you have thrown contains changing lines, these direct you to a 'follow-up' hexagram.

Like life itself, the *I Ching* is a hermetic labyrinth of wonders from which you can only escape by closing the book.

The Follow-Up Hexagram
Once you have changed the strong and weak lines into their opposites, a new 'follow-up' hexagram is created which provides information about a future phase of life. The information on the left-hand page is the most useful for studying this hexagram, since follow-up hexagrams contain no changing lines.
The information on the right-hand page can, of course, be useful for clarifying your study of the follow-up hexagram.

These hexagrams are components of the starting hexagram and offer directions for successfully dealing with your present situation.

The lines of the hexagram correspond to various parts of the body. The instructions you find there provide insight into your current physical and spiritual state.

: Strong Changing Line
: Weak Changing Line

復 24

Heaven	
Wind	
Mountain	
Thunder	

WÛ WANG (Innocence)

The characters Wû and Wang indicate a timid retreat after you have seen that the realization of one of your ideas is too much for you. As long as your failure is due to unfamiliarity with heavenly or earthly laws, you have acted with perfect innocence and need not be ashamed of this learning process.

The play of forces in the hexagram can help you with this learning process. The infinite depth of the heavens, from where the wind or your flow of thoughts originates, indicates that nothing is too crazy to contemplate and that your thoughts are essentially sincere. The stable mountain reaching up to the heavens symbolizes not only an overview, through which you learn to take into account the heavenly influences you cannot control, but also the inner peace you will need to bring your ideas to fruition. The thunder rolling up the mountain is the symbol of your physical capabilities, which turn your thoughts into actions and thereby show you what material resources are, or are not, within your reach.

A man exerts all his force in a vain attempt to overcome an obstacle. The character indicates negation

A girl sheltering in a refuge. Therefore, a mistake or disorder

Innocence
The infinite depth of the heavens is food for all the realistic and unrealistic thoughts that you, in your innocence, may have. By testing the feasibility of these ideas in practice, you discover that you can control many factors, but not all. The following directions *(reading from bottom to top)* may help you in those situations you can control.   (25)

A Mature Relationship
Now that you have immersed yourself deeply in the material world and discovered that there are factors you cannot control, you no longer attach importance to results. The only things that counts, from now on, is the adventure of the road, which you travel with light feet.   44

Withdrawal
Practical experience teaches you when it is time to withdraw and digest your experiences. Once you realize that the path you have travelled is more important than where you end up, you have learned more than you intended.   33

The Blessed Marriage
Regularly take distance from your actions and study their effects on your environment. On the basis of these observations, determine when and when not to act.   53

Increase
Force nothing. By steadily translating your thoughts into deeds and giving each result its due, you can avoid making big mistakes.   42

Nourishment
You take in the food of experience by translating a thought into practice and getting your teeth into it.   27

WÛ WANG

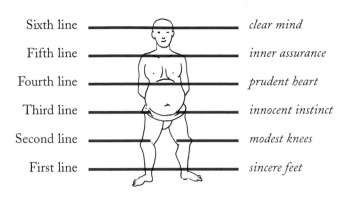

Sixth line ———— *clear mind*

Fifth line ———— *inner assurance*

Fourth line ———— *prudent heart*

Third line ———— *innocent instinct*

Second line ———— *modest knees*

First line ———— *sincere feet*

The Individual Lines

Sixth line
The outer limits of the heavens indicate that you have unerring insight into the heavenly and earthly factors in a given situation. You realise that some matters just have to run their course because everyone is right in his or her way; do not interfere and maintain your innocence.

Fifth line
The heart of the heavens, and the beginning of the wind or your subconscious, suggest a vague thought you cannot quite grasp but keep mulling over anxiously. If you simply admit in all sincerity that for the moment you are at a loss, you will feel relieved and pleased.

Fourth line
The beginning of the heavens, the top of the mountain, and the core of the wind (or the moment between breathing in and breathing out), all denote a period of peace and quiet during which you can study the heavenly and earthly circumstances. Put your thoughts in order so that you can gauge the most favorable time for action.

Third line
The thunder below the top of the mountain rolls back towards you, bringing with it a reaction triggered by the sincere thoughts you have put into action. All actions have unpredictable consequences. You lead away an ox that has been left unattended, and someone with cow dung on his shoe gets the blame. The good deed you do today will be condemned tomorrow.

Second line
The rumbling of the thunder at the foot of the mountain indicates that you have no overview of your situation, but you can gain experience by getting your teeth into a project. Then you can continuously adjust your original line of thought and, in time, master the laws of heaven and earth.

First line
The start of the thunder symbolizes both your lower jaw and your feet, which are the essence of innocence because they do not move of their own accord. If you, as their master, can be just as innocent and ignorant as these subjects, you will not make intentional mistakes and need not be ashamed of anything.

Introduction
The Wû Wang hexagram is determined by *Nourishment (27)*.
The eager lower jaw (first line) lifts the food of experience to the upper jaw, where the result of your action is tasted with a clear mind (sixth line), inner assurance (fifth line) and a prudent heart (fourth line) before new instructions are given.

Strong and Weak Changing Lines
Extra attention should be paid to strong and weak lines in the hexagram you have thrown. A strong line signifies that you are addressing the situation with too much force, whereas a weak line calls for a bolder attitude.

The Hermetic *I Ching*
The answer to your specific question is not found only in the starting hexagram. For a deeper insight, you can also study the various separate hexagrams that make up the starting hexagram. The number next to these hexagrams indicates the page where you can find their complete interpretation. If the hexagram you have thrown contains changing lines, these direct you to a 'follow-up' hexagram.

Like life itself, the *I Ching* is a hermetic labyrinth of wonders from which you can only escape by closing the book.

The Follow-Up Hexagram
Once you have changed the strong and weak lines into their opposites, a new 'follow-up' hexagram is created which provides information about a future phase of life. The information on the left-hand page is the most useful for studying this hexagram, since follow-up hexagrams contain no changing lines.
The information on the right-hand page can, of course, be useful for clarifying your study of the follow-up hexagram.

 These hexagrams are components of the starting hexagram and offer directions for successfully dealing with your present situation.

The lines of the hexagram correspond to various parts of the body. The instructions you find there provide insight into your current physical and spiritual state.

▬▬◦▬▬ : Strong Changing Line
▬▬✕▬▬ : Weak Changing Line

 无妄 25

Mountain
Thunder
Marsh/Moon
Heaven

A mature person. Also: big and tall —— 大畜

Yin, female and instinctive. Also: profound, mysterious, —— 大畜
to nurture, to feed, docility. Cattle in a field, earthly life

TÂ KHÛ (The Power of Strength)

The combined action of the characters Tâ and Khû indicate that you are only really mature when you are able to serve your environment and know how to exert your physical and spiritual force in a measured way.

In the hexagram, this is depicted by the stable mountain rising up out of the infinite, creative energy of the heavens. The marsh/moon embedded in the heavens attests to profound insight into earthly life, which ensures that energy is distributed with perfect regularity. This power is never excessive, as the thunder rolling up the mountain confirms. The greatest strength of a wise person is a helpfulness derived from the knowledge that acquiring insight is a gradual and laborious process. You may want to lead others to the vantage point on the mountain top which offers an overview of life, but this does not imply that you can spare them the steep climb. Everyone has to make their own ascent, at their own pace.

The Power of Strength
You will know the master by his restraint. Being of service is not the same as being servile. Always remember that another can only be proud of achievements brought about by his or her own efforts. The following steps may help you to come down from your ivory tower.

 (26)

Nourishment
Providing others with spiritual food in order to help them is one thing. Making them dependent on you is quite another.

 27

Relaxation
A person cannot be permanently tensed for action. You should know this, having slackened the reins often enough during your own learning process. If not, you have understood nothing of the laws of heaven and earth.

 41

Fertility
Observe the movement of the moon. Once she is full, she wanes and if she is dark you know for certain she will become full again. Anyone with insight knows exactly when someone is thirsting for knowledge and when he or she is drunk with it.

 54

Vital Energy
Whenever you have to force yourself to be of service to another, you are at fault. Genuine vital energy, which is at one with the power of the heavens, is characterized by a minimal waste of energy.

 34

Fulfilment
Do not allow yourself to be guided by sentiments that entangle you in earthly affairs. Hold on to the thought that you want to enjoy the earthly game without losing yourself in illusions.

 43

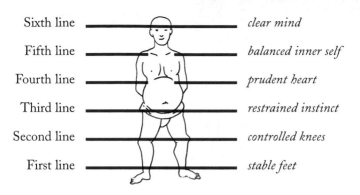

Sixth line ——————— *clear mind*
Fifth line ——————— *balanced inner self*
Fourth line ——————— *prudent heart*
Third line ——————— *restrained instinct*
Second line ——————— *controlled knees*
First line ——————— *stable feet*

The Individual Lines

Sixth line

The top of the mountain indicates that you have an overview of your surroundings. If you are a worthy exponent of the heavens' creative energy you will know just how to dose the distribution of your knowledge on earth and see exactly when and where your services are or are not needed.

Fifth line

The upwardly rolling thunder that is concentrated below the top of the mountain symbolizes a decisive approach that maintains inner balance so that your clear mind is not swamped by anger or emotions. Keep in mind that the teeth of a castrated boar will still command respect as long as nobody knows the boar has been castrated.

Fourth line

The heart of the thunder, the foot of the mountain, and the waxing moon show that you have not yet achieved the height of your powers; moreover, you have no overview. You can be of service to others, but be careful, for you are like a young bull whose horns should be covered before he becomes dangerous.

Third line

The thunder rising from heaven and the new moon indicate great strength and the right motivation, but experience is lacking. By calmly observing someone who has gone before you, you can learn how to use your energy in a balanced way, without becoming a slave or a despot.

Second line

The dark moon in the infinite depth of the heavens is like an empty wagon ready for departure. You so want to be taken seriously that you seize every opportunity to volunteer your services, even though you are not ready. Once you appreciate that you are in a period of relaxation, you will understand why no one is paying any attention to you.

First line

The outer limits of heaven attest to great strength, but stay far away from earthly bustle. Like your feet, which have no innate motivation to take you anywhere, you would be wise not to interfere actively with your surroundings.

Introduction

The Tâ Khû hexagram is determined by *Nourishment (27)*. The upper jaw (sixth line) denotes a clear mind, which moderates your eager lower jaw, or your instinct (third line), and so carefully doses your consumption. Your mouth is filled with a balanced inner self (fifth line) and a prudent heart (fourth line).

Strong and Weak Changing Lines

Extra attention should be paid to strong and weak lines in the hexagram you have thrown. A strong line signifies that you are addressing the situation with too much force, whereas a weak line calls for a bolder attitude.

The Hermetic *I Ching*

The answer to your specific question is not found only in the starting hexagram. For a deeper insight, you can also study the various separate hexagrams that make up the starting hexagram. The number next to these hexagrams indicates the page where you can find their complete interpretation. If the hexagram you have thrown contains changing lines, these direct you to a 'follow-up' hexagram.

Like life itself, the *I Ching* is a hermetic labyrinth of wonders from which you can only escape by closing the book.

The Follow-Up Hexagram

Once you have changed the strong and weak lines into their opposites, a new 'follow-up' hexagram is created which provides information about a future phase of life. The information on the left-hand page is the most useful for studying this hexagram, since follow-up hexagrams contain no changing lines. The information on the right-hand page can, of course, be useful for clarifying your study of the follow-up hexagram.

} These hexagrams are components of the starting hexagram and offer directions for successfully dealing with your present situation.

 The lines of the hexagram correspond to various parts of the body. The instructions you find there provide insight into your current physical and spiritual state.

══⊙══ : Strong Changing Line
══×══ : Weak Changing Line

大畜  **26**

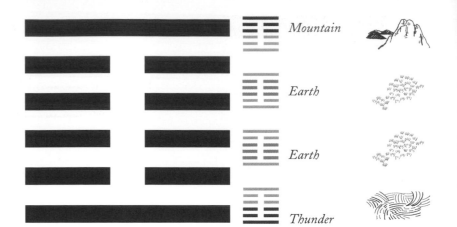

Mountain

Earth

Earth

Thunder

*A rough sketch of a face, with emphasis on the chin
or the lower jaw*

頤

*A head on a body
The meaning is generally restricted to head*

Î (Nourishment)

The emphasis on the head's lower jaw in the character Î signifies the taking in of food. This refers not only to physical nourishment, but also to spiritual food.

In the hexagram, the mountain towering over the earth symbolizes a stable person who calmly surveys the surroundings and decides what nourishment will enable him or her to grow physically and spiritually. The mountain can be compared with the upper jaw, which shows the lower jaw where it should sink its teeth. The lower jaw is represented by the thunder moving towards the mountain. It follows that the mobile lower jaw is comparable with your body, which translates into action the information gathered by your head. The earth, which brings forth all things, lies clamped between the mountain (or upper jaw) and the thunder (or lower jaw), indicating that all possible nourishment is available to you. It is up to you to decide what you will or will not take in.

Nourishment
All the information you take in is digested and assumes a particular significance. Whatever is useful to you is translated into ready knowledge and the rest is ignored. Remember that while the waste products from your physical nourishment are excreted, the impressions left by your experiences linger on in your body, either consciously or subconsciously. The following steps *(reading from bottom to top)* outline the process of digesting experiences.

(27)

The Destruction of the Past
Inner surety concerning your possessions often stands in the way of dealing with your past. Once you have digested a problem that has occupied you daily, you are overwhelmed by a physical and spiritual emptiness that is very frightening. You are not yet ready for something new and you almost crave the old situation in which you were sure of nourishment. If you do not want to live in the past any longer, try to taste something new.

23

Restrained Energy
The earth brings forth all things. Nevertheless, you will cling to eating habits that you developed in your youth in order to survive — even when they are no longer necessary. Letting go of these habits opens up the possibility that you can enjoy the things you crave.

2

Winter Solstice, Awakening
From the moment your senses are activated, information floods in. Gradually, a frame of reference forms in your mind, giving significance to your impressions. Since you are initially dependent on the experiences offered by your upbringing, these are the impressions that shape your mind.

24

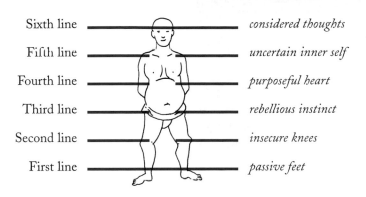

Sixth line ——————— *considered thoughts*

Fifth line ——————— *uncertain inner self*

Fourth line ——————— *purposeful heart*

Third line ——————— *rebellious instinct*

Second line ——————— *insecure knees*

First line ——————— *passive feet*

The Individual Lines

Sixth line

The top of the mountain, or the upper jaw, represents your mind, which decides what you will get your teeth into. Your intellect and the signals supplied by your senses cannot ensure that the food you take in will be to your taste, but try it anyway.

Fifth line

This line below the top of the mountain and at the earth's surface denotes the here and now. You know what you have, but not what you will get. You may choose to hang on to your present situation, but once you realize that your inner assurance can never be taken away, you clamber confidently towards new prospects.

Fourth line

The foot of the mountain, which lies both under the earth and on its surface, represents the stirring of your heart. A heart that craves mouth-watering things is like the covetous eye a tiger fixes on its prey. There is generally nothing suspect about a natural desire for food.

Third line

Beneath the earth, the thunder has reached its climax. The lower jaw stops moving towards the upper jaw. This indicates that instead of biting the bullet you are hanging on to survival strategies you have absorbed in the past. Trust your heart, your inner assurance and your current insights, and tear yourself free.

Second line

The thunder rumbles deep below the earth, suggesting that you are afraid of breaking with your old survival strategies; you turn for help to the first line or lower jaw, which has nothing to say. Do not allow the past to weigh you down; straighten your back and get your teeth into something new.

First line

The beginning of the thunder, or the lower jaw which can do nothing of its own accord and which is, like your feet, completely dependent on instructions from above, indicate your current state of mind. You have a tortoise mentality — but it can turn in the blink of an eye into a tiger's mentality if you follow your heart straight away.

Introduction

In the Î hexagram, each of the open lines influences the decision made by the upper jaw (sixth line) as to whether the lower jaw (first line) will bite into new food from the earth's ☷ abundant array, or whether you will again force down a morsel that has been on the menu for years.

Strong and Weak Changing Lines

Extra attention should be paid to strong and weak lines in the hexagram you have thrown. A strong line signifies that you are addressing the situation with too much force, whereas a weak line calls for a bolder attitude.

The Hermetic *I Ching*

The answer to your specific question is not found only in the starting hexagram. For a deeper insight, you can also study the various separate hexagrams that make up the starting hexagram. The number next to these hexagrams indicates the page where you can find their complete interpretation. If the hexagram you have thrown contains changing lines, these direct you to a 'follow-up' hexagram.

Like life itself, the *I Ching* is a hermetic labyrinth of wonders from which you can only escape by closing the book.

The Follow-Up Hexagram

Once you have changed the strong and weak lines into their opposites, a new 'follow-up' hexa-gram is created which provides information about a future phase of life. The information on the left-hand page is the most useful for studying this hexagram, since follow-up hexagrams contain no changing lines.

The information on the right-hand page can, of course, be useful for clarifying your study of the follow-up hexagram.

These hexagrams are components of the starting hexagram and offer directions for successfully dealing with your present situation.

The lines of the hexagram correspond to various parts of the body. The instructions you find there provide insight into your current physical and spiritual state.

⚊⚋⚊ : Strong Changing Line
⚊✕⚊ : Weak Changing Line

A mature person. Also: big and tall

Walking along, step by step

A skeleton. The character also indicates a deformed mouth caused by a cleft palate

TÂ KWO (Vigorous Mind)

The interplay of the characters Tâ and Kwo shows that as long as you allow your mouth to twist the truth that permeates you to your very bones, you are not moving through life in a mature way.

   In the hexagram, the marsh/moon embedded in the upper heaven portrays your mouth filled with concepts that are based on illusions. This is a sign that you are elevating earthly matter to heavenly bliss and concealing the infinite depth of the lower, true heaven, which is the skeleton of life. The wind blowing down from this heaven indicates that there is no ready answer to the question of what life is all about. The only surety you have is that your body will keep functioning as long as you keep breathing. Once you are aware of this, you will vigorously dismiss your illusions and, as a mature person, attune your vital rhythm to the creative energy of the universe. This enables you to confront the truth with your eyes wide open.

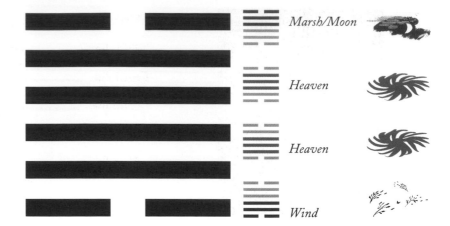

Marsh/Moon

Heaven

Heaven

Wind

Vigorous Mind

By clinging to illusions, you call down upon yourself more misfortune than pleasure. You will always be confronted by questions to which you have no answer or which entangle you more and more deeply in your own lies. The following directions *(reading from bottom to top)* may help you to face up to reality. (28)

Fulfilment

If you have understood the directions listed below, the only thought that remains is that you can enjoy the earthly game without losing yourself in illusions. 43

Creative Energy
The infinite depth of the heavens, which encircle the earth and in one way or another ensure a balance that keeps this pearl in her orbit, lends itself to being filled by every illusion imaginable. If you can, instead, manage to create within yourself a similar balance between giving and receiving, you will ultimately need no other reasons for existence. I

A Mature Relationship

Do not drown yourself in earthly worries. Study the power of the heavens which keep life in balance. Then, look around you and realize that every creature that becomes a link in the chain of life comes and goes. Try, therefore, to share your spiritual and physical wealth with others in the knowledge that everything you do not distribute loses its value and disappears. 44

TÂ KWO

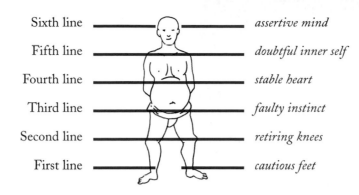

Sixth line —————— *assertive mind*

Fifth line —————— *doubtful inner self*

Fourth line —————— *stable heart*

Third line —————— *faulty instinct*

Second line —————— *retiring knees*

First line —————— *cautious feet*

The Individual Lines

Sixth line
The full moon symbolizes someone who is bathing shamelessly in earthly illusions. If you remember to break free of this fleeting enjoyment as soon as the moon wanes, no one can blame you for your behavior — although it is still somewhat suspect.

Fifth line
The new moon rising in the heavens is like a withered willow tree coming into flower again, or an old woman with a young bridegroom. The pleasure to be gained from such a situation is worth enjoying and will never disappoint, provided you do not pretend temporary things are eternal.

Fourth line
When the moon is dark, you are confronted with the infinite depth of the heavens. The moon will wax and drive away your loneliness, but the how and why of her return will always be hidden within the ocean of creative energy. Do not rack your brains about this; try to achieve an inner balance like the one you see before you.

Third line
The wind that originates in the infinite depth of the heavens represents the life force, whose workings you do not yet understand. You do not know what life is all about, and you are a little lost. Start by nurturing your will to survive so that you at least have something to hold on to.

Second line
The core of the wind, or your consciousness, at the base of the infinite depth of the heavens is like a withered willow tree that is sprouting anew, or an old man with a young bride. You realize that life's continuity depends on reproduction and you share your physical and spiritual wealth with others.

First line
The outermost line of the wind indicates that you weigh every word before offering any opinion about the workings of heaven's creative energy. If your mind cannot provide any explanation, how can you expect your feet to know?

Introduction
The Tâ Kwo hexagram points out the most secure way to approach life.
If you make earthly things your basis, you will sooner or later drown in your own illusions ☱. If you take your example from the wind ☴, you will always have recourse to a tangible reality, and its unknown outcome can only be better than you expected.

Strong and Weak Changing Lines
Extra attention should be paid to strong and weak lines in the hexagram you have thrown. A strong line signifies that you are addressing the situation with too much force, whereas a weak line calls for a bolder attitude.

The Hermetic *I Ching*
The answer to your specific question is not found only in the starting hexagram. For a deeper insight, you can also study the various separate hexagrams that make up the starting hexagram. The number next to these hexagrams indicates the page where you can find their complete interpretation. If the hexagram you have thrown contains changing lines, these direct you to a 'follow-up' hexagram.

Like life itself, the *I Ching* is a hermetic labyrinth of wonders from which you can only escape by closing the book.

The Follow-Up Hexagram
Once you have changed the strong and weak lines into their opposites, a new 'follow-up' hexagram is created which provides information about a future phase of life. The information on the left-hand page is the most useful for studying this hexagram, since follow-up hexagrams contain no changing lines.
The information on the right-hand page can, of course, be useful for clarifying your study of the follow-up hexagram.

} These hexagrams are components of the starting hexagram and offer directions for successfully dealing with your present situation.

The lines of the hexagram correspond to various parts of the body. The instructions you find there provide insight into your current physical and spiritual state.

⚊⊙⚊ : Strong Changing Line
⚋×⚋ : Weak Changing Line

大過 **28**

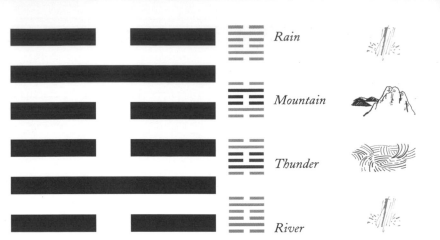

Rain

Mountain

Thunder

River

坎

The earth which brings forth all things

坎

A person breathing. The character also means: out of breath, becoming exhausted and failing in one's duty

KHAN (Water, the Giver of Life)

The complete character stands for a hole, a pit and a snare. The construction of Khan shows that the pit or the snare is earthly life, from which you cannot escape as long as you breathe.

In this hexagram, water symbolizes the cycle of life: it falls from the heavens and then streams to the sea, where it evaporates and returns again as rain. The mountain and the thunder symbolically indicate the eternal perpetuation of this cycle. On the other hand, the mountain also represents a stable person, who collects the fertile knowledge (the rainwater) and distributes it again, like the river tamed by the pulsating motion of the thunder. The ideal way to live is like a calmly flowing river, whose course brings it into contact with all the situations the earth brings forth. Without attaching to anything in particular, the river irrigates many fields and finally flows into the sea. Do not forget that the river bed has already been eroded by the current; many have preceeded you on this path. They, too, were aware that collecting knowledge, digesting it, and handing it on is the natural, inescapable course of life.

Water, the Giver of Life

Life is founded on the seas and sustained by its streams. Rain represents fertility, while the river — which springs forth so passionately and flows into the sea so calmly — symbolizes life's path. The following steps indicate the most fruitful way to move through life. **(29)**

Initial Difficulty

The rainwater forms a lake of fertile knowledge on the top of the mountain. When it overflows, the water continues on its way in the form of a river, which irrigates the fields. Similarly, you need to know what you are talking about if you want to have something to offer another. **39**

Confusion

Growth and confusion go hand in hand. The ideas and ideals you announced yesterday will be outdated tomorrow because you will have learned from experience. **3**

Nourishment

Nourish yourself with pieces of information whose eternal wisdom is proven. **27**

Youthful Innocence

When you are at the source of the river, do not think that you already know what rapids are waiting for you. After a superficial introduction to age-old wisdom, you would be unwise to pose as someone who has already traveled this way. **4**

Cutting the Knot

If the lake is completely full, it flows over. When you have the feeling that you need to make room in your spirit before you can receive anything new, the moment has come to distribute what you have learned. **40**

KHAN

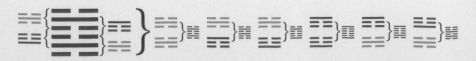

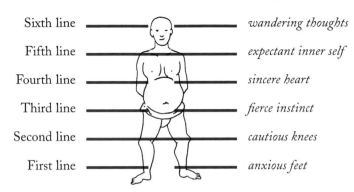

Sixth line ———————————— *wandering thoughts*

Fifth line ———————————— *expectant inner self*

Fourth line ———————————— *sincere heart*

Third line ———————————— *fierce instinct*

Second line ———————————— *cautious knees*

First line ———————————— *anxious feet*

The Individual Lines

Sixth line
The rainwater that collects on the top of the mountain and cannot flow away is like a head full of confused and obsessive thoughts. You have heard the bell toll, but you do not know what makes it ring. Make sure you are well-informed before you undertake anything.

Fifth line
The lake on the top of the mountain is not yet filled to the brim. You are on the verge of distributing your fertile knowledge. Do not throw yourself on others like a turbulent river. You need inner peace and self-control if you are to come across clearly.

Fourth line
Below the top of the mountain, the thunder keeps the river under control You are capable of distributing your knowledge in a form that is readily understandable, as if you were providing an easily digestible meal of rice and light wine, served up in simple earthenware. Universal truths have been handed out in this way since time immemorial.

Third line
The roar of the river as it plunges downwards and the rumble of the approaching thunder make the foot of the mountain tremble. This confus-ing situation indicates that any insights you may want to bestow on others are made redundant by new information that comes your way.
Hold yourself in, and wait until you have an overview of the situation.

Second line
The beginning of the thunder, or the eager lower jaw, is trying to get a hold on the river, or stream of life, as it flashes past. Making a choice out of all the abundance the earth brings forth seems difficult. By carefully setting your teeth into something, you will be able to move along until you encounter something else you would rather bite into.

First line
The river or stream of life, on which you can float peacefully along, brings you in contact with all things the earth brings forth and irrevocably dis-charges into the sea. Do not think that you can prevent life from ending by clinging to the bank. The only thing you will avoid are exquisite experiences.

Introduction
The Khan hexagram is determined by *Nourishment (27)*. The top of the mountain or the immovable upper jaw (fifth line) represent your inner assurance, which you develop by cautiously getting your teeth into things — as is symbolized by the pulsating movement of the thunder or lower jaw (second line) — and by first tasting them before you bite all the way through.

Strong and Weak Changing Lines
Extra attention should be paid to strong and weak lines in the hexagram you have thrown. A strong line signifies that you are addressing the situation with too much force, whereas a weak line calls for a bolder attitude.

The Hermetic *I Ching*
The answer to your specific question is not found only in the starting hexagram. For a deeper insight, you can also study the various separate hexagrams that make up the starting hexagram. The number next to these hexagrams indicates the page where you can find their complete interpretation. If the hexagram you have thrown contains changing lines, these direct you to a 'follow-up' hexagram.

Like life itself, the *I Ching* is a hermetic labyrinth of wonders from which you can only escape by closing the book.

The Follow-Up Hexagram
Once you have changed the strong and weak lines into their opposites, a new 'follow-up' hexa-gram is created which provides information about a future phase of life. The information on the left-hand page is the most useful for studying this hexagram, since follow-up hexagrams contain no changing lines.
The information on the right-hand page can, of course, be useful for clarifying your study of the follow-up hexagram.

} These hexagrams are components of the starting hexagram and offer directions for successfully dealing with your present situation.

The lines of the hexagram correspond to various parts of the body. The instructions you find there provide insight into your current physical and spiritual state.

▬●▬ : Strong Changing Line
▬✕▬ : Weak Changing Line

The yak — 離

A short-tailed bird —

LÎ (Fire, the Transforming Element)

Li as a whole means to separate, to leave, and to dissolve.
The construction of the character sheds light on these definitions.
The bird represents the freedom of your spirit which determines the
nourishment and motion of your material body, symbolized by the yak.
Once death moves in, the spirit leaves the body, and their pact
is dissolved.

In the hexagram, this dissolution is represented by the fire/sun
which transforms all things. This force is manifested by the moon's
cyclic transformation from a brilliant satellite into a dead rock. The sun,
the eternal center around which our planetary system turns, represents
insight and perspective. Similarly, you are a microcosm with an inner
source of light that is kept burning by your breath, or the wind, which
flies into you like the spirit of life. By feeding your body with earthly
experiences and mentally rising above matter like a bird, you develop
wisdom that gives you — like the sun — an overview of the material.
Remember that your body is transformed with each breath, because
your inner fire consumes you. On the other hand, the more inner light
you possess, the more youthful your radiance will be.

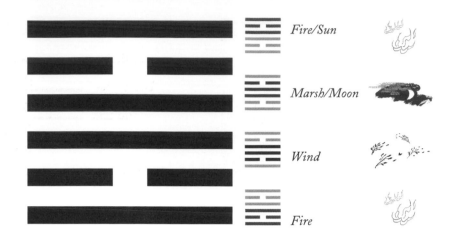

Fire/Sun

Marsh/Moon

Wind

Fire

Fire, the Transforming Element

Fire feeds on fuel. The light of the fire renders everything visible and the heat transforms the fuel into its
essential components. Once you are aware that your
inner fire is clear insight, you can understand the
value of your body as fuel. The following directions
(reading from bottom to top) may help you to burn like
a steady, clear flame.

(30)

Duality

The moon waxes and wanes again. After joy comes
grief, and after rain the sun will shine. The sun is
never extinguished. Do not think at the moments
when you see no light that there is no light at all.

38

Dissolving (Dissolution)

Be aware that you are constantly taking in and
digesting impressions. You should regularly submit
your body to a careful examination and analyze even
minor aches or pains you would normally repress.

50

Vigorous Mind

Let go of temporary, earthly illusions and attune your
life's rhythm to the eternal, creative energy of the
universe. In this way, you can confront the truth with
your eyes wide open.

28

Inner Change (Distillation)

Keep in mind that you cannot, and do not need to,
improve on creation. Only through inner change can
you develop the insight that everything is just as it is
meant to be.

49

The Management of the Inner Being

Breathe calmly, so that you can order your thoughts.
Then your inner fire will burn steadily, like a clear
flame, and will not be fanned or smothered by
emotions, anger, or exhausting impotence.

37

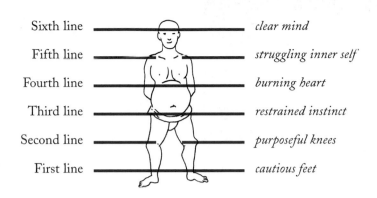

Sixth line	——————————	clear mind
Fifth line	——————————	struggling inner self
Fourth line	——————————	burning heart
Third line	——————————	restrained instinct
Second line	——————————	purposeful knees
First line	——————————	cautious feet

The Individual Lines

Sixth line
Like the ever-shining sun, your clear mind unifies your body and spirit by conscientiously driving out disturbing thoughts and the physical complaints associated with them. For the sun, everything is equal and one thing cannot be discordant with another.

Fifth line
The rose-red full moon, which is illuminated by the sun, bathes in the reflective surface of the marsh. The climax of a period has been reached, and once again you have to say goodbye to something that has given you much pleasure. Do not think, if you see no light at the moment, that there is no more light at all.

Fourth line
The sun and the beginning of the wind are submerged beneath the surface of the marsh/moon. Just as suddenly as life's light was kindled by your first breath, it will disappear with your last. Be aware that few people can reconcile themselves, deep in their hearts, to this fact.

Third line
The setting sun has disappeared below the bed of the marsh/moon and the core of the wind represents a breathing space. This situation indicates that you are behaving as if you are on the point of breathing your last breath, whereas in fact you have a whole life ahead of you. Enjoy it, and do not give up before your time has truly come.

Second line
The core of the inner fire, which is fueled by the wind or the breath, represents someone who thoroughly enjoys life. If you are like this, with your inner being in order, you can move calmly and purposefully through life like a clear flame which burns evenly.

First line
Your inner fire is kindled but you have not yet acquired much insight. Your first steps will be cautious. The more your inner self grows, the more you realize that simply continuing to breathe can offer you more insight.

Introduction
The Lî hexagram is dominated by *Vigorous Mind (28)*. Inner doubt (fifth line) about the correct use of your body (second line) will play tricks on you as long as you live. Even if you resolutely align yourself with the universal power-play, so that you move through life in the purest possible way, you cannot know the course your transformation will take.

Strong and Weak Changing Lines
Extra attention should be paid to strong and weak lines in the hexagram you have thrown. A strong line signifies that you are addressing the situation with too much force, whereas a weak line calls for a bolder attitude.

The Hermetic *I Ching*
The answer to your specific question is not found only in the starting hexagram. For a deeper insight, you can also study the various separate hexagrams that make up the starting hexagram. The number next to these hexagrams indicates the page where you can find their complete interpretation. If the hexagram you have thrown contains changing lines, these direct you to a 'follow-up' hexagram.

Like life itself, the *I Ching* is a hermetic labyrinth of wonders from which you can only escape by closing the book.

The Follow-Up Hexagram
Once you have changed the strong and weak lines into their opposites, a new 'follow-up' hexagram is created which provides information about a future phase of life. The information on the left-hand page is the most useful for studying this hexagram, since follow-up hexagrams contain no changing lines.
The information on the right-hand page can, of course, be useful for clarifying your study of the follow-up hexagram.

These hexagrams are components of the starting hexagram and offer directions for successfully dealing with your present situation.

The lines of the hexagram correspond to various parts of the body. The instructions you find there provide insight into your current physical and spiritual state.

▦▭ : Strong Changing Line
▦▭ : Weak Changing Line

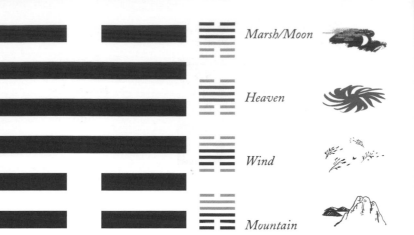

A kind of halberd (long-handled weapon)

The sickle-shaped, waxing moon, a wound, and a mouth.
Therefore: to wound with the mouth or to bite

HSIEN (The Game Of Love)

The current meaning of the character Hsien is: a whole, all and complete. The construction of the character indicates that you remain 'whole' by using the halberd to maintain your inner peace and cut yourself loose from destructive emotional situations at the right time. The wound caused by the mouth indicates that you have to stand firm in this, so that you are not later plagued by self-reproach.

In the hexagram, the movement of the marsh/moon points to the right time for harvesting experiences. The marsh/moon is embedded in the heavens, which represent inner strength. The core of the heavens (fourth line) is your heart, which you pawn for external physical and spiritual impressions. It is fed by your breath (or the wind) which is associated with the stable mountain. Taken as a whole, the hexagram indicates that you can maintain an overview and your inner peace through steady breathing. This peace does not stem from rigidity but from constantly moving past earthly matter (as the moon does) without getting bogged down in passions or undigested emotions. Love for yourself and for others depends on your zest for life, which you develop by continuously renewing yourself and lose by clinging on to finished business.

 Marsh/Moon

 Heaven

 Wind

 Mountain

The Game of Love
Earthly love is characterized by highs and lows. Heavenly love is constant. Through experience, you can develop the inner peace of the heavens, which means you can always be radiantly present. The following directions *(reading from bottom to top)* pave the way to a loving existence.

(31)

Fulfilment
If you have understood the preceding directions, the only thought that remains is that you can enjoy the earthly game peacefully and lovingly without losing yourself in illusions.

43

Vigorous Mind
Should an emotional love threaten to imprison you, concentrate on your breathing so that your inner peace is restored.

28

A Mature Relationship
Base your breathing on the power of the heavens, which sustain life in a loving and balanced way.

44

Withdrawal
Do not linger in a situation that has reached its climax. Draw back at the right time, and digest your experience focusing alternately on heaven and earth.

33

The Blessed Marriage
Summer, autumn, winter, spring, day, night, breathing in and breathing out; all these transitions mark the rhythm of earthly life. Each moment has its own beauty. If you lovingly move along with these moments, you will take action when the time is ripe and withdraw at the right moment.

53

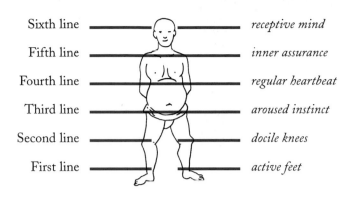

The Individual Lines

Sixth line — *receptive mind*
Fifth line — *inner assurance*
Fourth line — *regular heartbeat*
Third line — *aroused instinct*
Second line — *docile knees*
First line — *active feet*

Sixth line
The full moon influences your jaws and your tongue, so that you blather excitedly. Out of the abundance of the heart, the mouth overflows. Your harvest is great, but you must go on. Chew, swallow and move on to the next experience.

Fifth line
Beyond the reflective surface of the waxing moon lie the farthest reaches of the heavens. Here, you shrug your shoulders at the excitement that characterizes the sixth line. Inner surety and zest for life go hand in hand. Emotional excitement threatens this balance.

Fourth line
You have sold your heart, or the core of your inner heaven, to the new moon, or an illusion. The functioning of your heart depends on your breathing. As long as you can control your highs and lows by breathing calmly, your heart will beat steadily and manifest itself in a warm and joyful feeling.

Third line
The top of the mountain reaching to the heavens and the core of the wind, or the moment between breathing in and breathing out, represent the choice you have to make between keeping an overview or throwing yourself into earthly pleasures. Stay in control until you recognize the moment (sixth line) when you can briefly let yourself go.

Second line
Under the top of the mountain the wind, or your breathing, influences your attitude to life. You champ at the bit as soon as you scent the temptations of the earth. Inner peace and your zest for life may hold you back from completely immersing yourself in earthly things.

First line
At the foot of the mountain, you are moving your toes. Your feet have no say in which way they should go. Wait calmly for what will present itself and lovingly follow life's path without giving up your inner peace.

Introduction
The Hsien hexagram is determined by *Vigorous Mind (28)*. The sixth line indicates a receptive mind and the second line a stable attitude to life. Inner peace ☶ is maintained both by taking in and giving out (as the moon does ☱) and through regular breathing ☴.

Strong and Weak Changing Lines
Extra attention should be paid to strong and weak lines in the hexagram you have thrown. A strong line signifies that you are addressing the situation with too much force, whereas a weak line calls for a bolder attitude.

The Hermetic *I Ching*
The answer to your specific question is not found only in the starting hexagram. For a deeper insight, you can also study the various separate hexagrams that make up the starting hexagram. The number next to these hexagrams indicates the page where you can find their complete interpretation. If the hexagram you have thrown contains changing lines, these direct you to a 'follow-up' hexagram.

Like life itself, the *I Ching* is a hermetic labyrinth of wonders from which you can only escape by closing the book.

The Follow-Up Hexagram
Once you have changed the strong and weak lines into their opposites, a new 'follow-up' hexagram is created which provides information about a future phase of life. The information on the left-hand page is the most useful for studying this hexagram, since follow-up hexagrams contain no changing lines.
The information on the right-hand page can, of course, be useful for clarifying your study of the follow-up hexagram.

} These hexagrams are components of the starting hexagram and offer directions for successfully dealing with your present situation.

 The lines of the hexagram correspond to various parts of the body. The instructions you find there provide insight into your current physical and spiritual state.

 : Strong Changing Line
: Weak Changing Line

咸   **31**

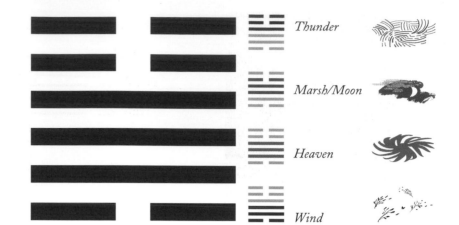

The human heart — 恒

An object that turns full circle. A cycle —

HÊNG (Continuity, Balanced Movement)

The character Hêng stands for continuity and, as the construction of the character indicates, this refers to the life span of the human heart. Your heart beats most regularly and longest if your breathing is attuned to the intensity of your physical effort, rather than being influenced by mental confusion. A long life depends on balanced physical satisfaction.

In the hexagram, the core of the heavens or your instinct (third line) is the seat of your physical well-being. This heaven is formed by the marsh/moon and the wind. On the one hand, this indicates a stable life cycle — like that of the waxing, waning moon — in which there is a timely release of the tension you have built up in your body. On the other hand, the wind, or your breathing, which is associated with the lower part of your body, suggests that your heartbeat is not affected by disturbing thoughts. Therefore, the thunder pulsates like a regularly beating heart—becoming excited by instinctive stirrings and quickening during physical exertion, but calming down again as soon as you are physically satisfied.

Thunder
Marsh/Moon
Heaven
Wind

Continuity, Balanced Movement
The regular release of physical tension contributes to one's zest for life and a longer life span. The following directions *(reading from bottom to top)* warn that by giving yourself over to physical satisfaction, you would only achieve the opposite.

(32)

Fertility
The most fertile time for physical release is initially sensed intuitively. As you dare to trust these feelings, they develop into an inner conviction.

54

Vital Energy
Keep in mind that whenever you have to force yourself to reach physical satisfaction, you are on the wrong track. True vital energy, which is connected to the heavens, is characterized by a minimal waste of energy.

34

Fulfilment
If you have understood the previous directions, the only thought that remains is that you can physically enjoy the earthly game without losing yourself in illusions.

43

Vigorous Mind
If you sense that letting yourself go may imprison you in physical addiction, concentrate on your breathing in order to restore your inner peace.

28

A Mature Relationship
Base your breathing on the power of the heavens, which sustain life in an impersonal, well-balanced, and loving way.

44

HÊNG

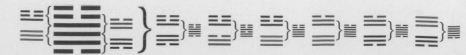

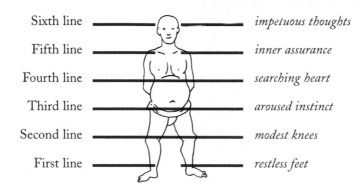

The Individual Lines

Sixth line ———— impetuous thoughts

Fifth line ———— inner assurance

Fourth line ———— searching heart

Third line ———— aroused instinct

Second line ———— modest knees

First line ———— restless feet

The Individual Lines

Sixth line
The uppermost line of the thunder indicates that you are struggling to think of a way to extend your life span. Your body indicates when it is hungry or thirsty and when it needs relief, so you should also trust it to signal its need for exercise and satisfaction.

Fifth line
The full moon and the disturbance in the core of the thunder point to a period of physical unrest. Giving yourself over to physical satisfaction at this moment can do no harm. But you should be aware that later you will have to restore your inner peace, just as surely as the moon will wane again.

Fourth line
Beyond the reflective surface of the waxing moon the outer limits of the heavens can be found, and the beginning of the thunder pulsates like a steadily beating heart. This situation indicates that you are not stimulated to physical satisfaction at the moment. It would appear that there is no exciting 'game' in your field of vision. Stop hunting!

Third line
The core of your inner heaven, or your instinct, is still balanced thanks to unconscious breathing, but the waxing of the new moon stirs you to seek physical fulfilment. You may find your instincts embarrassing and try to repress them, but this will not be to your advantage if you want to fully enjoy a long life.

Second line
The core of the wind, or the moment between breathing in and breathing out, is located at the border of the inner heaven, which suggests that you are waiting for action. Like your pliant and obedient knees, you await stimuli that will set you in motion. You will respond instinctively, without mentally screening these stimuli.

First line
The outermost line of the wind represents the uninterrupted rhythm of your breathing. This line is connected to your feet and indicates that you are constantly wanting to move, even though this movement (as opposed to steady breathing) is not conducive to a long life.

Introduction
The Hêng hexagram is determined by *Vigorous Mind (28)*. The fifth line stands for the inner surety that exercise and physical satisfaction are necessary for a long life span. This is confirmed by the first line, or your feet which are always itching to hit the road.

Strong and Weak Changing Lines
Extra attention should be paid to strong and weak lines in the hexagram you have thrown. A strong line signifies that you are addressing the situation with too much force, whereas a weak line calls for a bolder attitude.

The Hermetic *I Ching*
The answer to your specific question is not found only in the starting hexagram. For a deeper insight, you can also study the various separate hexagrams that make up the starting hexagram. The number next to these hexagrams indicates the page where you can find their complete interpretation. If the hexagram you have thrown contains changing lines, these direct you to a 'follow-up' hexagram.

Like life itself, the *I Ching* is a hermetic labyrinth of wonders from which you can only escape by closing the book.

The Follow-Up Hexagram
Once you have changed the strong and weak lines into their opposites, a new 'follow-up' hexagram is created which provides information about a future phase of life. The information on the left-hand page is the most useful for studying this hexagram, since follow-up hexagrams contain no changing lines.
The information on the right-hand page can, of course, be useful for clarifying your study of the follow-up hexagram.

These hexagrams are components of the starting hexagram and offer directions for successfully dealing with your present situation.

The lines of the hexagram correspond to various parts of the body. The instructions you find there provide insight into your current physical and spiritual state.

⬛─o─⬛ : Strong Changing Line
⬛─x─⬛ : Weak Changing Line

恒  **32**

Sacrificial meat. A suckling pig
Meat, the moon
Walking step by step
A male pig (a boar)

THUN (Withdrawal)

Thun means to flee, to hide and to withdraw. The construction of the character indicates that the illusory fantasies of the mindless masses (symbolized by meat) are gradually being exalted to 'truths'. If you do not want to offer up your inner world of ideas, as a suckling pig is sacrificed, have the courage to withdraw in time, head held high, and seek the solitude of the wild boar.

The two heavens in the hexagram point to a situation in which the infinite depth of the upper, true heaven is obscured by the lower, mythical heaven, which is a product of the human mind. The wind, or the realm of thought, which originates in the true heaven and blows through the imagined heaven, suggests the notion of filling in one's innate, inner emptiness with a belief that gives meaning to human existence. If you do not want to be steeped in these illusions, which are usually religious but may also stem from another form of naiveté, your only option is to courageously withdraw from the gullible crowd to the top of the mountain. Here, you can clearly see the interaction between yourself and the infinite depth of the heavens.

Heaven
Heaven
Wind
Mountain

Withdrawal
If you sense that you are in danger of becoming caught up in notions that are incompatible with your fundamental, inner truth, withdrawing from the situation is a mark of courage, for it means leaving behind your friends and relatives. This difficult path is laid out for you below *(reading from bottom to top)*. (33)

Creative Energy
There are no sufficient words for describing the universe, but you might experience something of this immense ocean of creative energy by allowing your consciousness to dissolve into it completely.
You can then return to human fancies with a shrug and a clear mind. I

A Mature Relationship
You are advised to undertake the confrontation with the infinite depth of the heavens, while finding a way to deal with the loss of friends and relatives. Withdrawing is hard, because you deny yourself much when you rise above humanity and adhere to concepts which, like the power of the heavens, feel balanced and affectionate but — above all — impersonal. 44

Withdrawal
Never disappear too hastily. Retain a well-balanced presence and finish the affairs in which you are involved. With your inner calm you will stand out from the crowd, and you will be seen — as the true heavens are seen — without attracting any real attention. (33)

The Blessed Marriage
Always keep an overview, and take care not to be unconsciously influenced by thoughts of duty or safety. Remain true to yourself, and stay involved as long as the situation is acceptable to you. Withdraw only when you feel it is time to do so. 53

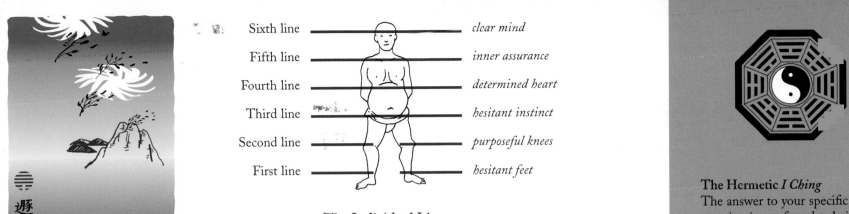

Sixth line ——————— *clear mind*

Fifth line ——————— *inner assurance*

Fourth line ——————— *determined heart*

Third line ——————— *hesitant instinct*

Second line ——————— *purposeful knees*

First line ——————— *hesitant feet*

The Individual Lines

Sixth line

This outermost line of the true heaven is not influenced by the invented universe. You have remained true to yourself and nobly withdrawn in order to stay in contact with your deepest, inner truth. As soon as you feel the time is ripe, you can re-enter the earthly arena with a clear mind.

Fifth line

The core of the true heaven is overshadowed by the outermost line of the invented universe. Your inner surety is so powerful that you withdraw no further than is strictly necessary, so that you do not have to turn your back on everyone and anyone who is dear to you.

Fourth line

The beginning of the true heaven lies hidden beneath the core of the invented universe. The wind that originates here is like your deepest, inner truth. You withdraw in order to preserve that pure feeling in yourself, but it tears at your heartstrings to abandon what is dear to you.

Third line

The top of the mountain is veiled by the beginning of the invented universe, while the middle of the wind, or the moment between breathing in and breathing out, indicates hesitant behavior. You will find it easier to overcome this hesitance if you are leaving only material security behind, rather than friends and relatives. Remain true to yourself!

Second line

The wind that rises in the infinite depth of the true heaven blows below the top of the mountain. As long as this energy is maintaining the purity of your inner being, you will be flexible enough to survive in the common herd and the inner peace you radiate will ensure that you (like the true heaven) are seen, but do not attract any attention.

First line

You are at the foot of the mountain and cannot reach the summit in time. The best thing to do is to mark time and maintain a profound inner calm until the tide of stupidity turns.

Introduction

In the Thun hexagram, the top of the mountain (third line) is the only place where you can escape ideas that threaten your inner peace.

By connecting your realm of thought ☷ directly to the infinite depth of the true, upper heaven ☰ you can stand firm and wait for the tide of stupidity to turn.

Strong and Weak Changing Lines

Extra attention should be paid to strong and weak lines in the hexagram you have thrown. A strong line signifies that you are addressing the situation with too much force, whereas a weak line calls for a bolder attitude.

The Hermetic *I Ching*

The answer to your specific question is not found only in the starting hexagram. For a deeper insight, you can also study the various separate hexagrams that make up the starting hexagram. The number next to these hexagrams indicates the page where you can find their complete interpretation. If the hexagram you have thrown contains changing lines, these direct you to a 'follow-up' hexagram.

Like life itself, the *I Ching* is a hermetic labyrinth of wonders from which you can only escape by closing the book.

The Follow-Up Hexagram

Once you have changed the strong and weak lines into their opposites, a new 'follow-up' hexagram is created which provides information about a future phase of life. The information on the left-hand page is the most useful for studying this hexagram, since follow-up hexagrams contain no changing lines.

The information on the right-hand page can, of course, be useful for clarifying your study of the follow-up hexagram.

} These hexagrams are components of the starting hexagram and offer directions for successfully dealing with your present situation.

 The lines of the hexagram correspond to various parts of the body. The instructions you find there provide insight into your current physical and spiritual state.

▬ⓞ▬ : Strong Changing Line
▬✕▬ : Weak Changing Line

 **33**

Thunder

Marsh/Moon

Heaven

Heaven

大
壯

A mature person. Also: big and tall ——⌐

The left half of a tree. Also: thick and strong ——| 大壯

A wise person or a scholar ——⌐

TÂ KWANG (Vital Energy)

The characters Tâ and Kwang indicate a mature way of dealing with
vital energy. The left half of the tree also symbolizes the left hand,
or strength. The wise person in possession of great strength uses the
right hand (or giving hand) to apply this power with diplomacy,
intelligence and self-control.

Vital energy, which is by nature balanced and impersonal, is symbolized in the hexagram by the lower, true heaven. This heaven is associated
with the lower part of the body, which implements your orders with as
much energy as you put into steering it. The reflective marsh/moon is
embedded in the true heaven and colors the upper heaven (that is, your
inner heaven). You have to attune your vital energy to the demands of
earthly existence, and if you expend this energy as the moon does you
will never overextend yourself. As soon as your inner strength approaches
boiling point, it starts to decline, and just when you think you feel weak,
it increases again. If you can deal with your vital energy in this way, your
heart will be filled with zest for life and pulsate as steadily as the thunder, whose rhythm is derived from the constant motion of the moon.

Vital Energy
You are truly strong only when you use your strength
wisely. Then great strength is a blessing rather than
a source of misery. The following directions *(reading
from bottom to top)* explain how you can optimize the
application of your vital energy.

(34)

Fertility
Observe the rhythm of the moon, which grows full
and wanes again, and never falters on her way.
Similarly, you will have to sense intuitively the most
fruitful time for applying your vital energy. The more
you dare to trust this sense, the more it will develop
into an inner conviction.

54

Vital Energy
Keep in mind that whenever you have to force yourself to achieve something, you are on the wrong track.
True vital energy which is connected to the heavens
opens more doors with diplomacy, intelligence, and
self-control than with brute force.

(34)

Fulfilment
If you want to maintain your zest for life you will
have to carefully conserve your inner balance.
Do not be tempted to think that material possessions
mean more than they do. By wasting your vital energy
on them you turn a source of pleasure into a pool
of misery.

43

Creative Energy
The infinite depth of the heavens, which encircle the
earth and in one way or another ensure a balance that
keeps this pearl in her orbit, serve as your great example of how cautiously you should use your strength.

1

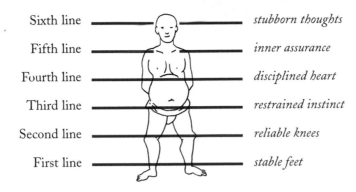

Sixth line ———————— *stubborn thoughts*

Fifth line ———————— *inner assurance*

Fourth line ———————— *disciplined heart*

Third line ———————— *restrained instinct*

Second line ———————— *reliable knees*

First line ———————— *stable feet*

The Individual Lines

Sixth line
The uppermost line of the thunder indicates that thought alone renders your vital energy useless. If you do not convert your thoughts into deeds, they keep churning around in your brain, so that you are like a frustrated ram battering his head aimlessly against the enclosure that prevents him from moving forwards or backwards.

Fifth line
In the core of the thunder, the moment of full moon has not yet been reached. This indicates the need to subtly expend your vital energy before your inner tension reaches a climax. You temper this power with wisdom, so that you are not like a ram in heat throwing himself on a docile ewe.

Fourth line
Your heartbeat is as steady as the thunder, which derives its rhythm from the constant motion of the moon. A vital heart is like the axis of a wheel whose tension is distributed evenly through its spokes. If you are spiritually and physically in balance, doors that brute force could never unlock will open for you.

Third line
The dark moon symbolizes your survival instinct, which is based on the naturally balanced and impersonal strength of the heavens and which is unconsciously activated in threatening situations. Consciously taking off the built-in brake on your instinct will lead to brutal explosions of power. A strong person exercises self-discipline in every situation.

Second line
By attuning yourself to the heart of the true heaven — the outstanding example of balance in motion and motion in balance — you develop an inner equilibrium and flexibility that allows you to adapt the use of your vital energy and adopt the appropriate attitude in any situation that life presents.

First line
The outermost border of the true heavens asserts great vital energy, but like your feet is not in a position to exert any influence on your motivation to do something with this power. For the moment, it would be unwise to use your vital energy for anything other than preserving your inner peace.

Introduction
The Tâ Kwang hexagram indicates that you, like any other living creature, are a source of unconscious vital energy (lines one to four, inclusive) which is directed first and foremost towards the survival of the species. Inner refinement (fifth line) and intelligence (sixth line) raise you above this behavior and help to channel this power within yourself.

Strong and Weak Changing Lines
Extra attention should be paid to strong and weak lines in the hexagram you have thrown. A strong line signifies that you are addressing the situation with too much force, whereas a weak line calls for a bolder attitude.

The Hermetic *I Ching*
The answer to your specific question is not found only in the starting hexagram. For a deeper insight, you can also study the various separate hexagrams that make up the starting hexagram. The number next to these hexagrams indicates the page where you can find their complete interpretation. If the hexagram you have thrown contains changing lines, these direct you to a 'follow-up' hexagram.

Like life itself, the *I Ching* is a hermetic labyrinth of wonders from which you can only escape by closing the book.

The Follow-Up Hexagram
Once you have changed the strong and weak lines into their opposites, a new 'follow-up' hexagram is created which provides information about a future phase of life. The information on the left-hand page is the most useful for studying this hexagram, since follow-up hexagrams contain no changing lines.
The information on the right-hand page can, of course, be useful for clarifying your study of the follow-up hexagram.

These hexagrams are components of the starting hexagram and offer directions for successfully dealing with your present situation.

The lines of the hexagram correspond to various parts of the body. The instructions you find there provide insight into your current physical and spiritual state.

⬛—o—⬛ : Strong Changing Line
⬛—x—⬛ : Weak Changing Line

大壯

34

Birds swoop down on the field looking for food ──

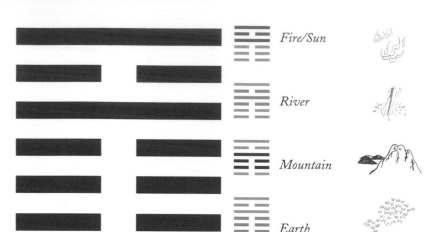

The sun rises above the horizon ──

CHIN (Advance, Approach)

The character Chin represents the sunrise, which makes visible all that the earth brings forth. The birds descending to earth are a sign that you are moving from a vantage point towards the things you need. Earthly life provides for everyone's needs and if you have an independent spirit you can choose from the abundance whatever suits you for the moment.

The sun, which shines impartially on all things, is above the mountain in this hexagram, indicating that you have an overview that is not colored by prejudices. Your fertile knowledge, which is stored as a lake on the top of the mountain, has been completely digested so that you can go out, unhindered by your past, to meet the future the earth lays out before you. These achievements mean you can move through earthly life with the inner peace of a stable mountain and the fluidity of water in a stream, which saturates everything in its path but attaches to nothing. If you can also digest the knowledge you collect along the way, you will develop into a sun which cheers everyone with its light.

Fire/Sun

River

Mountain

Earth

Advance, Approach
At first sunlight, what lies before you is made visible. At high noon, you have an overview of what you have and have not yet accomplished. And at sunset you know what the day has brought you. In the following directions it will become clear that 'approach' does not simply mean moving towards something, but also achieving insight or becoming more in touch with yourself. **(35)**

Restricted Movement
You move like a young fox that has wet its tail. If you want to know how to prevent this in future, you had better ask an old fox for advice. **64**

The Wise Man
The wise man is like the sun that crowns the top of the mountain. Equipped with inner peace and an overview, this old fox moves impartially over the earth. **56**

Initial Difficulty
Gravity forces the water on the top of the mountain to find its way downwards. Wise people know that if they want to be seen as a sun they also have to behave like one, bestowing their knowledge just as impartially and obligingly, every day. **39**

Union
Self-control, inner peace, and insight into others are the qualities that determine whether the knowledge you hand out falls on fertile ground. However wise you may be, do not forget that you, too, can learn something from the process of giving. **8**

The Destruction of the Past
If you digest at night the experiences gathered during the day, you will face the next day in a good mood and again be able to take your pick from the abundant impressions that present themselves. **23**

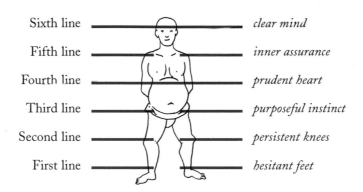

Sixth line ——————————— *clear mind*

Fifth line ——————————— *inner assurance*

Fourth line ——————————— *prudent heart*

Third line ——————————— *purposeful instinct*

Second line ——————————— *persistent knees*

First line ——————————— *hesitant feet*

The Individual Lines

Sixth line
The sun setting behind the mountain top suggests a head crowned with horns. This indicates that while you project consistent opinions to the outside world you are constantly beset by private doubts about what would have happened if you had made a different decision.

Fifth line
The sun is at its zenith and has united with the water, or your fertile knowledge. You have inner assurance and are ready to distribute what you have acquired. If you do, there is no point in worrying about whether you will succeed or fail. The sun never asks itself such a question.

Fourth line
The rising sun under the lake of fertile knowledge on the top of the mountain is a sign that you want to advance but you are behaving like a mole which shuns the daylight. If you have digested yesterday's experiences there is nothing stopping you from setting a goal for this new day.

Third line
Under the top of the mountain, fertile knowledge streams like water over the surface of the earth. Self-control, inner peace, and insight into the growth processes of others turn you into a sun that allows its light to shine on everyone around it.

Second line
Beneath the earth's surface, where the foot of the mountain lies hidden, you want to advance, but you have no overview. If you stand firm and keep looking around you to see how others are rooted in mother Earth, you will discover there is still a lot to learn.

First line
Deep beneath the earth's surface, your feet are ready to advance. Stand firm and always be willing (like your obedient feet) to treat everyone who approaches you kindly. You do not have to have an overview in order to learn your own lesson in life.

Introduction
The Chin hexagram is determined by *The Destruction of the Past (23)*. You can move through creation just like the sun ☰, which always bestows its light radiantly and impartially, if you re-examine at noon the goal you set yourself in the morning and digest the day's experiences at night.

Strong and Weak Changing Lines
Extra attention should be paid to strong and weak lines in the hexagram you have thrown. A strong line signifies that you are addressing the situation with too much force, whereas a weak line calls for a bolder attitude.

The Hermetic *I Ching*
The answer to your specific question is not found only in the starting hexagram. For a deeper insight, you can also study the various separate hexagrams that make up the starting hexagram. The number next to these hexagrams indicates the page where you can find their complete interpretation. If the hexagram you have thrown contains changing lines, these direct you to a 'follow-up' hexagram.

Like life itself, the *I Ching* is a hermetic labyrinth of wonders from which you can only escape by closing the book.

The Follow-Up Hexagram
Once you have changed the strong and weak lines into their opposites, a new 'follow-up' hexagram is created which provides information about a future phase of life. The information on the left-hand page is the most useful for studying this hexagram, since follow-up hexagrams contain no changing lines.
The information on the right-hand page can, of course, be useful for clarifying your study of the follow-up hexagram.

} These hexagrams are components of the starting hexagram and offer directions for successfully dealing with your present situation.

The lines of the hexagram correspond to various parts of the body. The instructions you find there provide insight into your current physical and spiritual state.

▬●▬ : Strong Changing Line
▬✕▬ : Weak Changing Line

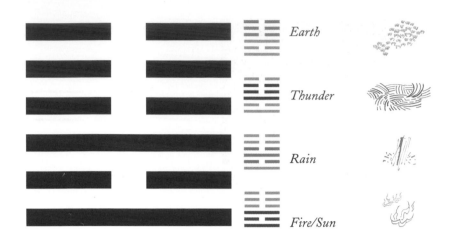

Earth

Thunder

Rain

Fire/Sun

明夷

The sun — 明

A man armed with a bow. A barbarian, uncivilized, to kill.

The character can also denote a peaceful feeling. — 夷

The moon which reflects the sunlight. Light, clarity, insight —

MING Î (Hidden Insight)

The interplay of the characters Ming and Î indicates the emergence of a dark force that drives out light and insight. If intolerance rules your environment, you would be wise to hide your wisdom for the time being. With a peaceful feeling you can accept the fact that just as the sun and the moon periodically disappear and reappear, the time will come when you can let your light shine again.

In the hexagram, the disappearance of the light is symbolized by the dense rainclouds which block the sun from view and by the earth turning away from the sun. This situation is not hopeless, however, as indicated by the thunder beginning at the third line (your survival instinct). The pulsating thunder suggests, on the one hand, that the earth constantly rotates, ensuring that the sun becomes visible again. On the other hand, that you keep your inner light and fertile knowledge hidden until the time is ripe to chase away the darkness that dominates your surroundings like a cloud veiling the sun.

Hidden Insight

If a regime that shuns the daylight assumes power, keep your clear insight hidden; your inscrutable exterior will safeguard your freedom to act. The following directions can shed light on your path in dark times.

(36)

Winter Solstice, Awakening

Just as there comes a time when the sun can let its power be felt once again, the moment will come when you can manage to drive out the darkness that dominates your environment.

24

The Army

Follow your survival instinct, seek allies, base your strategy on the common good, and do not allow yourself to be carried away by egotism, anger, or other emotions.

7

Cutting the Knot

Now that your strength is increasing and the dark force is beginning to show its weakness, it is time to strike.

40

Completion

When the sun reaches its highest point, it starts to descend. The sun keeps on shining but cannot prevent the night. Be aware, therefore, that you can temporarily dispel a dark force, but you cannot destroy it forever.

55

Successful Movement

In time, the sun always breaks through a layer of clouds. If you are aware of this, you will be able to confront each dark situation by shrouding your clear insight in mystery, knowing that your pure inner being is not dependent on external appearances.

63

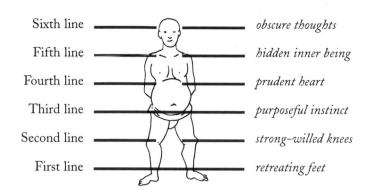

Sixth line	—	*obscure thoughts*
Fifth line	—	*hidden inner being*
Fourth line	—	*prudent heart*
Third line	—	*purposeful instinct*
Second line	—	*strong-willed knees*
First line	—	*retreating feet*

The Individual Lines

Sixth line

The surface of the earth is shrouded in darkness. The dark force that now rules to the farthest reaches of the heavens shall soon disappear below the earth. Darkness will always be driven out by light, and, in the same way, all forms of tyranny will come to an end if they are constantly undermined.

Fifth line

The thunder rumbles beneath the surface of the earth. Many 'trees' that tolerated nothing in their shadow and thought that they could grow to reach the heavens have been felled by people who steadily gnawed at their roots while carefully concealing their intentions.

Fourth line

Deep beneath the earth's surface, the core of the pulsating thunder raises a curtain of mist. If you assume an outward appearance that hides your inner intentions, you can cautiously leave your hiding place and explore the enemy position by entering the dark force and leaving it again.

Third line

The start of the thunder, or your survival instinct, allows your inner light to shine like the midday sun. The dark force that has shrouded you like a layer of clouds is broken up and driven away. Realize that in a dualistic world you can temporarily ban evil, but you can never destroy it forever.

Second line

The red layer of clouds that obscures the rising sun indicates that the dark force offends your sense of what is right and proper. Be like the sun, which seems to disappear behind the clouds but in reality is always ready to let its light shine.

First line

The sun has set. You would be well advised to stay on the alert, like the sun, and hide your insight. No one will hear you if you go knocking on doors, for they are all asleep. Wait for the right moment before you speak the saving words that will expel the force causing the darkness.

Introduction

The Ming Î hexagram is determined by *Winter Solstice, Awakening (24)*. You need to realize that, just as the sun is regularly banned by the force of darkness, there are periods in which it is better to hide until the moment arrives when you are called upon to act.

Strong and Weak Changing Lines

Extra attention should be paid to strong and weak lines in the hexagram you have thrown. A strong line signifies that you are addressing the situation with too much force, whereas a weak line calls for a bolder attitude.

The Hermetic *I Ching*

The answer to your specific question is not found only in the starting hexagram. For a deeper insight, you can also study the various separate hexagrams that make up the starting hexagram. The number next to these hexagrams indicates the page where you can find their complete interpretation. If the hexagram you have thrown contains changing lines, these direct you to a 'follow-up' hexagram.

Like life itself, the *I Ching* is a hermetic labyrinth of wonders from which you can only escape by closing the book.

The Follow-Up Hexagram

Once you have changed the strong and weak lines into their opposites, a new 'follow-up' hexagram is created which provides information about a future phase of life. The information on the left-hand page is the most useful for studying this hexagram, since follow-up hexagrams contain no changing lines. The information on the right-hand page can, of course, be useful for clarifying your study of the follow-up hexagram.

These hexagrams are components of the starting hexagram and offer directions for successfully dealing with your present situation.

The lines of the hexagram correspond to various parts of the body. The instructions you find there provide insight into your current physical and spiritual state.

— o — : Strong Changing Line
— x — : Weak Changing Line

明夷 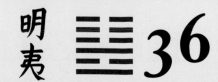 **36**

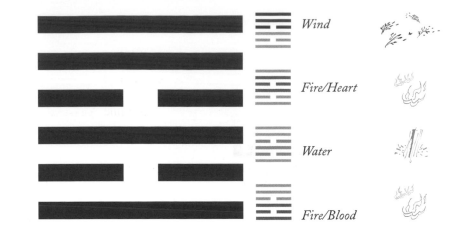

Pigs living in and around a house. Also: a man in his house ——

The legs of a person. Standing erect or with a straight back ——

家人

KÎA ZÂN

(The Management of the Inner Being)

The characters Kîa and Zân indicate the fair management of a household (or the inner being). Your male aspect, or your spiritual disposition, is first and foremost responsible for your female aspect, or your physical well-being. If you are sincere and your outward appearance radiates the peace of your inner being, you will serve as an example to those around you.

The hexagram shows that the right attitude to life stems from your breath, or the wind. The wind also stands for your realm of thought, and it is obvious that if you harbor sincere thoughts your breathing will have a rhythm that is in tune with your spiritual peace. Steady breathing ensures that your inner fire is kept alight by a regularly beating heart. The blood running through your veins keeps your body — of which about eighty percent is water — at the right temperature. The blood is also connected with your temperament and your sexual instinct. These characteristics, too, are determined by your degree of inner peace, and it is worth ensuring that the periodic tension they cause is diffused in time.

Wind

Fire/Heart

Water

Fire/Blood

The Management of the Inner Being
Your outward behavior depends on your spiritual disposition. The more you are tormented by frustrations, the more anger and uncontrolled emotion will drive you to behave like a wild boar and estrange yourself from those around you. This is not to say that you should simply roll in the mud like a fattened pig and then let yourself be led to the slaughter. If you want to follow a middle way, you can learn how to do so from the following directions.

(37)

Redemption
If you first calmly weigh up what you think, and then not only say what you think but also do what you say, you win the trust of those around you. If you simply say whatever comes into your head without putting your words into effect, you have lost before you have even begun.

59

Restricted Movement
You are still moving like a young fox that has wet its tail. You have given up your inner peace in order to satisfy your physical instincts.

64

Fire, the Transforming Element
Once you bring your inner fire to consciousness in the form of clear insight, you can understand the value of your body as the fuel for this fire and you know that you have to treat it with care. Do not be too cautious, though. If your inner thermostat is never turned up to full enjoyment, zest for life is out of the question.

30

Successful Movement
Now that you are moving like an old fox, you know precisely when and how you can satisfy your physical needs without overstepping the bounds of courtesy.

63

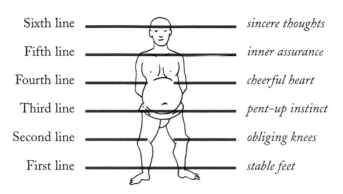

Sixth line ———————— *sincere thoughts*

Fifth line ———————— *inner assurance*

Fourth line ———————— *cheerful heart*

Third line ———————— *pent-up instinct*

Second line ———————— *obliging knees*

First line ———————— *stable feet*

The Individual Lines

Sixth line

The beginning of the wind is like your — still unconscious — realm of thought, which by nature is not colored by external impressions and is as sincere as the mind of a newborn child. If you can keep on dealing in an unprejudiced way with your surroundings, you are truly an upright person.

Fifth line

The core of the wind, or your consciousness, keeps your inner fire burning confidently. You are your body's sovereign, a master who senses the needs of all his subjects and does not neglect a single function. If you radiate this sort of assurance, you are an example to all.

Fourth line

Fed by your breathing, your heart beats regularly and keeps your body, which is predominantly water, at the right temperature. This keeps you cheerful, so that you can always approach those around you in a friendly way and do not have to lash out at anyone in frustration.

Third line

The inner fire controls the water to its very core. This means that you have your temper and instincts under control. Take care that your spiritual regime is not too rigid. If your body cannot release tension at the appropriate time, your zest for life disappears and those around you will mock you for being exaggeratedly righteous.

Second line

The inner fire, or the blood running through your veins, keeps your body at the right temperature. By respecting your body's needs and providing it with the quantities of air, light, water, food and action it naturally requires, you ward off physical ailments that can influence your spirit.

First line

The fire that activates your feet is kindled in your spirit. If you think with your feet, restlessness will dominate you all your life. Once you are aware that each part of the body has a specific function, you can discover what 'moves' other people, and in this way assess what they are like.

Introduction

The Kîa Zân hexagram is determined by your breathing ☴, which enables you to regulate your inner fire ☲. Your outward behavior, or your physical presentation, symbolized by the water ☵, becomes slow and uninterested when it is cooled down too much, and emotional and aggressive when it is overheated.

Strong and Weak Changing Lines

Extra attention should be paid to strong and weak lines in the hexagram you have thrown. A strong line signifies that you are addressing the situation with too much force, whereas a weak line calls for a bolder attitude.

The Hermetic *I Ching*

The answer to your specific question is not found only in the starting hexagram. For a deeper insight, you can also study the various separate hexagrams that make up the starting hexagram. The number next to these hexagrams indicates the page where you can find their complete interpretation. If the hexagram you have thrown contains changing lines, these direct you to a 'follow-up' hexagram.

Like life itself, the *I Ching* is a hermetic labyrinth of wonders from which you can only escape by closing the book.

The Follow-Up Hexagram

Once you have changed the strong and weak lines into their opposites, a new 'follow-up' hexagram is created which provides information about a future phase of life. The information on the left-hand page is the most useful for studying this hexagram, since follow-up hexagrams contain no changing lines.

The information on the right-hand page can, of course, be useful for clarifying your study of the follow-up hexagram.

These hexagrams are components of the starting hexagram and offer directions for successfully dealing with your present situation.

The lines of the hexagram correspond to various parts of the body. The instructions you find there provide insight into your current physical and spiritual state.

▬o▬ : Strong Changing Line
▬x▬ : Weak Changing Line

家人 ䷤ **37**

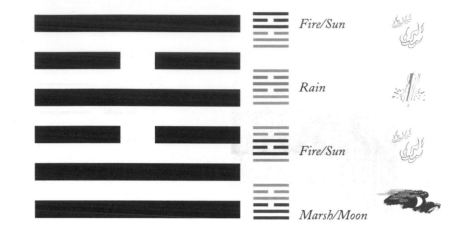

Fire/Sun

Rain

Fire/Sun

Marsh/Moon

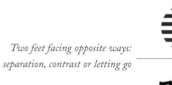

*Two feet facing opposite ways:
separation, contrast or letting go*

The human eye

*An arrow in the bull's-eye of a target.
An action ends when the arrow hits the target.*

睽

KHWEI (Duality)

The character Khwei means to see double, to see cross-eyed, and contrast. The construction of the character indicates that you only see things clearly when you possess enough self-knowledge to know the right course through life. If you cannot find the target within yourself, you wander from left to right, steered by conflicting thoughts rather than inner assurance. Because you are also unable to see the inner motives behind other people's outward display, you are always having to adjust your view.

In the hexagram, the upper, true sun makes matter visible. The lower sun is your inner light, while the rainclouds and the marsh/moon stand for your outward appearance. As you gather fertile knowledge (rain), you come to know yourself. This, in turn, equips you to love yourself so that you maintain your zest for life (the marsh/moon) and do not have to pretend to be someone you are not. By developing awareness of your inner self, you also learn to sense the motives of others so that you know exactly with whom you are dealing.

Duality

Your outward behavior depends primarily on your inner impulses. Developing self-knowledge saves you from assuming a facade to mask your insecurity, and also teaches you to estimate the true worth of others. The following directions may help you to see yourself clearly. (38)

Restricted Movement

As long as you move through life like a young fox that has wet its tail, you are too reliant on outward appearances. You see no further than the end of your nose. 64

Fire, the Transforming Element

Once you are aware that your inner fire is clear insight, you realize that outward appearance is a facade to hide your inner impotence. 30

Successful Movement

To move like an old fox, uphold an appearance that reflects your inner peace in every situation. 63

Regular and Orderly
When there is too much rain, the marsh floods; when there is too little, it dries up. Your zest for life depends on your degree of self-knowledge. If, out of insecurity, you pretend to be more or less than what you are, you violate your true self. In that case, there can be no question of a truly enjoyable life. 60

Duality

The moon waxes and wanes again. Grief follows joy, and sunshine follows rain. As long as you live you are dependent on duality, but if you more consciously make use of your inner light, your view of life is less likely to be confused. (38)

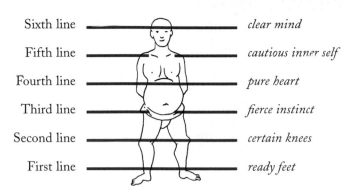

Sixth line ——————————— *clear mind*

Fifth line ——————————— *cautious inner self*

Fourth line ——————————— *pure heart*

Third line ——————————— *fierce instinct*

Second line ——————————— *certain knees*

First line ——————————— *ready feet*

The Individual Lines

Sixth line
The sun is at its highest point. If you penetrate to the core of your existence you can see through the outward show of others. By presenting yourself as you really are, you can make them aware of the process you have been through, so that they no longer have to hide themselves from you.

Fifth line
The core of the sun has the power to dispel the raincloud. You are on the right path to self-discovery. You cannot go wrong if you now throw off the last shreds of mist veiling your inner truth, knowing that you can freely adopt the outward appearance that is appropriate for a given situation.

Fourth line
Your inner light connects with the rising sun, but is still hidden behind the center of the raincloud. You experience contact with your inner truth, and you meet others who have the same goal. You did feel like an orphan, but it now appears that you have relatives.

Third line
The outward reflection of your inner light is like the full moon, which is veiled in wisps of mist. This suggests that you are presenting yourself to others as more than you really are. Worse still, you continue to hide behind all sorts of delusions and thereby make yourself even more ridiculous.

Second line
The waxing moon reflects your inner light. All beginnings are difficult but if you try to adopt an outward appearance that you think fits your inner being, others will — or will not — see through it, and in this way you will gradually come to know yourself.

First line
The dark moon, which is waiting for the sunlight to reach her once again, is a sign that it will not be time for you to undertake anything until some-one crosses your path. Stay calm and model yourself on others. Anything that you are capable of observing in another must also be part of yourself, so you can adjust it in your own behavior.

Introduction
The Khwei hexagram is determined by the fire/sun. By gathering insight ☲ (lower fire/sun) you obtain an overview ☲ (upper fire/sun) and you do not have to veil yourself in deceptive mists ☵. Through self-knowledge you can also read the inner state of others from their outward appearance ☲.

Strong and Weak Changing Lines
Extra attention should be paid to strong and weak lines in the hexagram you have thrown. A strong line signifies that you are addressing the situation with too much force, whereas a weak line calls for a bolder attitude.

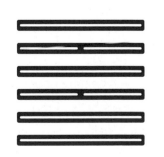

The Hermetic *I Ching*
The answer to your specific question is not found only in the starting hexagram. For a deeper insight, you can also study the various separate hexagrams that make up the starting hexagram. The number next to these hexagrams indicates the page where you can find their complete interpretation. If the hexagram you have thrown contains changing lines, these direct you to a 'follow-up' hexagram.

Like life itself, the *I Ching* is a hermetic labyrinth of wonders from which you can only escape by closing the book.

The Follow-Up Hexagram
Once you have changed the strong and weak lines into their opposites, a new 'follow-up' hexa-gram is created which provides information about a future phase of life. The information on the left-hand page is the most useful for studying this hexagram, since follow-up hexagrams contain no changing lines.
The information on the right-hand page can, of course, be useful for clarifying your study of the follow-up hexagram.

} These hexagrams are components of the starting hexagram and offer directions for successfully dealing with your present situation.

 The lines of the hexagram correspond to various parts of the body. The instructions you find there provide insight into your current physical and spiritual state.

⚍ : Strong Changing Line
⚏ : Weak Changing Line

睽  38

Rain

Fire/Sun

River

Mountain

KIEN (Initial Difficulty)

The character Kien means to limp, crippled, and unmanageable or stubborn. Spiritual and physical exhaustion is forcing you to close a chapter in your life. It is obviously time to digest your past experiences and recuperate physically. If you turn away from the world in frustration it will be difficult to get moving again.

This situation is symbolized in the hexagram by the mountain, which you have climbed with difficulty in order to achieve an overview and find inner peace. Now that you have arrived, it is time to digest your experiences. This is indicated by the sun covered by the raincloud, which is a sign that your outward appearance is affected by the impressions you have gathered because you have not yet processed them internally. Because you are determined not to continue on the same footing, you do not offer what is inside you to others, and your pent-up energy — like rainwater that cannot flow away — forms a reservoir on the top of the mountain. It is natural for water to flow, but you will have to overcome initial difficulty in order to bring this about. Close off this period in your life so the new will not be laced with old habits.

An empty space, closed off with stones or other materials
To build in, to wall in and to close off

A resting foot. The closed circle indicates immobility.

寒

Initial Difficulty

 (39)

If you are so exhausted that you have to retreat, you have gone wrong somewhere and feel daunted by the prospect of throwing yourself back into life. The following steps can help you prevent this blockade and lead you down from the top of the mountain.

Successful Movement

63

The sun dispels the clouds. If you want to move through life like an old fox, you will not take on more than you can handle.

Water, the Giver of Life

29

Rain represents fertility, while the river — which springs forth so passionately and flows into the sea so calmly — symbolizes life's path. The beginning of this path is unavoidable, so it should not be ignored.

Restricted Movement

64

You are moving through life like a young fox that has wet its tail. You have thrown yourself too passionately into a situation that you cannot handle.

The Wise Man

56

The wise man is like the radiant sun crowning the top of the mountain. If you regularly withdraw to contemplate your experiences and translate them into inner wisdom, you will always be able to face the earthly adventure in good spirits.

Initial Difficulty

 (39)

Gravity forces water to find its way downwards. You know that the sun reappears every day and disappears when it is not welcome, and you know that running water does not attach to anything. In the same way, you should distribute your wisdom without imposing yourself on others. This will save you from getting bogged down in situations.

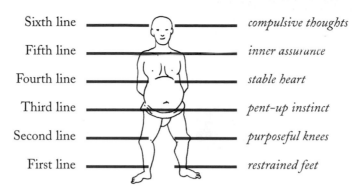

Sixth line ———————— *compulsive thoughts*

Fifth line ———————— *inner assurance*

Fourth line ———————— *stable heart*

Third line ———————— *pent-up instinct*

Second line ———————— *purposeful knees*

First line ———————— *restrained feet*

The Individual Lines

Sixth line
The outermost edge of the raincloud in the hexagram stands for your mind, which cannot free itself from the period that is behind you. A train of compulsive thoughts flashes through your brain. Calm your breathing, process your past, and then confidently close that chapter.

Fifth line
At its zenith, the sun is covered by the center of the raincloud. This is the crucial moment for processing the period behind you. By concentrating your remaining energy on the inner surety that you do not want to go on in the old way, you can break down the wall you are hiding behind.

Fourth line
The rising sun has almost dispelled the bank of clouds, yet you remain as inactive as the water forming a lake on the top of the mountain. The wisest course is to keep building up your inner assurance with vital energy until the spell of your past is broken and you can start again with a clean slate.

Third line
The sun casts its first rays over the lake on the top of the mountain. Your survival instinct indicates that you need to flow, like the water, but you are not yet sure of yourself. Wait until you have the inner peace and surety that comes from knowing that you will not attach to anything and that you will disappear when you are not welcome.

Second line
Below the top of the mountain, the water flows away. Because the past is still playing on your mind, you are fighting the current as you strive not to slip back into your old approach to life. At this time, when your behavior is still laced with old habits, it is important to keep standing on your own two feet and avoid clinging to anything.

First line
At the foot of the mountain, there is nothing to do but wait. You do not have the strength to withdraw to the top of the mountain, and if you continue as before you will find yourself in the same problematic situations you have just escaped. Be aware that freeing yourself spiritually from an intolerable situation is the first step towards something new.

Introduction
In the Kien hexagram, the sun ☷ which rises behind the mountain ☶ and breaks through the layer of clouds ☵ (above) indicates that you are putting an end to the situation on the other side of the mountain.
Like a brook ☵ (below) twinkling in the sunlight, you come down the mountain with a feeling of inner peace and head for the sunset where a new phase of life awaits you.

Strong and Weak Changing Lines
Extra attention should be paid to strong and weak lines in the hexagram you have thrown. A strong line signifies that you are addressing the situation with too much force, whereas a weak line calls for a bolder attitude.

The Hermetic *I Ching*
The answer to your specific question is not found only in the starting hexagram. For a deeper insight, you can also study the various separate hexagrams that make up the starting hexagram. The number next to these hexagrams indicates the page where you can find their complete interpretation. If the hexagram you have thrown contains changing lines, these direct you to a 'follow-up' hexagram.

Like life itself, the *I Ching* is a hermetic labyrinth of wonders from which you can only escape by closing the book.

The Follow-Up Hexagram
Once you have changed the strong and weak lines into their opposites, a new 'follow-up' hexagram is created which provides information about a future phase of life. The information on the left-hand page is the most useful for studying this hexagram, since follow-up hexagrams contain no changing lines.
The information on the right-hand page can, of course, be useful for clarifying your study of the follow-up hexagram.

These hexagrams are components of the starting hexagram and offer directions for successfully dealing with your present situation.

The lines of the hexagram correspond to various parts of the body. The instructions you find there provide insight into your current physical and spiritual state.

▬▬o▬▬ : Strong Changing Line
▬▬x▬▬ : Weak Changing Line

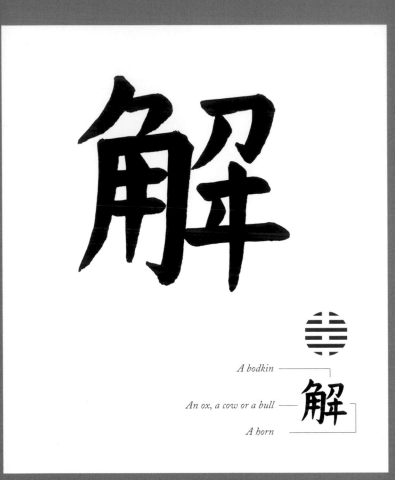

A bodkin

An ox, a cow or a bull

A horn

解

KIEH (Cutting the Knot)

The character Kieh represents a bodkin made from the horn of an ox, a cow, or a bull, and means to disentangle, to explain, or to rectify. This suggests that you are facing a complicated situation which you can disentangle with the patience of an ox or a cow or break through with the fierce strength of a bull.

   The play of forces in the hexagram indicates that the sun, or your inner light, is caught up in an all-consuming problem that will be as difficult to dispel as a thick layer of clouds. The thunder originating from the sun symbolizes that you can either disentangle a knot with analytical patience or cleave it and put an end to the situation with lightning speed. The cloudburst that is then released may be fierce, but it cleanses the sky. Behave like the sun, which tries to evaporate the clouds during the day before apparently disappearing in the southwest, though in reality it stands firm in the heavens. If you do not succeed in the actions you undertake during the day, cut the knot at night with the force of lightning so that you can be radiantly present the following morning.

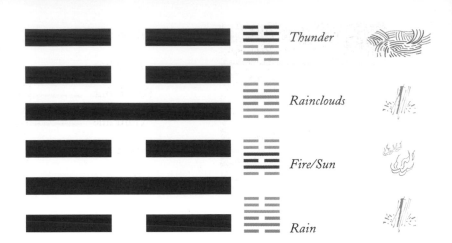

Thunder

Rainclouds

Fire/Sun

Rain

Cutting the Knot
If you are persistently shrouded in dark clouds (and there is no sign of rain or action), it is healthy to decisively throw off the millstone around your neck before it exhausts you physically and spiritually. The following directions show you the way to a cloudless sky.

(40)

Completion
When the sun reaches its highest point, it starts to descend. Once you are aware that the sun keeps on shining and it is always possible for you to see your surroundings, you will not allow your view to be blocked for long.

55

Successful Movement
Just as the sun always dispels the clouds, an old fox ensures that he keeps a grip on every situation. If he finds he has misjudged a situation, he gets out in time. If, in a weak moment, he allows himself to become entangled, he will always find a way to free himself, graciously or ungraciously, from the problem.

63

Water, the Giver of Life
Rain represents fertility, while the river — which springs forth so passionately and flows into the sea so calmly — symbolizes life's path. An old fox is wise through experience, but in an emergency will not refrain from being as fierce as he was in his youth.

29

Restricted Movement
You move like an old fox that has wet its tail. You have forced your way out of a situation that you could not tolerate any longer. Wait calmly until your tail has dried before you start on something new.

64

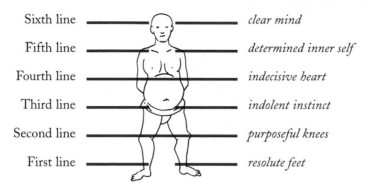

Sixth line —————— *clear mind*

Fifth line —————— *determined inner self*

Fourth line —————— *indecisive heart*

Third line —————— *indolent instinct*

Second line —————— *purposeful knees*

First line —————— *resolute feet*

The Individual Lines

Sixth line
The thunder is at its height, which denotes that your clear mind is fully aware of what is causing the impasse, but you cannot think of any rational arguments that would demolish the wall. As soon as you perceive the core of the problem, you should lash out with a tongue that is as sharp as a crackling flash of lightning.

Fifth line
The core of the thunder cleaves apart the layer of clouds. You search determinedly for a way to break through the power restraining you. You do not know the precise ins and outs of the situation, and deep in your heart you are still looking for a peaceful solution, but it can do no harm to make it obvious that your patience is coming to an end.

Fourth line
The sun at its zenith cannot break through the layer of clouds. That is why the beginning of the thunder beats like an indecisive heart weighed down by sorrows. You cannot achieve an overview, so you are best off picking away at the tangled roots of the problem until you find like-minded companions.

Third line
The rising sun shines through the gap between two clouds. Your survival instinct is not yet totally awakened, so you do not experience the situation as being so threatening that you need to escape. This sort of complacency may get you up to your ears in problems that you could solve now.

Second line
The sun casts its first rays on a thick layer of clouds. You are aware of the danger hanging over your head, and you still have time to escape it. Move on cunningly, like an old fox, and outsmart the young foxes trying to entangle you in their problems.

First line
The rain falls. If you move calmly with the current and do not attach to anything, you will not be caught up in problems.

Introduction
In the Kieh hexagram, the layer of clouds ☵ disturbs your rhythm of life (lines two to four, inclusive). The sun ☲ associated with these lines indicates that you have the calm patience to solve the situation, but the thunder ☳ is a sign that you cannot wait around endlessly and will, at a given moment, demolish the wall blocking your view.

Strong and Weak Changing Lines
Extra attention should be paid to strong and weak lines in the hexagram you have thrown. A strong line signifies that you are addressing the situation with too much force, whereas a weak line calls for a bolder attitude.

The Hermetic *I Ching*
The answer to your specific question is not found only in the starting hexagram. For a deeper insight, you can also study the various separate hexagrams that make up the starting hexagram. The number next to these hexagrams indicates the page where you can find their complete interpretation. If the hexagram you have thrown contains changing lines, these direct you to a 'follow-up' hexagram.

Like life itself, the *I Ching* is a hermetic labyrinth of wonders from which you can only escape by closing the book.

The Follow-Up Hexagram
Once you have changed the strong and weak lines into their opposites, a new 'follow-up' hexagram is created which provides information about a future phase of life. The information on the left-hand page is the most useful for studying this hexagram, since follow-up hexagrams contain no changing lines.
The information on the right-hand page can, of course, be useful for clarifying your study of the follow-up hexagram.

These hexagrams are components of the starting hexagram and offer directions for successfully dealing with your present situation.

The lines of the hexagram correspond to various parts of the body. The instructions you find there provide insight into your current physical and spiritual state.

━━━o━━━ : Strong Changing Line
━━x━━ : Weak Changing Line

A hand seen from the side.

*A small shell used as money in early times in China.
Here, the shell is round, so the meaning is: closed off,
round, ended and the finishing of a ritual.*

SUN (Relaxation)

The character Sun means to diminish, to decrease and to contract. The construction of the character indicates that a period of hard work is coming to an end and a time of relaxation is dawning, when you can reap the harvest of your efforts.

In the hexagram, the stable mountain enthroned above the earth is a sign that you have gained an overview and inner peace. The thunder which originates from the marsh/moon and brings to life everything the earth can bring forth indicates that you are now in a period when earthly fruits extend to the heavens. Because you have an overview and show sincerity, you are incapable of making a wrong decision and, as the hexagram indicates, you can open yourself completely to the beauty the earth has to offer.

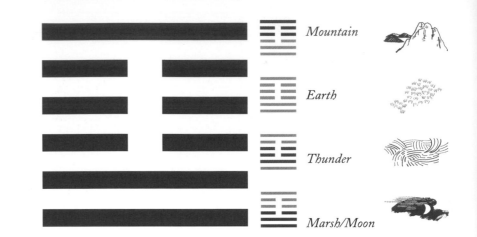

Mountain

Earth

Thunder

Marsh/Moon

Relaxation
You have struggled to climb the mountain and, now that you have achieved an overview and inner peace, it is time to enjoy the material things that formerly weighed you down. However, in this situation, too, there are rules you should be aware of, as the following directions indicate.

(41)

The Destruction of the Past
If you want to relax without a care in the world, you will have to put the worries that lie behind you out of your mind.

23

Nourishment
Do not go so far as to forget the flavor of the problems you have already tasted. Otherwise, you will bite into affairs you have spat out in disgust in the past.

27

Winter Solstice, Awakening
Stay calm and keep your eyes open. Do not rush into a situation whose outcome is uncertain for you.

24

Attraction
Show yourself as you are and hide nothing; only then will you attract situations in which you can fully relax.

19

Fertility
When the moon is full, she wanes again. A wise person therefore knows exactly when a period of relaxation is drawing to a close.

54

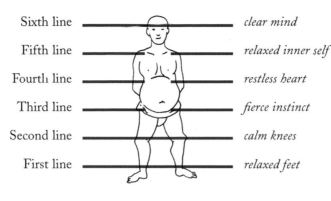

The Individual Lines

Sixth line		clear mind
Fifth line		relaxed inner self
Fourth line		restless heart
Third line		fierce instinct
Second line		calm knees
First line		relaxed feet

Sixth line
The top of the mountain indicates that you have an overview and inner peace, so that you will not become physically or spiritually dependent on situations you will later find difficult to let go of. Keep clearly in mind that you are not looking for security, but for temporary relaxation.

Fifth line
Beneath the top of the mountain, the luxuriant surface of the earth which brings forth all things lies open to you. Be aware of the temporary nature of this superficial beauty, and enjoy it to the full. Do not look under the shell of the tortoise, for then you would be going more deeply into things than is really necessary.

Fourth line
At the foot of the mountain hidden under the earth's surface, the thunder pounds like a restlessly beating heart. The moon has disappeared, and you have no overview. You are in danger of losing your heart to the feelings you experienced during your period of relaxation. Relish the memory, bring your heart to rest, and move on to the order of the day.

Third line
The full moon disappears behind the earth before the thunder reaches its peak. For the moment you have given yourself over to the feeling that you are not of this world. Do not let yourself be tempted to relax even more because you will then have to make a great effort to come back to earth.

Second line
The beginning of the thunder and the waxing moon are associated with the eager lower jaw, which is controlled by the clear mind symbolized by the upper jaw. It is clear that you should not initiate anything at the moment and should not fasten your teeth into anything. Stay calm and keep your eyes open.

First line
The dark moon waits calmly until the sunlight reaches her. For you, too, this is a period to relax and see what comes your way. If you encounter something that feels good, do not hesitate to go with it — but keep in the back of your mind that when the moon is full, it starts to wane again.

Introduction
The Sun hexagram is determined by *Nourishment (27)*. The immovable upper jaw (sixth line) is like a clear mind prescribing which spiritual and physical food is salutary for your inner relaxation (lines three to five, inclusive) so that the eager lower jaw (second line) does not set its teeth into the wrong affairs.

Strong and Weak Changing Lines
Extra attention should be paid to strong and weak lines in the hexagram you have thrown. A strong line signifies that you are addressing the situation with too much force, whereas a weak line calls for a bolder attitude.

The Hermetic *I Ching*
The answer to your specific question is not found only in the starting hexagram. For a deeper insight, you can also study the various separate hexagrams that make up the starting hexagram. The number next to these hexagrams indicates the page where you can find their complete interpretation. If the hexagram you have thrown contains changing lines, these direct you to a 'follow-up' hexagram.

Like life itself, the *I Ching* is a hermetic labyrinth of wonders from which you can only escape by closing the book.

The Follow-Up Hexagram
Once you have changed the strong and weak lines into their opposites, a new 'follow-up' hexagram is created which provides information about a future phase of life. The information on the left-hand page is the most useful for studying this hexagram, since follow-up hexagrams contain no changing lines.
The information on the right-hand page can, of course, be useful for clarifying your study of the follow-up hexagram.

These hexagrams are components of the starting hexagram and offer directions for successfully dealing with your present situation.

The lines of the hexagram correspond to various parts of the body. The instructions you find there provide insight into your current physical and spiritual state.

═o═ : Strong Changing Line
═x═ : Weak Changing Line

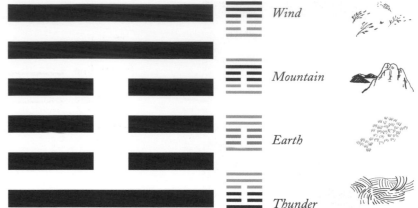

Wind

Mountain

Earth

Thunder

Water —

A vessel that is so full of water it overflows
Therefore: abundance, profit, and filling up

Yî (Increase)

The character Yî represents material abundance, which enables you to turn your attention to your inner being.

The wind blowing over the top of the mountain in the hexagram symbolizes the stream of thoughts with which you analyze all things the earth brings forth. The earth spreads itself out before you, in full bloom, as denoted by the thunder which symbolically actualizes the potential of matter. The mountain enthroned above the earth is both a sign that you have inner peace and an overview of all the different forms and behaviors adopted by earthly beings. These signs indicate that in times of abundance, when you do not have to fight so hard for life's basic necessities like food, shelter, and protection, you will have time and energy left over. You can use this to develop yourself spiritually, by carefully observing the world and getting to the bottom of how it functions. Beware of the temptation, at such times, to pursue even more material riches and so throw away this unique opportunity for spiritual development.

Increase
The combination of material wealth and spiritual poverty in one person is a danger to the world. Genuine fertility is based on an awareness of the value of material possessions in combination with spiritual awareness. The growth process outlined below *(reading from bottom to top)* shows how you can achieve this.
(42)

The Blessed Marriage
Keep drawing back, at the right time, from the abundance of impressions you have gathered, and contemplate them calmly and quietly.
53

Observation, Contemplation
In general, one sees only what one wants to see. Your preconceptions filter out the information you think will be useful to you, and you fail to notice the rest. Try to change your points of view so that you develop a new perspective on life.
20

The Destruction of the Past
If you have achieved a certain level of material well-being, take another look back over your life in order to appreciate the true worth of material possessions. Do not allow them to hinder your spiritual growth.
23

Nourishment
The more independent you become, the more you discover how much effort is required to secure the basic necessities of life, and what material possessions are really worth. Your means of supporting yourself will not always be enjoyable.
27

Winter Solstice, Awakening
Early in life, your survival depends on the food you are supplied. It makes no difference whether you lie in a wooden crib or a golden cradle.
24

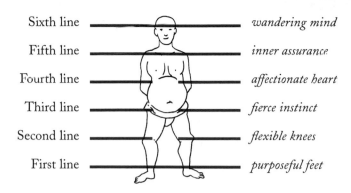

Sixth line —————————— *wandering mind*

Fifth line —————————— *inner assurance*

Fourth line —————————— *affectionate heart*

Third line —————————— *fierce instinct*

Second line —————————— *flexible knees*

First line —————————— *purposeful feet*

The Individual Lines

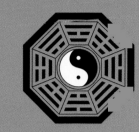

Sixth line
The beginning of the wind indicates that you are still unaware of spiritual norms and values and focus solely on accumulating all the material possessions your heart desires. Your insatiable material hunger contributes nothing to your environment and will cause much resentment.

Fifth line
The core of the wind, or your consciousness, is connected to the top of the mountain. An overview and inner peace are essential for a contemplative way of life. You consume no more than you need, and with your insight and sincerity, you are a fertile source for those around you.

Fourth line
Under the top of the mountain, the surface of the earth lies open to you, and you enjoy its abundance to the full. You have all that your heart desires. If you strive for true inner surety, you would be wise to now turn your attention to your spiritual development.

Third line
Beneath the earth, the thunder rumbles at the foot of the mountain. Out of a survival instinct, you have accumulated material security by means that do not bear examination in the cold light of day. Work through your past and concentrate on spiritual development so you can walk the path of the golden mean, which offers escape from the earthly mire.

Second line
Deep beneath the earth's surface, the thunder shakes at the roots of your existence. You become aware of the miracle of life. This is something deeper than the accumulation of material possessions, which are a millstone around your neck. Now that you know what lies under the shell of the turtle, you straighten your back and disseminate your knowledge.

First line
The beginning of the thunder represents awakening and supporting oneself. Stand on your own two feet, with both eyes open, and fight addiction to earthly matter. Keep in mind that true growth is an interplay between the accumulation of material possessions and the search for spiritual development.

Introduction
The Yî hexagram is determined by *Nourishment (27)*. The immovable upper jaw (sixth line) is associated with your inner surety, which is dependent on both material and spiritual wealth. Therefore, it does not merely live off physical nourishment (lines two to four, inclusive) but also ensures that your eager lower jaw (first line) sets its teeth into the roots of your spiritual existence.

Strong and Weak Changing Lines
Extra attention should be paid to strong and weak lines in the hexagram you have thrown. A strong line signifies that you are addressing the situation with too much force, whereas a weak line calls for a bolder attitude.

The Hermetic *I Ching*
The answer to your specific question is not found only in the starting hexagram. For a deeper insight, you can also study the various separate hexagrams that make up the starting hexagram. The number next to these hexagrams indicates the page where you can find their complete interpretation. If the hexagram you have thrown contains changing lines, these direct you to a 'follow-up' hexagram.

Like life itself, the *I Ching* is a hermetic labyrinth of wonders from which you can only escape by closing the book.

The Follow-Up Hexagram
Once you have changed the strong and weak lines into their opposites, a new 'follow-up' hexagram is created which provides information about a future phase of life. The information on the left-hand page is the most useful for studying this hexagram, since follow-up hexagrams contain no changing lines.
The information on the right-hand page can, of course, be useful for clarifying your study of the follow-up hexagram.

These hexagrams are components of the starting hexagram and offer directions for successfully dealing with your present situation.

The lines of the hexagram correspond to various parts of the body. The instructions you find there provide insight into your current physical and spiritual state.

▬o▬ : Strong Changing Line
▬x▬ : Weak Changing Line

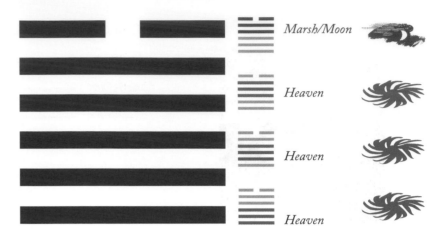

Marsh/Moon

Heaven

Heaven

Heaven

A hand holding the right side of a two-sided object,
from which the left side has disappeared.
By extension, the character means: to decide, surety
or to take up residence somewhere

KWÂI (Fulfilment)

Left and right stand for material gain and spiritual development, respectively. The character Kwâi indicates that a decision has been made: preference is being given to the right side of the object. This shows that fulfilment is achieved through the development of inner wisdom which offers more surety than does outward appearance.

    The hexagram is made up of three heavens on which the marsh/moon rests, indicating that in order to achieve inner wisdom you have to let go of the illusory thoughts that have, until now, given meaning to your life. The only Truth on which you can base your existence is the infinite depth of the lower, true heaven, about which you know as much as your feet do. Do not lose yourself, therefore, in the illusion of a heaven on earth which starts at your knees (second line) and which places physicality and material gain above all. You should also reject the upper heaven, which springs from your survival instinct (third line); it symbolizes a mythical universe which offers the illusion of surety by bestowing meaning on your innate, inner emptiness.

Fulfilment

If you believe in a heaven on earth and glorify material gain and physicality, you will feel cruelly deceived if you sink into poverty or become sick and weak. Similarly, if out of fear or uncertainty you take refuge in a mythical universe, there will come a time when you will be assailed by doubts. You can only truly enjoy the earthly game once you are free of illusions. By day, base your insights on the eternal sun which illuminates the earth in all her changing seasons. By night, dare to confront the unfathomable depth of the true heaven.

 (43)

Creative Energy

The infinite depth of the heavens, which encircle the earth and in one way or another ensure a balance that keeps this pearl in her orbit, lends itself to being filled by every illusion imaginable. If you strive for spiritual development and steadfastly reject all illusion, you translate the universal power-play into an inner balance of offering and receiving. Then you can be like the earth and moon, rotating rhythmically and blissfully in the sunlight, and you will find your fulfilment in whatever they bring forth through the creative energy of the heavens.

1

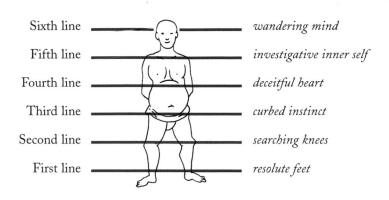

Sixth line ———————— *wandering mind*

Fifth line ———————— *investigative inner self*

Fourth line ———————— *deceitful heart*

Third line ———————— *curbed instinct*

Second line ———————— *searching knees*

First line ———————— *resolute feet*

The Individual Lines

Sixth line

The full moon is in the heavens and will soon wane. As long as you elevate its illusory light (representing material gain and/or myth) to the level of Truth, you will be sadly deceived. Focus on the thought that you want to enjoy the earthly game without losing yourself in illusions.

Fifth line

The waxing moon rises in the mythical heaven. Your inner surety is sorely tested, because you are surrounded by illusions. It is as if you are faced with the task of weeding a bed of seedlings, in which the weeds are barely distinguishable from the plants you later want to harvest.

Fourth line

The new moon appears in the illusory heaven. Do not pretend to be the sun, while everyone can see that your real thoughts are as dark as a ripe fruit found rotten once peeled. You want everything your heart desires, and you justify this with the dogmatic assertion that outward display is the true light.

Third line

The true heaven is hidden behind the illusory heaven. You put on an apparently decisive outward display, in an attempt to diminish your fear of the innate emptiness inside you. If you are sensible, you will put an end to this behavior because it deceives your survival instinct.

Second line

The core of the true heaven is overshadowed by the idea that material gain is everything. If you are confronted at night by the infinite depth of the true heaven, you are shocked by the vacuous idea that earthly possessions and exaggerated attention to outward appearances can offer you more surety.

First line

At the outer limits of the true heaven you are still wondering whether there might be some convincing evidence that would explain the infinite depths encircling you. It is as if you assume you can move forward just by moving your toes, while deep down you know that what you are attempting is absurd.

Introduction

The Kwâi hexagram is determined by the sixth line, which represents your mind that is clinging on to illusions ☱. You are seeking inner justification ☰ for your behavior. Learn from your feet (first line), which are not motivated to carry you by self-interest, fear, or uncertainty, but serve you as impartially as the universe provides you with its energy.

Strong and Weak Changing Lines

Extra attention should be paid to strong and weak lines in the hexagram you have thrown. A strong line signifies that you are addressing the situation with too much force, whereas a weak line calls for a bolder attitude.

The Hermetic *I Ching*

The answer to your specific question is not found only in the starting hexagram. For a deeper insight, you can also study the various separate hexagrams that make up the starting hexagram. The number next to these hexagrams indicates the page where you can find their complete interpretation. If the hexagram you have thrown contains changing lines, these direct you to a 'follow-up' hexagram.

Like life itself, the *I Ching* is a hermetic labyrinth of wonders from which you can only escape by closing the book.

The Follow-Up Hexagram

Once you have changed the strong and weak lines into their opposites, a new 'follow-up' hexagram is created which provides information about a future phase of life. The information on the left-hand page is the most useful for studying this hexagram, since follow-up hexagrams contain no changing lines.

The information on the right-hand page can, of course, be useful for clarifying your study of the follow-up hexagram.

} These hexagrams are components of the starting hexagram and offer directions for successfully dealing with your present situation. The lines of the hexagram correspond to various parts of the body. The instructions you find there provide insight into your current physical and spiritual state.

▬●▬ : Strong Changing Line
▬x▬ : Weak Changing Line

 **43**

 Heaven

 Heaven

 Heaven

 Wind

A prince bends towards his subjects
and issues his orders.

A young woman

KÂU (A Mature Relationship)

The character Kâu means to couple and reproduce. From its structure, one can see that there is a relationship between reproduction and the transfer of knowledge. The young woman gives birth to new life, which is endowed with the prince's insights.

The hexagram is made up of three heavens and the wind, or realm of ideas, which is allied with the lower half of the body. This suggests the first phase of life, in which thinking is focused solely on physical survival. You are warned not to always keep your thoughts attuned to the lower heaven, which begins at the knees and signifies outward display and material gain. Equally, do not lose yourself in the middle heaven, which begins at the underbelly or instinct, where the wind originates. This heaven symbolizes a mythical universe from which you derive ostensible security by concentrating on procreation, in order to bestow meaning on your innate, inner emptiness. Survival of the species is important, but a civilized and adult relationship with earthly life is dependent on the degree of spiritual insight you develop. This means allowing your heart to connect with the infinite depth of the upper, true heaven, and incorporating the knowledge you gather there into the raising of your offspring.

A Mature Relationship

The earth is the source of all life. Yet it is unwise to become attached to this strong and ever-fruitful female force. The mark of a mature relationship with the earth is that you focus on the infinite depth of the heavens, from which the earth derives her creative energy, and regard earthly matter as the wet nurse from whose breast you will, sooner or later, be torn. This relationship has been part of wise teaching for thousands of years. Here is how to achieve it.

(44)

Creative Energy

The infinite depth of the heavens, which encircle the earth and in one way or another ensure a balance that keeps this pearl in her orbit, lends itself to being filled by every illusion imaginable. If you strive for spiritual development and steadfastly reject all illusion, you translate the universal power play into an inner balance of offering and receiving. This means you will not always be in step with those around you, but you will be true to yourself and others.

I

A Mature Relationship

Reproduction and the transfer of knowledge go hand in hand. Once you recognize that every heavenly body moves independently through the universe and has developed its own, unique way of staying in balance, you will give your 'children' the chance to secure a position for themselves, on the basis of their own capabilities. Individuals who have found themselves can become attached to others without being intrusive or completely losing themselves. If you must lose yourself in anything, let it be the infinite depth of the heavens. This will teach you to free yourself from material things.

(44)

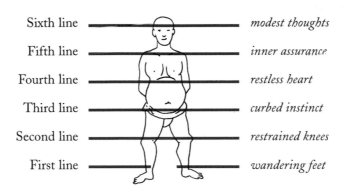

Sixth line ——————— *modest thoughts*

Fifth line ——————— *inner assurance*

Fourth line ——————— *restless heart*

Third line ——————— *curbed instinct*

Second line ——————— *restrained knees*

First line ——————— *wandering feet*

The Individual Lines

Sixth line
The outer limit of the true heaven — which is impossible to capture in thoughts, let alone words — is a sign that you are fooling yourself and others if you try to make any conclusive statements about it. It is unwise to boast of your spiritual potency if words are all you have to back it up.

Fifth line
The core of the true heaven, which is overshadowed by the last wisps of the mythical heaven, is like a ripe fruit covered by the leaves of a tree. This implies that you would be better off using metaphors to convey insights that are difficult to put into words.

Fourth line
The true heaven is hidden behind illusory heavens. You lay your nets to capture a partner, but your predilection for outward display makes you unsure of what you have to offer others. Stop pushing, and turn your attention inwards so that the mists around you lift and you can see what you really want.

Third line
The wind rises in the illusory heaven. You show off your physical potency, but behind that facade your motivations are primitive. Your human skin has, as it were, been stripped from your back. Survival instinct is only half the story. Make sure that you also have something to offer spiritually.

Second line
In the middle of the wind, or your consciousness, you are almost free from the idea that outward display is heaven on earth. Still, you would be better off turning to the true heaven to gather more spiritual insight before using your physical potency.

First line
The end of the wind indicates that you want to scream out your desire to cling to the earth forever and — like air itself — force your way into all around you. If you are conscious that every breath may be your last and that you always have one foot in the grave, you will find it easier to free yourself from material things.

Introduction
The Kâu hexagram is determined by the first line: your feet, which place you on solid ground. This quest for stability, which stems from a survival instinct (third line), is part of you from your first breath ☴. Straighten your back (second line) as you grow to adulthood, and turn your attention to the upper, true heaven ☰ with a quiet heart (fourth line), inner surety (fifth line), and cautious judgment (sixth line).

Strong and Weak Changing Lines
Extra attention should be paid to strong and weak lines in the hexagram you have thrown. A strong line signifies that you are addressing the situation with too much force, whereas a weak line calls for a bolder attitude.

The Hermetic *I Ching*
The answer to your specific question is not found only in the starting hexagram. For a deeper insight, you can also study the various separate hexagrams that make up the starting hexagram. The number next to these hexagrams indicates the page where you can find their complete interpretation. If the hexagram you have thrown contains changing lines, these direct you to a 'follow-up' hexagram.

Like life itself, the *I Ching* is a hermetic labyrinth of wonders from which you can only escape by closing the book.

The Follow-Up Hexagram
Once you have changed the strong and weak lines into their opposites, a new 'follow-up' hexagram is created which provides information about a future phase of life. The information on the left-hand page is the most useful for studying this hexagram, since follow-up hexagrams contain no changing lines.
The information on the right-hand page can, of course, be useful for clarifying your study of the follow-up hexagram.

} These hexagrams are components of the starting hexagram and offer directions for successfully dealing with your present situation.

The lines of the hexagram correspond to various parts of the body. The instructions you find there provide insight into your current physical and spiritual state.

⚊⊙⚊ : Strong Changing Line
⚋✕⚋ : Weak Changing Line

 **44**

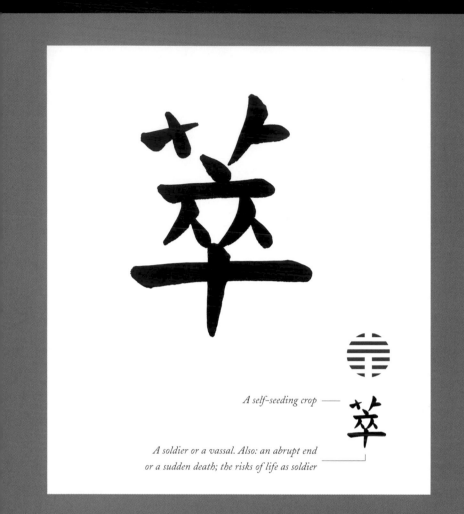

A self-seeding crop —

A soldier or a vassal. Also: an abrupt end
or a sudden death; the risks of life as soldier

TZHUI (Unity of Body and Soul)

The character Tzhui means to bundle or harvest grain. The soldier stands for physical strength. The grain he carries on his shoulders represent his life experiences, harvested in the battle with earthly matter. The true warrior goes into battle with full concentration and is prepared for death. This is why he sorts things out for himself before the battle, separating his experiences into wheat and chaff so that he can stand firmly in the here and now, unhindered by the past. So purified, he faces the future.

In the hexagram, the mountain symbolizes a remote temple, high above the earth, to which you retreat. The marsh/moon and the wind on the top of the mountain suggest that you call up every memory of your past and speak out all the things you have on your chest. You can achieve deep insight by turning to the heavens with your supposed truths and finding out whether they withstand the test of eternity. If they do, you can throw off illusions — the chaff from your harvest of corn — like the moon, which abruptly wanes once it is full. All that is really valuable is translated into inner assurance, or the fifth line, which is the starting point for the wind that blows over the earth. This is a sign that after your retreat you will return with the wisdom you have acquired and sow this golden grain on earth.

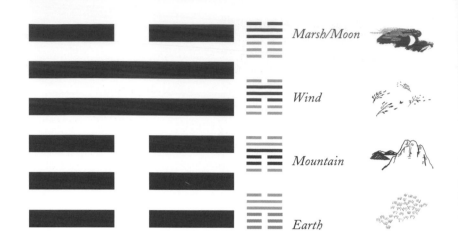

	Marsh/Moon	
	Wind	
	Mountain	
	Earth	

 Unity of Body and Soul
If you live in the here and now, you enjoy each and every moment. You are not hindered by your past and you are aware of the temporary nature of your existence. The following directions *(reading from bottom to top)* lead to unity in the temple of your personality. (45)

 Vigorous Mind
Once you are aware that your notion of friend or foe is a projection, you forge unity between your body and spirit. You can achieve this by turning your attention to the heavens, which sustain life impartially and continuously, and by realizing that you can let go of all illusion as easily as the full moon wanes. 28

 The Game of Love
If you are a true warrior, you will make peace with everyone you have hurt, betrayed, or deserted along the way and also thank everyone who has hurt, betrayed, and deserted you — for it is this past that has led you to insight. 31

 The Blessed Marriage
Try to find inner peace so that you can fully appreciate the preceding truth and recall the past without prejudice. 53

 Observation, Contemplation
In general, you only see what you want to see. It is your preconceptions that make friends or enemies of others. Realize that enemies were kind enough to teach you this lesson. 20

 The Destruction of the Past
After a fight, you withdraw from the battleground to contemplate and put into perspective either the euphoria of victory or the licking of your wounds. 23

TZHUI

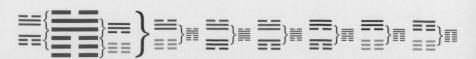

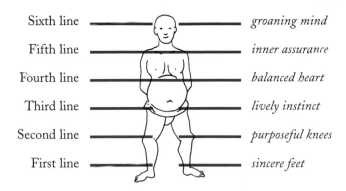

Sixth line ——————— *groaning mind*

Fifth line ——————— *inner assurance*

Fourth line ——————— *balanced heart*

Third line ——————— *lively instinct*

Second line ——————— *purposeful knees*

First line ——————— *sincere feet*

The Individual Lines

Sixth line
As is indicated by the full moon, which will wane again, you are letting go — albeit reluctantly — of ideas and ideals dear to your heart. All thought is founded on duality. If you love darkness, you reject light and vice versa. Do not get permanently attached to anything and always be open to change.

Fifth line
The waxing moon and the beginning of the wind, or your breathing, represent the inner certainty that you can begin to let go of anything you cherish before it is fully established in your life. Steady, contemplative breathing will save you from becoming physically attached to something that will lead you into spiritual trouble.

Fourth line
The new moon rises over the top of the mountain provocatively, but the core of the wind, or your breathing in and breathing out, keeps your heart beating steadily. If you can keep on breathing calmly, you will not easily sell your heart to things that disturb the unity between your body and soul.

Third line
Under the top of the mountain, the wind, or your breathing, plays over the surface of the earth which brings forth all things. Sighing, you try to achieve unity of body and soul on the basis of what you see around you. However, you have no overview, and when you concentrate on one thing, you have to let another go. One learns by doing!

Second line
At the foot of the mountain which is hidden beneath the earth's surface, you can see the very roots of existence. Once you perceive that everything and everyone is seeking the light, you will reject your prejudiced ideas about friends and enemies. A new spring will dawn for you because you will have found unity of body and soul.

First line
You are like your feet, which are anchored deep in the earth and form part of a unity they cannot comprehend. Look around you at the roots, which all move towards the light. You, too, can find your way in life by seeking illumination from others.

Introduction
The Tzhui hexagram is determined by *Vigorous Mind (28)*. If you have given your heart to an illusion ☱, look to your inner assurance ☵ to retrieve the situation. In this way, you can achieve a unity of body and soul ☷ which enables you to stay in the here and now.

Strong and Weak Changing Lines
Extra attention should be paid to strong and weak lines in the hexagram you have thrown. A strong line signifies that you are addressing the situation with too much force, whereas a weak line calls for a bolder attitude.

The Hermetic *I Ching*
The answer to your specific question is not found only in the starting hexagram. For a deeper insight, you can also study the various separate hexagrams that make up the starting hexagram. The number next to these hexagrams indicates the page where you can find their complete interpretation. If the hexagram you have thrown contains changing lines, these direct you to a 'follow-up' hexagram.

Like life itself, the *I Ching* is a hermetic labyrinth of wonders from which you can only escape by closing the book.

The Follow-Up Hexagram
Once you have changed the strong and weak lines into their opposites, a new 'follow-up' hexagram is created which provides information about a future phase of life. The information on the left-hand page is the most useful for studying this hexagram, since follow-up hexagrams contain no changing lines.
The information on the right-hand page can, of course, be useful for clarifying your study of the follow-up hexagram.

} These hexagrams are components of the starting hexagram and offer directions for successfully dealing with your present situation.

 The lines of the hexagram correspond to various parts of the body. The instructions you find there provide insight into your current physical and spiritual state.

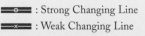 : Strong Changing Line

——— : Weak Changing Line

45

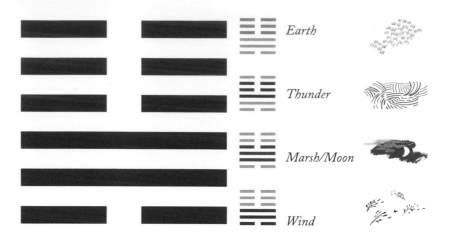

Earth

Thunder

Marsh/Moon

Wind

SHÊNG (Flowering /Calcination)

The character Shêng signifies rising through the ranks. In ancient China, the number ten, written as +, was the perfect number, containing the idea of 'to be' and 'not to be' as well as the five cardinal points of creation (east, west, south, north and center). These signs imply that you have your life in your own hands and that you develop through doing.

The hexagram is capped by the earth, which brings forth all things. This indicates that all your opportunities for development, or flowering, are latently present. In the early phase of your life you are focused solely on survival, so the wind, or your consciousness, remains closely connected with your survival instinct until you develop another frame of reference. Everything that has a will to live seeks the light, which is at its zenith above the earth in the south. This is why the upwardly moving thunder, which symbolizes the driving force behind development or flowering, begins with your survival instinct (third line). The marsh/moon rests on your knees (second line), symbolizing the joyful pursuit of the light. This is an attitude to life that will ultimately bear fruit. In this very early phase of development, however, there is nothing wrong with giving your heart to the illusion of the full moon, for as you blossom you will learn to distinguish outward display from reality.

Ten handfuls

A hand — 升

Ten —

Flowering (Calcination)

Your survival instinct, which is oriented towards growth, turns to every spark of light. When one dies down, it immediately focuses on another, rather than wait for the first to flare up again. In this way, you move closer and closer to the true source of light. As soon as your consciousness takes the helm, you tend to ignore this wise lesson. By way of reminder, therefore, the way of the instinct is laid out for you below *(reading from bottom to top)*.

(46)

Winter Solstice, Awakening

Awakening represents turning yourself to the sun, which you can only recognize as the true source of all light once you perceive life's duality.

24

Attraction

Apart from the true light, every outward appearance has an attractive and an unattractive side.
Do not linger in unattractive circumstances once the attraction is over.

19

Fertility

A fruitful period lasts only as long as you have the feeling that you are becoming 'fuller', and is over as soon as you feel that you are being diminished in some way.

54

Continuity, Balanced Movement

Pursuing a will-o'-the-wisp will eventually cause physical tension which is not beneficial for your growth process.

32

Vigorous Mind

In the earliest phase of life, when you cannot see the difference between outward display and reality, there is no harm in following a will-o'-the-wisp as long as you let it go as soon as its light dies down.

28

SHÊNG

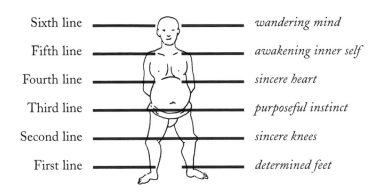

Sixth line ———— *wandering mind*

Fifth line ———— *awakening inner self*

Fourth line ———— *sincere heart*

Third line ———— *purposeful instinct*

Second line ———— *sincere knees*

First line ———— *determined feet*

The Individual Lines

Sixth line

Without a frame of reference, your thoughts wander aimlessly over the surface of the earth, which brings forth all things. In this phase of your life, when you cannot distinguish between outward display and reality, it is not advisable to cling on to anything — unless your instinct urges you to do so.

Fifth line

The thunder comes rolling along under the earth. You have seen the roots of your existence and freed yourself from the illusory moonlight, which has lost its attraction. Instead of giving way to irritation, focus your budding inner assurance on the true light, which rises above duality.

Fourth line

The full moon which will wane again and the pulsating of the thunder deep beneath the earth's surface indicate that you have let yourself be guided — with a steadily beating heart — by an illusory light. Now that you see through the illusion, you let go of its glitter with sincere gratitude for its contribution to your development.

Third line

The beginning of wind and thunder and the waxing moon are signs that you are instinctively following something that brings light into your inner darkness. Take care to let go of this light as soon as it dies down or loses its attraction.

Second line

The core of the wind and the new moon indicate that you are allowing yourself, sincerely and unconsciously, to be led by your physical impulses and that you follow any weak glimmer that appears. This is the way to develop a frame of reference, but it also implies that as you become more conscious, a new spring will arrive, and your choices will become more difficult.

First line

The wind plays around your feet which are always ready to move on. Nothing is stopping you from setting out and following a light that will lead you to more consciousness than your feet demonstrate.

Introduction

The Shêng hexagram is determined by *Vigorous Mind (28)*. In the earliest phase of life, your consciousness ☴ is connected with your survival instinct (third line), which follows every light ☴ that stimulates development. This growth is ultimately directed ☷ towards finding the true light of life, which nourishes earthly matter ☷.

Strong and Weak Changing Lines

Extra attention should be paid to strong and weak lines in the hexagram you have thrown. A strong line signifies that you are addressing the situation with too much force, whereas a weak line calls for a bolder attitude.

The Hermetic *I Ching*

The answer to your specific question is not found only in the starting hexagram. For a deeper insight, you can also study the various separate hexagrams that make up the starting hexagram. The number next to these hexagrams indicates the page where you can find their complete interpretation. If the hexagram you have thrown contains changing lines, these direct you to a 'follow-up' hexagram.

Like life itself, the *I Ching* is a hermetic labyrinth of wonders from which you can only escape by closing the book.

The Follow-Up Hexagram

Once you have changed the strong and weak lines into their opposites, a new 'follow-up' hexagram is created which provides information about a future phase of life. The information on the left-hand page is the most useful for studying this hexagram, since follow-up hexagrams contain no changing lines.
The information on the right-hand page can, of course, be useful for clarifying your study of the follow-up hexagram.

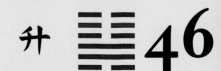

} These hexagrams are components of the starting hexagram and offer directions for successfully dealing with your present situation.

The lines of the hexagram correspond to various parts of the body. The instructions you find there provide insight into your current physical and spiritual state.

══●══ : Strong Changing Line
══×══ : Weak Changing Line

46

A camp (originally a foot) ——

A firmly rooted tree ——

K'UN (Dying Off /Putrefaction)

The character K'un represents tiredness, which forces someone to rest under a tree. A tree grows towards the sunlight, and its branches and leaves do not reach further into the sky than its roots allow. This is a sign that you should take your example from the tree's balanced and tireless growth, which allows everyone to find peace and shelter under its shady crown.

The hexagram indicates that you think you have found wisdom and inner assurance by focusing on the unstable light of the marsh/ moon. Because your breath, or the wind, is also connected with this light, your inner fire burns unevenly. As a result, your path through life (the flowing river) follows the rhythms of the moon: one moment you are trying too hard to please others and the next you are collapsing in exhaustion. You are a tree that has reached out further than its roots can support. It offers no one rest or good example because it is constantly on the point of toppling over — rather like an overfull bookcase laden with books that contain nothing but empty pages.

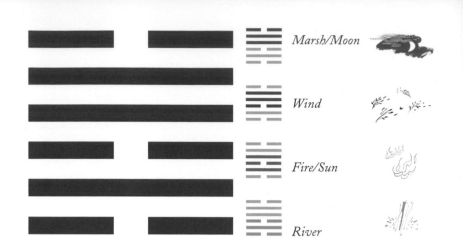

Marsh/Moon

Wind

Fire/Sun

River

Dying Off (Putrefaction)
Dying off or transposition is an alchemical process that keeps the body and the soul in perfect balance. When you transform all your spiritual food into physical action, your 'sublime wisdom' is continuously tested against reality, and you are firmly grounded. The following directions show you how to root yourself in life.
(47)

Vigorous Mind
Shake off the concepts you have adopted as soon as you notice that they diminish your physical functioning and zest for life.
28

Inner Change (Distillation)
Bear in mind that your attitude to life is transformed through every new insight you develop, even though the physical requirements for life stay the same.
49

The Management of the Inner Being
Your spiritual attitude is responsible for your physical well-being. When you ignore your physical needs, you are behaving as if you are not of this earth.
37

Redemption
By carefully studying your physical needs, you learn to match your actions to these needs. You cannot tell anyone anything about life if you think that you are above it.
59

Restricted Movement
As you translate your knowledge into action, you will feel like a young fox that has wet its tail when someone else does not believe you or assails you with other arguments. This will happen often. No one knows what life is all about, so you should not store away your impressions as if they were higher wisdom.
64

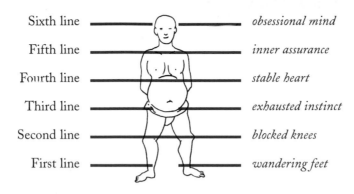

Sixth line		*obsessional mind*
Fifth line		*inner assurance*
Fourth line		*stable heart*
Third line		*exhausted instinct*
Second line		*blocked knees*
First line		*wandering feet*

The Individual Lines

The Hermetic *I Ching*
The answer to your specific question is not found only in the starting hexagram. For a deeper insight, you can also study the various separate hexagrams that make up the starting hexagram. The number next to these hexagrams indicates the page where you can find their complete interpretation. If the hexagram you have thrown contains changing lines, these direct you to a 'follow-up' hexagram.

Like life itself, the *I Ching* is a hermetic labyrinth of wonders from which you can only escape by closing the book.

Sixth line
Your mind clings to the illusion of the full moon, which is about to wane. By making a 'truth' of outward display, you have gotten yourself into a difficult situation. Do not keep on arrogantly asserting that you have found truths when, in fact, these are melting like snow in the sun.

Fifth line
The waxing moon and the beginning of the wind, or your breathing, indicate that you are fooling yourself and that you are unstable if you elevate your impressions to the level of 'truths' without first testing them in practice. It is only by translating your thoughts into words and deeds that you can see what they are worth.

Fourth line
The new moon symbolizes an attractive light that can encourage zest for life and growth, as long as you do not sell your heart to it. Use your breathing (the middle of the wind) to keep your inner fire burning evenly so that you do not find yourself running breathlessly after something transient.

Third line
The core of the inner fire which is barely glowing because the wind, or your breathing, is exhausted, indicates that you are ignoring your survival instinct and therefore letting your body's vital energy drain away like sap from a dying tree. Put aside illusions and concentrate on your breathing so that you can once again meet your physical requirements.

Second line
The core of the water, which is flowing away, and the beginning of the inner fire, which is reaching upwards, symbolizes a powerless attitude to life. Spiritual overexertion makes you weak at the knees. Pause for rest under a tree, and take it as your example.

First line
The water flows, but is not being fed by vital energy. You try to stand on your feet but fall over backwards and lie like a tree blown over by the wind, with its roots in the air. You should be ashamed that you have neglected your physical self.

Introduction
The K'un hexagram is determined by *Vigorous Mind (28)*. Because your mind (sixth line) latches on to the moon ☷, which grows full and wanes again, the surety you thought you had achieved vanishes. As a result, your breath ☴ catches in your throat and your inner fire ☲ cannot burn optimally, which interrupts your rhythm of life ☵.

Strong and Weak Changing Lines
Extra attention should be paid to strong and weak lines in the hexagram you have thrown. A strong line signifies that you are addressing the situation with too much force, whereas a weak line calls for a bolder attitude.

The Follow-Up Hexagram
Once you have changed the strong and weak lines into their opposites, a new 'follow-up' hexagram is created which provides information about a future phase of life. The information on the left-hand page is the most useful for studying this hexagram, since follow-up hexagrams contain no changing lines.
The information on the right-hand page can, of course, be useful for clarifying your study of the follow-up hexagram.

These hexagrams are components of the starting hexagram and offer directions for successfully dealing with your present situation.   The lines of the hexagram correspond to various parts of the body. The instructions you find there provide insight into your current physical and spiritual state.

▬▬●▬▬ : Strong Changing Line
▬▬✕▬▬ : Weak Changing Line

47

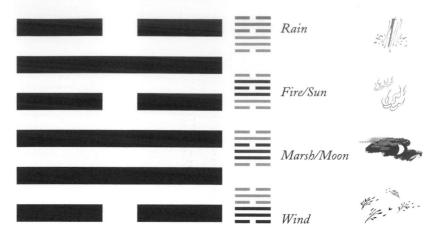

A piece of land divided into eight fields which are owned by eight families. The middle section, where the well is situated, is for communal use.

CHING (Inner Growth /Sublimation)

In the Ching character, the eight fields symbolize the eight trigrams on which the I Ching is founded and from which the 64 hexagrams can be derived. The idea behind this is that the rain that falls on the fields, or the trigrams, absorbs their particular energies, which mix underground and can be drawn up out of the well. Once you have acquired the knowledge underlying the I Ching you, too, can become a living source of information.

In the hexagram, your inner assurance and your survival instinct are determined by the fire/sun, so that your heart and mind can sincerely and impartially distribute your knowledge.
The marsh/moon, which is warmed by the fire/sun, represents an inexhaustible zest for life because it is constantly supplemented by the rain. This also indicates that temporary illusions always remain subordinate to reality. Because the wind, or your breathing, is connected with your survival instinct, you move through life in a relaxed but alert way. All these qualities make you an unlimited source of inspiration to others.

Rain

Fire/Sun

Marsh/Moon

Wind

Inner Growth (Sublimation)
By studying the basic principles of life, you become a source of inspiration to others so that everyone who crosses your path can quench his or her thirst for knowledge. If someone asks your advice and finds your answer unsatisfying, do not add anything in order to justify yourself. You can draw wisdom from the following directions *(reading from bottom to top).* (48)

Successful Movement
The mark of wisdom based on experience is that you do not lose yourself in a situation your inner surety cannot deal with. 63

Regular and Orderly
When there is too much rain, the marsh floods; when there is too little, it dries up. If, out of insecurity, you pretend to be more or less than you are, you violate your true self and become implausible. 60

Duality
The moon becomes full and wanes again. As long as you live you are bound to duality, and every answer you come up with will be ambiguous. As your self-knowledge increases, your inner perception will become clearer. 38

Dissolving (Dissolution)
By pointing to the fact that your breath and the sun are of vital importance, you demonstrate life's fundamental principles. 50

Vigorous Mind
You can never offer a clear-cut answer to the question of what life is all about, but you can try to shed more light on your own reality. 28

CHING

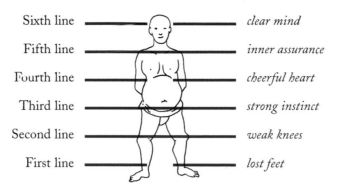

Sixth line ——————— *clear mind*

Fifth line ——————— *inner assurance*

Fourth line ——————— *cheerful heart*

Third line ——————— *strong instinct*

Second line ——————— *weak knees*

First line ——————— *lost feet*

The Individual Lines

Sixth line

The fertile rainwater which streams freely indicates that you are an over-flowing source of knowledge that can quench everyone's thirst. Therefore, you should not shut yourself off — as if your were covering the well — because then you would run the risk of suffocating in your own wisdom.

Fifth line

The center of the running water and the flames of your inner fire suggest that you possess an inner assurance which allows you to speak refreshing words from a warm heart. Take care not to lose yourself in a situation that demands more energy than you possess.

Fourth line

At full moon, there is a risk that you will ignore your true insight and your fertile knowledge. The purity of the well is restored as soon as you stop selling your heart to illusions. Once you are aware of the value of outward display and reality, you will not need — out of insecurity — to present yourself as more or less than you really are.

Third line

The waxing moon, and the beginning of both the inner fire and the wind, suggest that you are a clear source of wisdom, but you are turning away instinctively from the confrontation with an illusion that can make your heart run wild. As long as you keep breathing calmly and maintain clear insight, you will not disappoint yourself or others.

Second line

The new moon which is connected to the middle of the wind, or your breathing in and breathing out, determines your attitude to life. You cling to the illusory light, and you are as implausible as a leaky bucket which is empty by the time it reaches the top of the well. You are fooling yourself if you give others the hope that you can quench their thirst.

First line

The end of the wind represents a muddy well. You are like your feet, which have no answers and are only suitable for moving you through earthly life. Therefore, you should not try to be a source of inspiration for others — unless they want to know something about ignorance.

Introduction

The Ching hexagram is determined by *Successful Movement (63)*. Your inner fire ☲ is so powerful that no cloud veils your mind (sixth line) and you will always come across clearly ☱. Your heart (fourth line) beats joyfully because your breathing ☴ is attuned to the earthly rhythm ☶, which means you can move fluidly through life.

Strong and Weak Changing Lines

Extra attention should be paid to strong and weak lines in the hexagram you have thrown. A strong line signifies that you are addressing the situation with too much force, whereas a weak line calls for a bolder attitude.

The Hermetic *I Ching*

The answer to your specific question is not found only in the starting hexagram. For a deeper insight, you can also study the various separate hexagrams that make up the starting hexagram. The number next to these hexagrams indicates the page where you can find their complete interpretation. If the hexagram you have thrown contains changing lines, these direct you to a 'follow-up' hexagram.

Like life itself, the *I Ching* is a hermetic labyrinth of wonders from which you can only escape by closing the book.

The Follow-Up Hexagram

Once you have changed the strong and weak lines into their opposites, a new 'follow-up' hexagram is created which provides information about a future phase of life. The information on the left-hand page is the most useful for studying this hexagram, since follow-up hexagrams contain no changing lines.
The information on the right-hand page can, of course, be useful for clarifying your study of the follow-up hexagram.

These hexagrams are components of the starting hexagram and offer directions for successfully dealing with your present situation.

The lines of the hexagram correspond to various parts of the body. The instructions you find there provide insight into your current physical and spiritual state.

━━o━━ : Strong Changing Line

━━x━━ : Weak Changing Line

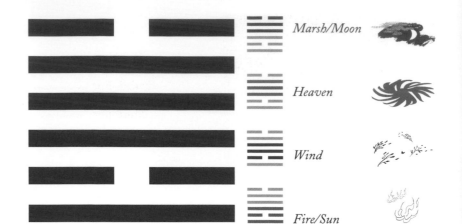

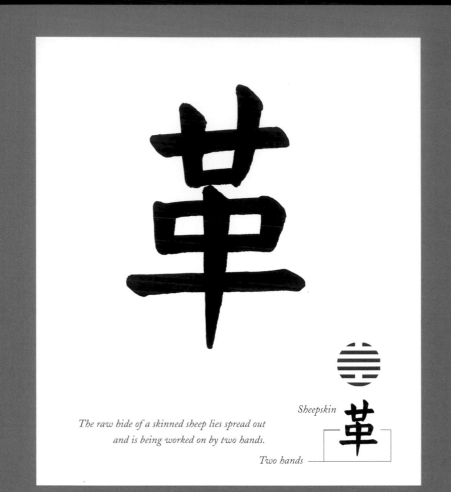

The raw hide of a skinned sheep lies spread out and is being worked on by two hands.

Sheepskin 革

Two hands

KO Inner Change (Distillation)

The character Ko means to skin, and indicates inner change in the sense that a skin (or external covering) is donned like clothing by a new inner being. Symbolically, this suggests that as you become more conscious, you change from a docile 'sheep' into an intelligent human being with a different view of the world while creation and its conditions remain the same.

The hexagram shows that by widening your frame of reference you can assign a new meaning to what you see happening. As you realize what the external world entails, your inner self becomes aware of the creative energy of the heavens, and you no longer have to cling to the illusions of the marsh/moon. Your feelings become progressively more attuned to the fire/sun, or the true light of life, and the wind, or your breathing—both of which are hidden at this stage. Once you become aware of these vital energies, they enable you to stand firmly and fully in the world with a calmly beating heart. You may then feel that your surroundings, which were initially colored by your illusions, have changed. In fact, your inner self has been purified, and your perception of life has changed. Life itself has stayed essentially the same since its inception.

Marsh/Moon

Heaven

Wind

Fire/Sun

Inner Change (Distillation)

By looking for the truth behind every dualistic form you encounter, you approach reality. Realize that you do not need to, and indeed cannot, improve upon creation. Only through inner change can you achieve the insight that everything is as it should be. The following directions *(reading from bottom to top)* show you the path of change, in which you will believe only when your inner self has experienced it. **(49)**

Fulfilment

The only thought you are left with now is that you want to enjoy the earthly game without giving yourself over to illusions. **43**

Vigorous Mind
Free yourself from concepts as soon as you notice that they are disturbing your physical functioning or diminishing your zest for life. **28**

A Mature Relationship

You demonstrate a mature relationship with the earth when you turn your attention to the infinite depth of the heavens, from which the earth derives its creative energy. If you can easily let go of material things, you will always be open to the unknown. **44**

Unanimous Purpose
Who am I, where do I come from, and where am I going? You will find the answers to these questions by looking within yourself. Keep looking until you have developed a view of life that is as authentic and impartial as the heavens and the sun. **13**

The Management of the Inner Being

Attune your breathing to the deep peace radiated by the heavens. Do not allow your inner fire to be fanned by fear of the unknown or to be dimmed by illusions. **37**

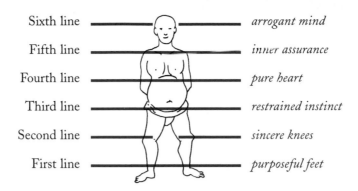

Sixth line ———————— *arrogant mind*

Fifth line ———————— *inner assurance*

Fourth line ———————— *pure heart*

Third line ———————— *restrained instinct*

Second line ———————— *sincere knees*

First line ———————— *purposeful feet*

The Individual Lines

Sixth line
The full moon which is about to wane indicates that when you see through illusion and let it go, your inner self changes — like a leopard moving from sleepy equanimity to action in a split second. If you do not do so, you change outwardly — like the moon — but your inner being is still deluded.

Fifth line
The waxing moon and the outermost limit of the heaven suggest that once you have inner assurance, you can enjoy earthly life without having to change yourself any more than the stripes on a tiger skin. It makes no difference, either inwardly or outwardly, whether a tiger's stripes are black on yellow or yellow on black.

Fourth line
The endearing light of the new moon rising in the center of the inner heaven represents a harmless illusion that touches your heart and gives you zest for life so that your breathing (the beginning of the wind) unconsciously quickens. There is no great problem with letting yourself go, as long as you can distinguish outward display from reality.

Third line
Your survival instinct is based on two heavenly certainties: the middle of the wind (your breathing in and breathing out) and the sun (your inner fire, which is burning evenly). This indicates that, at this stage, you would be wise to carefully consider and reconsider any change you might be contemplating, before taking any action.

Second line
The end of the wind, or the moment just before breathing in when your inner fire is smouldering quietly, indicates a period of contemplation before you decide to change your attitude to life. Since your knees are ready to move, straighten your back after a pause for rest and make the right decision!

First line
The source of the fire, which is connected with your feet, points to the fact that this is not the time for change. Hold on to what you have, and do not think that change can offer you anything at this stage. In your childlike ignorance, you would follow any illusion that presents itself.

Introduction
The Ko hexagram is determined by *Vigorous Mind (28)*. By letting go of illusions (sixth line) and transforming them into inner assurance (fifth line), you can experience the creative energy of the heavens ☰ deep within you and stand as securely in life as the sun ☲. As a result, your breathing ☴ is calm and you can enjoy the earthly game with a pure heart (fourth line).

Strong and Weak Changing Lines
Extra attention should be paid to strong and weak lines in the hexagram you have thrown. A strong line signifies that you are addressing the situation with too much force, whereas a weak line calls for a bolder attitude.

The Hermetic *I Ching*
The answer to your specific question is not found only in the starting hexagram. For a deeper insight, you can also study the various separate hexagrams that make up the starting hexagram. The number next to these hexagrams indicates the page where you can find their complete interpretation. If the hexagram you have thrown contains changing lines, these direct you to a 'follow-up' hexagram.

Like life itself, the *I Ching* is a hermetic labyrinth of wonders from which you can only escape by closing the book.

The Follow-Up Hexagram
Once you have changed the strong and weak lines into their opposites, a new 'follow-up' hexagram is created which provides information about a future phase of life. The information on the left-hand page is the most useful for studying this hexagram, since follow-up hexagrams contain no changing lines. The information on the right-hand page can, of course, be useful for clarifying your study of the follow-up hexagram.

These hexagrams are components of the starting hexagram and offer directions for successfully dealing with your present situation.

The lines of the hexagram correspond to various parts of the body. The instructions you find there provide insight into your current physical and spiritual state.

▬⊖▬ : Strong Changing Line
▬✕▬ : Weak Changing Line

革

49

A cooking pot on a tripod

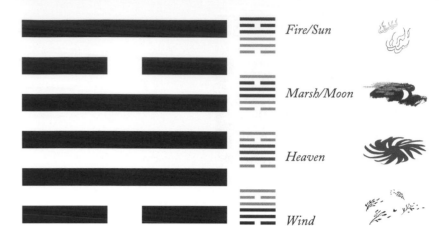

Fire/Sun

Marsh/Moon

Heaven

Wind

TING (Dissolving/Dissolution)

The character Ting represents a cooking pot and symbolizes the body, which extracts vital energy from food and processes sensory impressions into clear insight. When food is dissolved, its nutritional value is released. In the same way, sensory impressions have to be purified in the inner self so that the truth is separated off from outward display.

In the hexagram, the fire/sun and the wind, or your inner surety and breathing, are fundamental to the process of dissolution. An evenly burning inner fire is based on deep and concentrated breathing. Test spiritual nourishment, or your thoughts, in your inner heaven — where deep peace should reign — in order to detect any influences that might disturb your heart, your instinct or attitude to life. In this way, you can find out what is cooking. Both the marsh/moon and the wind originate in the core of the heaven (third line), or your instinct. Your instinct is directed towards survival and warns you as soon as illusions threaten, by making your breathing irregular. As long as you take notice of these signals, you will always know what to do.

 ### Dissolving (Dissolution)
Fire and air transform fuel into its essential components. By concentrating on linking your breathing to your inner surety, you can reveal the cause of physical and spiritual complaints and solve them. The following steps can help you on your way.

 (50)

 ### Duality
By testing a duality in your inner self, you learn to recognize its nutritional value.

38

Profound Insight, Great Possession
In order to develop profound insight, you need to know that you can resolve every duality you take in by becoming aware that the conflict you perceive is actually your own projection.

14

Fulfilment
Stay focused on the thought that you want to enjoy the earthly game without losing yourself in illusions.

43

 ### Vigorous Mind
Let go of concepts as soon as you notice that they disturb your breathing and hinder your physical functioning, which diminishes your zest for life.

28

A Mature Relationship
The mark of a mature relationship with the earth is that you focus on the infinite depth of the heavens, from which the earth derives her creative energy. If you can easily let go of material things, you will always live in a relaxed way.

44

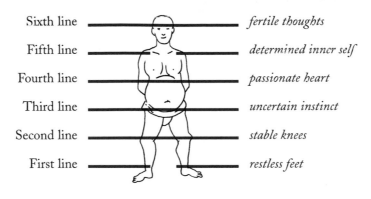

Sixth line ———————— *fertile thoughts*

Fifth line ———————— *determined inner self*

Fourth line ———————— *passionate heart*

Third line ———————— *uncertain instinct*

Second line ———————— *stable knees*

First line ———————— *restless feet*

The Individual Lines

Sixth line
The flames of the fire indicate that once Truth is freed from outward display, it provides the energy for generating clear thoughts. You are like a cooking pot with jade handles, representing spiritual riches and fertile knowledge. If you can see through illusions, you can live in a relaxed way.

Fifth line
The full moon and the core of the heavens, or your inner surety, struggle for control of your mind. You are like a cooking pot with golden handles hung with metal rings (so the pot can be carried). Do not let illusions run rings around you and carry you away. Take in the information that is valuable to you and realize that outward appearances inevitably lose their brilliance.

Fourth line
The smoldering fire is outshone by the waxing moon, which disturbs the peace of your inner heaven. You are making a truth of outward display, which disturbs your breathing. Do not sell your heart to an illusion. If even one of the legs supporting the cooking pot breaks, the wisdom you have acquired will flow away ineffectively.

Third line
The new moon rising at the core of your inner heaven, or your cooking pot, does not weaken your survival instinct but alerts the beginning of the wind, or your breathing, which unconsciously quickens. Before you can succumb to something that inevitably turns out to be illusory, you see through it.

Second line
The beginning of the inner heaven symbolizes a full cooking pot whose contents are explored by the middle of the wind, or your breathing in and breathing out. Your attitude to life is determined by your knees, and as long as you have the feeling that they are vigorously supporting you, nothing can daunt you and you remain free of illusions.

First line
The end of the wind, or being out of breath, indicates exhaustion. If you are choosy about what might be good or bad for you, you are turning the cooking pot upside down and behaving as if your wisdom can be found in your feet. Just breathe in for now, even if the air is filled with illusions.

Introduction
The Ting hexagram is determined by *Vigorous Mind (28)*. Through deep and concentrated breathing ☴, which is attuned to your survival instinct (third line), you can test the true value ☰ of spiritual nourishment. In this way, your inner surety ☰ sees through all illusions ☳ and you can produce fertile thoughts (sixth line).

Strong and Weak Changing Lines
Extra attention should be paid to strong and weak lines in the hexagram you have thrown. A strong line signifies that you are addressing the situation with too much force, whereas a weak line calls for a bolder attitude.

The Hermetic *I Ching*
The answer to your specific question is not found only in the starting hexagram. For a deeper insight, you can also study the various separate hexagrams that make up the starting hexagram. The number next to these hexagrams indicates the page where you can find their complete interpretation. If the hexagram you have thrown contains changing lines, these direct you to a 'follow-up' hexagram.

Like life itself, the *I Ching* is a hermetic labyrinth of wonders from which you can only escape by closing the book.

The Follow-Up Hexagram
Once you have changed the strong and weak lines into their opposites, a new 'follow-up' hexagram is created which provides information about a future phase of life. The information on the left-hand page is the most useful for studying this hexagram, since follow-up hexagrams contain no changing lines.
The information on the right-hand page can, of course, be useful for clarifying your study of the follow-up hexagram.

These hexagrams are components of the starting hexagram and offer directions for successfully dealing with your present situation.

The lines of the hexagram correspond to various parts of the body. The instructions you find there provide insight into your current physical and spiritual state.

▬●▬ : Strong Changing Line
▬×▬ : Weak Changing Line

鼎 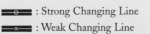 50

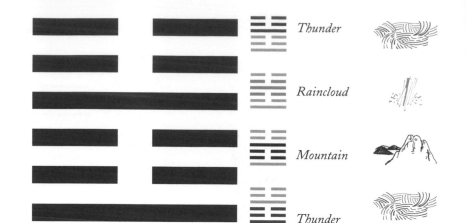

Heavenly order ——

Rain ——

A woman bending over to hide her menstruation. ——
By implication, therefore: time, period, and era

CHEN Confirmation (Coagulation)

The character Chen means to shake or shock. Its construction indicates that the cyclic occurrence of events that provide relief makes you uneasy because you cannot predict exactly when they will occur, even though their arrival is heralded by a certain degree of tension. This unease is a premonition which can only shake you as long as you are not familiar with it; once you recognize it for what it is, it merely confirms what you already suspect.

In the hexagram, the lower thunder, which originates at the foot of the mountain, symbolizes something indecipherable that is imposing itself on you and making you uneasy. The raincloud enveloping the top of the mountain indicates a coming period of growth which you cannot influence in advance. By preserving your inner peace and undertaking meticulous self-examination, you can find confirmation of your feelings and wait calmly until the natural tension, or the upper thunder, is released.

 Thunder

 Raincloud

 Mountain

 Thunder

 Confirmation (Coagulation)
Uneasy feelings are portents of forceful release. If you stay calm and focus on your inner self, you will begin to glimpse the cause of the tension you feel. Confirmation of these premonitions will shake you, but also bring relief. You can learn how to cushion the shock by reading the following directions *from bottom to top*. (51)

 Cutting the Knot
In this situation it is not advisable to use either force or patient analysis to free yourself from uneasy feelings. You will have to let nature take its course without allowing your uneasiness to develop into fear and then panic. 40

 Repression
If you begin to suspect that you are in a situation that has to run its course, direct your energy — for better or for worse — towards other things demanding your attention. 62

 Initial Difficulty
Since you do not know where your uneasiness comes from or how to get rid of it, it would be wise to retreat to a quiet place where you can investigate your spiritual and physical condition. 39

 Confusion
When you are assailed by feelings that you vaguely recognize but cannot clearly define, you become uneasy. 3

 Nourishment
All the information you take in is digested and given meaning within your frame of reference. 27

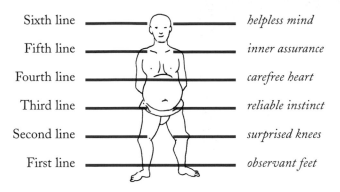

Sixth line		*helpless mind*
Fifth line		*inner assurance*
Fourth line		*carefree heart*
Third line		*reliable instinct*
Second line		*surprised knees*
First line		*observant feet*

The Individual Lines

Sixth line
The end of the thunder indicates that the breakthrough has occurred. The marriage between conjecture and certainty takes place here. If you have had an uneasy feeling of foreboding that you have not expressed, you will be as shocked as an ignorant girl seeing her menstrual blood for the first time.

Fifth line
The thunder pounding against the raincloud indicates that the air is pregnant with a mighty tension. Deep down, you are sure that something is about to happen. You have your suspicions as to what that is, but you know that worrying about it is a waste of energy. You would benefit from talking about it and then returning to your daily business.

Fourth line
The thunder originates at the top of the mountain where the rain forms a lake. This suggests that you are conscious of a threatening disruption and believe you have sufficient wisdom to deal with it. Do not make that mistake. Pour out your heart now, so that you will not later find yourself floundering, badly shocked, in the mire.

Third line
Below the top of the mountain, the thunder comes rolling up through a haze of rain. You have no overview and you feel that uneasiness is getting the better of you. You run the least risk of being overwhelmed by fear if you can translate the fertile knowledge others offer you into words and deeds.

Second line
In the heart of the thunder at the foot of the mountain, you are weighed down by such violent anxiety that you fear you will lose your mind. Stop worrying. Straighten your back and find a peaceful, quiet place where you can meditate on the cause of your anxiety. When the shock comes, you will realize that you had nothing to lose.

First line
The beginning of the thunder indicates the beginning of uneasiness. Do not drop or clench your lower jaw, but speak out. It may be that another can already tell you what is in the air so that you can laugh off your worries. If not, you have at least aired your feelings.

Introduction
The Chen hexagram is determined by *Nourishment (27)*. By speaking out ☳ (lower jaw/first line and upper jaw/fourth line), you lighten your heart (fourth line) and allow your fertile knowledge ☷ to flow a little, thereby reducing the tension. It is unclear when the shock ☷ (upper trigram) will come, but you will not be so badly shaken by it if you are calm inside.

Strong and Weak Changing Lines
Extra attention should be paid to strong and weak lines in the hexagram you have thrown. A strong line signifies that you are addressing the situation with too much force, whereas a weak line calls for a bolder attitude.

The Hermetic *I Ching*
The answer to your specific question is not found only in the starting hexagram. For a deeper insight, you can also study the various separate hexagrams that make up the starting hexagram. The number next to these hexagrams indicates the page where you can find their complete interpretation. If the hexagram you have thrown contains changing lines, these direct you to a 'follow-up' hexagram.

Like life itself, the *I Ching* is a hermetic labyrinth of wonders from which you can only escape by closing the book.

The Follow-Up Hexagram
Once you have changed the strong and weak lines into their opposites, a new 'follow-up' hexagram is created which provides information about a future phase of life. The information on the left-hand page is the most useful for studying this hexagram, since follow-up hexagrams contain no changing lines. The information on the right-hand page can, of course, be useful for clarifying your study of the follow-up hexagram.

 These hexagrams are components of the starting hexagram and offer directions for successfully dealing with your present situation.

The lines of the hexagram correspond to various parts of the body. The instructions you find there provide insight into your current physical and spiritual state.

━⊙━ : Strong Changing Line
━×━ : Weak Changing Line

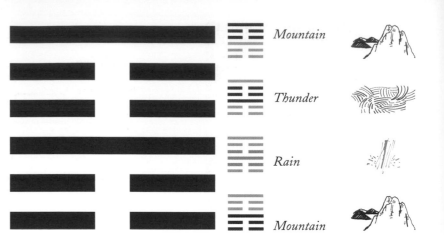

*Suddenly turning around
and looking someone straight in the eye.*

	Mountain	
Thunder		
Rain		
Mountain		

KÊN At Rest and Impassive

The character Kên means indomitable, to oppose, impassive and challenging. These are qualities clearly conveyed by a mountain. You, too, can develop awareness along these lines, so that your inner power is evoked by your outward appearance.

The hexagram is made up of two mountains: the one in the foreground is veiled by a raincloud which symbolizes fertile knowledge, while the one in the background is assailed by the rolling thunder, representing restlessness. You are like the mountain in the foreground if you possess knowledge that enables you to veil your appearance in mist and so adapt yourself to any situation. This also explains why you have the confidence to suddenly turn around and look someone straight in the eye. You can develop this sort of indomitable self-confidence by retreating to meditate at the foot of the mountain in the background. There, you realize that your thoughts are as restless as thunder because you are trying to escape the here and now by imagining what you will face at the top of the mountain. Once you realize that the only way to find out is to climb it, you will also understand that you can regard the future impassively if you are at peace in the present. Then you are like the mountain in the foreground.

At Rest and Impassive

When you are at rest, you are like your spinal column: a bundle of nerve fibres which impassively supports and directs your body. Once you have developed the same peace in your head, chest, and stomach, your ego disappears and the most you can say about yourself is that you are consciousness that is conscious of itself. Move down through the following directions to discover how to achieve this. **(52)**

Nourishment

Do not feed on thoughts of the next meal while you have not finished the food that is in front of you. **27**

Youthful Innocence

Do not act like a turbulent flood of water rushing blindly towards the future. Show curiosity, but move like a babbling brook which irrigates fields and is a joy to itself and others. **4**

Cutting the Knot

If you are enveloped in dark clouds, calmly take the time to untangle the problem, but cut the knot when your patience is exhausted.
Only real mountains have endless patience. **40**

Repression

If you radiate peace, others will see you as a challenge, just like a mountain that has to be climbed and conquered. Sometimes you are better off if people perceive you as a hill. **62**

Initial Difficulty

Withdraw when you need to digest your experiences, and throw yourself back into life when the time is right so that your knowledge does not become a pent-up chaos demanding release, whatever the cost. **39**

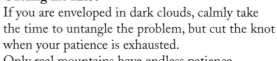

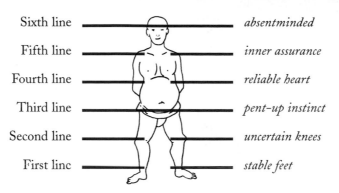

Sixth line —————————— *absentminded*

Fifth line —————————— *inner assurance*

Fourth line —————————— *reliable heart*

Third line —————————— *pent-up instinct*

Second line —————————— *uncertain knees*

First line —————————— *stable feet*

The Individual Lines

Sixth line

You have been a good student and have become like the top of the mountain: a beacon of inner and outward peace. Remain aware that only the here and now matters. Do not run ahead of events, and do not boast that you can solve all problems at once.

Fifth line

The end of the thunder under the top of the mountain indicates that the lower jaw, or the beginning of the thunder (third line), is kept in check. This means you should not burden others with endless chatter just so you can show off your knowledge. Only speak when you have the inner assurance that you have something worthwhile to say.

Fourth line

The fertile rain and the pulsating core of the thunder at the foot of the mountain represent a steadily beating heart which will not sell itself to the first illusion that comes along. Through meditation you develop peace and impassivity, but beware of the temptation of pride.

Third line

The thunder rises out of the lake at the top of the mountain. This indicates that your meditation is disturbed because you do not have your physical impulses under control. Your instinct is crying out for movement, while your heart is focused on inner peace. Water has to flow, so do not torment yourself: shake yourself loose.

Second line

Below the top of the mountain, the water flows away. You do not have your knees under control and you want to race down the mountain like water. You may be unhappy about this desire, but at this stage it may not be so foolish to first satisfy your urge to move before making a new attempt to meditate.

First line

The foot of the mountain is a sign that you are at rest from head to toe. Deep meditation places you firmly in the here and now and you are just like your feet, which still have no idea of where they are about to be sent.

Introduction

The Kên hexagram is determined by *Nourishment (27)*. Meditation is the food that provides you with peace, from your head (sixth line) to the belly (third line). As soon as you possess inner assurance (fifth line) and a reliable heart (fourth line) that does not sell itself to anything, you turn this acquisition into your attitude to life (first and second lines).

Strong and Weak Changing Lines

Extra attention should be paid to strong and weak lines in the hexagram you have thrown. A strong line signifies that you are addressing the situation with too much force, whereas a weak line calls for a bolder attitude.

The Hermetic *I Ching*

The answer to your specific question is not found only in the starting hexagram. For a deeper insight, you can also study the various separate hexagrams that make up the starting hexagram. The number next to these hexagrams indicates the page where you can find their complete interpretation. If the hexagram you have thrown contains changing lines, these direct you to a 'follow-up' hexagram.

Like life itself, the *I Ching* is a hermetic labyrinth of wonders from which you can only escape by closing the book.

The Follow-Up Hexagram

Once you have changed the strong and weak lines into their opposites, a new 'follow-up' hexagram is created which provides information about a future phase of life. The information on the left-hand page is the most useful for studying this hexagram, since follow-up hexagrams contain no changing lines.
The information on the right-hand page can, of course, be useful for clarifying your study of the follow-up hexagram.

} These hexagrams are components of the starting hexagram and offer directions for successfully dealing with your present situation.

 The lines of the hexagram correspond to various parts of the body. The instructions you find there provide insight into your current physical and spiritual state.

⚊⊚⚊ : Strong Changing Line
⚊×⚊ : Weak Changing Line

艮 **52**

Running water

漸

A carriage
An axe
To wield an axe. Also to cleave, split and cut loose

KIEN (The Blessed Marriage)

The character Kien stands for becoming slowly saturated, to climb up, and moving slowly along. The various symbols indicate that you are moving calmly on the stream of life and can avoid drowning in it because you are able to free yourself from any whirlpool that threatens to suck you down.

In the hexagram, the mountain and the wind represent an overview, inner peace, and relaxed breathing that is attuned to the rhythm of the heavens. Because the wind is connected to the fire/sun and the fertile rain, you also have a clear mind, inner assurance, a balanced heart, and a vigorous instinct. With these capacities, you are the ideal inhabitant of the earth. If you want to unite with her in true matrimony you should follow her rhythm, being active in the summer and resting in the winter, appearing in spring and disappearing in autumn. This implies that your marriage with the earth is only blessed if you respect the seasons in yourself and in others and know when it is time to plough, to sow, to harvest, and to rest.

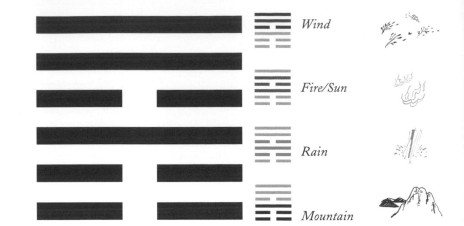

Wind

Fire/Sun

Rain

Mountain

The Blessed Marriage
The earth is like a wise old woman with an eternally youthful appearance. If you want to enjoy life as she does, do not hang on to situations that conflict with her nature. The path to a long and healthy life is laid out for you below.

(53)

The Management of the Inner Being
Calm breathing ensures that your inner fire burns purely and evenly and is not fanned or smothered by all-consuming anger or exhausting impotence.

37

Redemption
By studying your physical requirements, you learn to attune your actions to these needs.

59

Restricted Movement
If you do not want to move like a young fox that has wet its tail, do not be seduced into action if you feel the time is not ripe.

64

The Wise Man
The wise man is like the sun crowning the top of the mountain. This old fox moves over the earth impartially and with inner peace.

56

Initial Difficulty
The seasons are your guide to overcoming these difficulties. Plough when it is time to plough, sow if it is time for sowing, harvest when the crop is ready, and rest when nature rests.

39

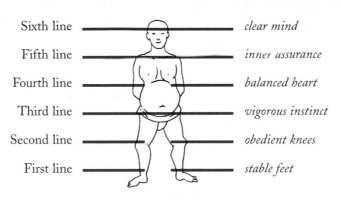

Sixth line	*clear mind*
Fifth line	*inner assurance*
Fourth line	*balanced heart*
Third line	*vigorous instinct*
Second line	*obedient knees*
First line	*stable feet*

The Individual Lines

Sixth line
The beginning of the wind suggests awakening from a deep sleep. If you are like a wild goose, you ready yourself to expand your activities and to depart for the 'breeding grounds'. Do not take wing while you are still half asleep, for then you would run the risk of falling into a situation for which you are not yet ready.

Fifth line
The middle of the wind, or your breathing in and breathing out, ensures that your inner fire burns like a pure flame. If you are like a wild goose, you land on a hill where you are a beacon for others. You open yourself to your environment, but do not allow yourself to become so impregnated by it that you can no longer escape.

Fourth line
The core of the fire/sun lies behind the last shreds of the raincloud, and the wind dies down. If you are a wild goose, you take notice of the trees and know that as soon as the leaves fall, it is high time to depart. Do not linger. You will waste energy and never be able to take your leave.

Third line
The beginning of the fire barely influences the snow on the top of the mountain. If you are like a wild goose, you know that your instinct is liberated in times of danger. Therefore, you can leave your physical being behind in deep peace and ascend into your spirit through meditation.

Second line
Below the top of the mountain, the water flows as a clear, fresh mountain stream. If you are like a wild goose, you know that it is now time to enjoy life to the full—without going so far that you plunge from a high peak into a deep valley from which you will never emerge.

First line
At the foot of the mountain you are like a wild goose nearing the coast after a long journey, or someone emerging from deep meditation. Be aware that, whatever happens, you must first get back your strength. At this stage, you have no more to report than your feet, which are happy simply to have reached solid ground.

Introduction
The movement in the Kien hexagram is determined by water ☵, which begins to flow as soon as the sun ☲ melts the snow on the mountain ☶. The wind ☴ indicates that you are following the rhythms of nature, like a wild goose that moves over the earth with the seasons and does not allow itself to be seduced into staying any longer than nature dictates.

Strong and Weak Changing Lines
Extra attention should be paid to strong and weak lines in the hexagram you have thrown. A strong line signifies that you are addressing the situation with too much force, whereas a weak line calls for a bolder attitude.

The Hermetic *I Ching*
The answer to your specific question is not found only in the starting hexagram. For a deeper insight, you can also study the various separate hexagrams that make up the starting hexagram. The number next to these hexagrams indicates the page where you can find their complete interpretation. If the hexagram you have thrown contains changing lines, these direct you to a 'follow-up' hexagram.

Like life itself, the *I Ching* is a hermetic labyrinth of wonders from which you can only escape by closing the book.

The Follow-Up Hexagram
Once you have changed the strong and weak lines into their opposites, a new 'follow-up' hexagram is created which provides information about a future phase of life. The information on the left-hand page is the most useful for studying this hexagram, since follow-up hexagrams contain no changing lines. The information on the right-hand page can, of course, be useful for clarifying your study of the follow-up hexagram.

These hexagrams are components of the starting hexagram and offer directions for successfully dealing with your present situation.

The lines of the hexagram correspond to various parts of the body. The instructions you find there provide insight into your current physical and spiritual state.

━o━ : Strong Changing Line
━x━ : Weak Changing Line

漸

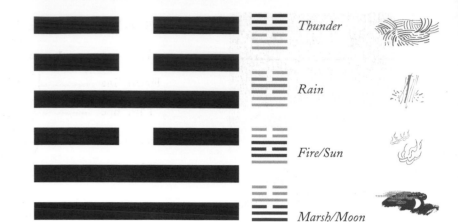

	Thunder
	Rain
	Fire/Sun
	Marsh/Moon

The arrival of the bride at the groom's house, where she ——
will live as a married woman. Marriage

歸妹

A girl

A tall tree. Also: a cycle and negation.

The younger sister: seductive but immature

KWEI MEI (Fertility)

The characters Kwei and Mei represent a succession of weddings involving a young, immature woman. This is not so strange once you realize that it refers to the sun's cyclic marriage with the moon, which waxes and wanes and does not possess the fertility of her older sister, the earth.

In the hexagram, the marsh/moon is illuminated by the sun and supplied with water by the rain so that it does not dry out or flood, and zest for life is preserved. The thunder symbolizes the continuous rhythm of the moon's completed cycle. The moon affects the water balance on earth and thereby also the flow of bodily fluids. Her false — but very seductive — light awakens sexual desires which conquer reason and elevate the value of the physical above that of the spiritual. The earth's younger sister is extremely enticing and can be useful to you as long as you accord her energy the right place in your life.

Fertility
The subtle energy of the moon has an almost intangible influence on earthly activities and works like a mirror which exposes your physical and spiritual weaknesses. Initially, the most fruitful time to learn from this energy is sensed intuitively and as you dare to trust these feelings, they develop into an inner conviction. The way to control this energy is explained by the following directions *(reading from bottom top).* (54)

Cutting the Knot
After this explanation it should be obvious that the moon had something to offer you, but no longer has. It is time to free yourself from this millstone around your neck. 40

Completion
When the sun reaches its highest point, it starts to descend. If you realize that the sun keeps on shining, you know that you can maintain a radiant appearance by not admitting the darkness into yourself. 55

Succesful Movement
Move like an old fox, and, whatever the situation, maintain an appearance that mirrors your inner peace. 63

Regular and Orderly
The moon waxes and wanes again. By concentrating on outward display and trying to see what remains of it after it is unmasked, you get at the truth. 60

Duality
The moon waxes and wanes again. The sun is never extinguished. Do not rely on outward display, and keep on searching for the true light behind this luminescence. 38

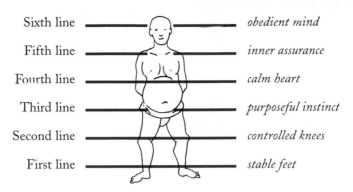

Sixth line ——————— *obedient mind*

Fifth line ——————— *inner assurance*

Fourth line ——————— *calm heart*

Third line ——————— *purposeful instinct*

Second line ——————— *controlled knees*

First line ——————— *stable feet*

The Individual Lines

Sixth line

The end of the thunder, or the dark moon, is like a woman carrying an empty basket. If your head is as empty as the basket, you have not been left with compulsive thoughts. You have withstood the test of your experiences because you have not raised illusions to 'truths'.

Fifth line

The core of the thunder where the water reaches its highest point represents the full moon which, like a seductive young woman, surpasses her older sister — the earth — in terms of attractiveness. By holding on to your inner assurance, you can freely and playfully learn from illusion.

Fourth line

The beginning of the thunder, which make the water rise, and the last rays of the setting sun suggest the waxing moon which makes your heart beat perceptibly. You are not yet in danger of selling out to illusion, but be wary and do not allow your true light to be suppressed. Seduction fills the air.

Third line

The core of the fire/sun and the pelting rain keep the reflective surface of the marsh/moon in balance. If you can make the true light the light of your life, outward display will become a welcome stimulus that will never permanently overwhelm you.

Second line

The early sunlight below the reflective surface of the marsh, or the waxing moon that has cast a longing eye at the sun, indicate that you are closing off a dark period in your life and heading for the true light. Beware of illusions which could make you lose your sincere attitude to life.

First line

The new moon is like a crippled woman who still easily manages to get around. Following her is not a problem, as long as you stand more firmly in life than she does. A new cycle is dawning. Even though you do not know what this cycle will bring, you can move along with it in order to discover the truth behind outward display.

Introduction

The Kwei Mei hexagram is determined by the movement ☳ of the moon ☱. If you attune your survival instinct (third line) to the true light ☲, or your spiritual development, you will not be led primarily by your sexual impulses and will be able to learn from outward appearances which is the basis of your physical desire ☱.

Strong and Weak Changing Lines

Extra attention should be paid to strong and weak lines in the hexagram you have thrown. A strong line signifies that you are addressing the situation with too much force, whereas a weak line calls for a bolder attitude.

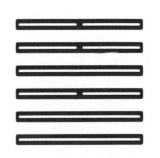

The Hermetic *I Ching*

The answer to your specific question is not found only in the starting hexagram. For a deeper insight, you can also study the various separate hexagrams that make up the starting hexagram. The number next to these hexagrams indicates the page where you can find their complete interpretation. If the hexagram you have thrown contains changing lines, these direct you to a 'follow-up' hexagram.

Like life itself, the *I Ching* is a hermetic labyrinth of wonders from which you can only escape by closing the book.

The Follow-Up Hexagram

Once you have changed the strong and weak lines into their opposites, a new 'follow-up' hexagram is created which provides information about a future phase of life. The information on the left-hand page is the most useful for studying this hexagram, since follow-up hexagrams contain no changing lines.

The information on the right-hand page can, of course, be useful for clarifying your study of the follow-up hexagram.

} These hexagrams are components of the starting hexagram and offer directions for successfully dealing with your present situation.

The lines of the hexagram correspond to various parts of the body. The instructions you find there provide insight into your current physical and spiritual state.

▬▬▬●▬▬ : Strong Changing Line
▬▬▬x▬▬ : Weak Changing Line

歸妹 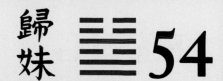 **54**

The harvested corn is displayed ——

A serving dish for meat ——

FÊNG (Completion)

The character Fêng represents the harvest and means exuberant, abundant, and luxuriant. From the construction of the character, it is obvious that the meat-dish, or your physical being, is restricted by upper and lower lines. This suggests that you are weighed down by the corn, or your spiritual riches. You are urged, therefore, to stop pretending to be less than what you are and to let your wisdom shine like the eternal sun.

The hexagram indicates that your attitude to life is based on the fire/sun, but you hide your inner surety behind the reflective appearance of the marsh/moon because you are afraid to display your knowledge to the external world. You can free your heart (fourth line) of the shadow you have called up out of fear by liberating your breathing (the wind) from the influence of the moon. Then your inner fire will keep burning evenly. When your beating heart is once again as regular and sincere as the approaching thunder, you are completely yourself. In extreme circumstances you can, as free will or survival instinct dictates, use outward appearance as a smokescreen to hide your inner assurance.

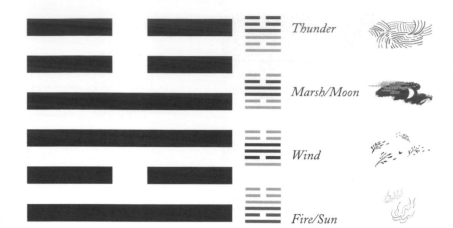

Thunder

Marsh/Moon

Wind

Fire/Sun

Completion

Do not be afraid that when you hand out your knowledge you are casting pearls before swine just because others do not believe you, ignore you, react emotionally, or become angry. Be yourself completely and — like the sun — let your inner light shine calmly and impartially, regardless of whether others ask this of you. The following directions *(reading from bottom to top)* can lead you to the point where you no longer hide your light under a bushel.

(55)

Fertility

Now that you know the effect of outward display, you can make good use of it as a mask in situations that you either do not like or find threatening.

54

Continuity, Balanced Movement

Your heart beats most regularly and longest if your breathing is attuned to the intensity of your physical effort, rather than is influenced by an unbalanced mental attitude.

32

Vigorous Mind

Free yourself of concepts as soon as you notice that they weigh you down physically and, therefore, diminish your zest for life.

28

Inner Change (Distillation)

Be aware that you do not need to — and cannot — improve on creation. Only through inner change can you develop the insight that everything is as it should be.

49

The Management of the Inner Being

Attune your breathing to the intense peace radiated by the sun so that your fear of rejection does not make your heart shrink like the waning moon.

37

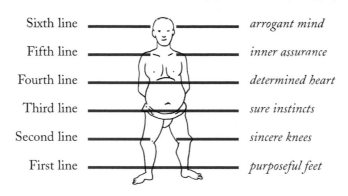

Sixth line ——————————— *arrogant mind*

Fifth line ——————————— *inner assurance*

Fourth line ——————————— *determined heart*

Third line ——————————— *sure instincts*

Second line ——————————— *sincere knees*

First line ——————————— *purposeful feet*

The Individual Lines

Sixth line

The end of the thunder symbolizes the waning moon which you elevate to the status of true light. Your realm of thought is like a ruin with a pompous facade which hides your lack of inner assurance. You watch hopefully for someone to come knocking at your front door, but no one rises to the bait.

Fifth line

The middle of the thunder and the full moon, which is about to wane, suggest that your heart will beat regularly once you stop selling it to illusions. Now that you know how to deal with outward display, you can use it as a mask in situations you either do not like or find threatening.

Fourth line

The waxing moon and the beginning of both the thunder and the wind indicate that you are still veiling yourself in illusion as a front for your insecurity, but that you are slowly becoming aware of the absurdity of your behavior. A sincere heart beats the longest.

Third line

The middle of the wind, or regular breathing in and breathing out, enable your inner fire to burn like the sun, which stands firmly in the heavens and illuminates the new moon. If you want to be impassive and impartial, you would be wise to hide your instincts behind a simple and inconspicuous exterior.

Second line

The end of the wind, or the moment of breathing in, indicates that the core of your inner fire is glowing as weakly as a distant star. You are not in a position to allow your inner fire to shine through in your attitude towards life. Use outward display as a smokescreen to hide your inner assurance.

First line

The beginning of the fire, which is actually as passive as your feet, smolders until it is raked up. As long as you keep breathing and possess inner assurance, you can choose to let your fire blaze. Do not be afraid to be completely yourself and to let your inner light shine like the sun.

Introduction

The Fêng hexagram is determined by the wind ☴ which, like the thunder ☳, originates at the fourth line, or your heart. When you have freed the wind, or your breathing, from the rhythm of the marsh/moon ☱, you will radiate inner certainty (second line) like the sun at high noon because you no longer see the fire/sun ☲ as a necessary evil.

Strong and Weak Changing Lines

Extra attention should be paid to strong and weak lines in the hexagram you have thrown. A strong line signifies that you are addressing the situation with too much force, whereas a weak line calls for a bolder attitude.

The Hermetic *I Ching*

The answer to your specific question is not found only in the starting hexagram. For a deeper insight, you can also study the various separate hexagrams that make up the starting hexagram. The number next to these hexagrams indicates the page where you can find their complete interpretation. If the hexagram you have thrown contains changing lines, these direct you to a 'follow-up' hexagram.

Like life itself, the *I Ching* is a hermetic labyrinth of wonders from which you can only escape by closing the book.

The Follow-Up Hexagram

Once you have changed the strong and weak lines into their opposites, a new 'follow-up' hexagram is created which provides information about a future phase of life. The information on the left-hand page is the most useful for studying this hexagram, since follow-up hexagrams contain no changing lines.

The information on the right-hand page can, of course, be useful for clarifying your study of the follow-up hexagram.

These hexagrams are components of the starting hexagram and offer directions for successfully dealing with your present situation.

The lines of the hexagram correspond to various parts of the body. The instructions you find there provide insight into your current physical and spiritual state.

━●━ : Strong Changing Line
━✕━ : Weak Changing Line

豐  **55**

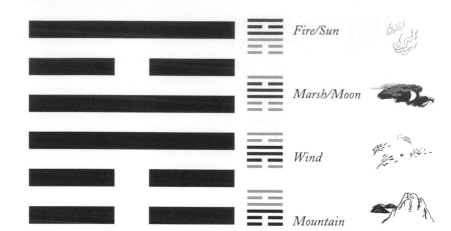

Fire/Sun

Marsh/Moon

Wind

Mountain

LÜ (The Wise Man)

The character Lü represents temporary lodgings, travelers, strangers or soldiers. The traveler who joins others along the way should behave as a guest. You are obviously wise if you behave modestly, do not speak out of turn or about things you know nothing about, do not meddle in others' affairs, and know that speech is silver and silence is golden.

In the hexagram, the fire/sun indicates that you possess inner assurance which is only partially hidden behind the outward brilliance of the marsh/moon. The wind, or your breathing, is associated with your inner fire and is based on the peace exuded by the stable mountain. You move through life in a calm and dignified way, and your attitude to life reveals that when it suits you, you are not as naive as you pretend to be. Like a tall tree that catches a great deal of wind, you may fall into the trap of pride, and this would mean your downfall.

Trees

Men camping under trees

Men or travelers

The Wise Man
A wise person is like the sun crowning the top of the mountain. When others indicate that they want your advice, you give it to them — impartially, and with inner calm. You are advised to show modesty and not to offer your opinion before you are asked, but to speak when others show they are open to hearing from you. You can learn how to become so wise by moving down through the following directions. **(56)**

Duality
Self-awareness is your defence against outward display based on insecurity, and it teaches you to gauge the true worth of others. **38**

Dissolving (Dissolution)
Use your inner surety to test the impression someone makes on you. If you breathe calmly and regularly, you will be able to sense what sort of person you are dealing with. **50**

Vigorous Mind
Do not pursue other people's concepts when you notice that this disturbs your breathing. Concentrate on your own affairs. **28**

The Game of Love
Love for yourself and others depends on your zest for life, which is based on inner surety and ensures that you do not, out of feelings of impotence, feel the need to cut others down to size. **31**

The Blessed Marriage
This marriage is only truly blessed if you know — in relation to yourself and to others — when it is time to plough, to sow, to harvest, and to rest. **53**

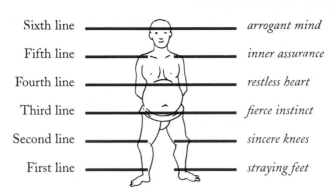

Sixth line ———————— *arrogant mind*

Fifth line ———————— *inner assurance*

Fourth line ———————— *restless heart*

Third line ———————— *fierce instinct*

Second line ———————— *sincere knees*

First line ———————— *straying feet*

The Individual Lines

Sixth line
The sun is at its highest point and confuses your dualistic mind.
You imagine yourself to be far above others. You try to cut everyone
around you down to size, but as soon as you are given some of your own
medicine you fall off your pedestal, shrieking. Pride goes before a fall.

Fifth line
The core of the fire/sun, or your inner surety, does not hide behind the full
moon, which is about to wane. This suggests that you are confronting
another, purposefully and impartially, with the truth. Initially, this will win
you no thanks, but later, your sincerity will be appreciated.

Fourth line
The beginning of your inner fire and the wind, or your breathing, which
are overshadowed by the waxing moon, indicate that you behave like
a courteous guest when in company, but the conversation, which is based
on illusions, makes you anxious. Withdraw in polite silence.

Third line
The new moon controlling the top of the mountain and the middle
of the wind, or your breathing in and breathing out, suggest that you are
insecure and that you behave rudely by pestering others with your words.
Because you cannot keep your mouth shut, you throw away any chance
you have of being accepted by those around you.

Second line
This position below the top of the mountain and at the end of the wind,
or the moment of breathing in, points to a modest attitude to life and,
to correct behavior. You know when it is time to listen, to speak, and
to withdraw.

First line
At the foot of the mountain you have no overview, and you step on many
sore toes. You interfere unasked in other people's affairs and behave like
a bull in a china shop, which turns everyone against you.

Introduction
The Lü hexagram is determined
by *Vigorous Mind (28)*. Do not fix your
mind ☷ on the illusion evoked
by the marsh/moon ☱, for then you
may become caught up in the idea that
you could be the true representative of
the fire/sun ☲. Take your example
from the mountain ☶ so that you
can stand with both feet firmly on the
ground.

Strong and Weak Changing Lines
Extra attention should be paid to strong and
weak lines in the hexagram you have thrown.
A strong line signifies that you are addressing
the situation with too much force, whereas
a weak line calls for a bolder attitude.

The Hermetic *I Ching*
The answer to your specific
question is not found only in the
starting hexagram. For a deeper
insight, you can also study the
various separate hexagrams that
make up the starting hexagram.
The number next to these
hexagrams indicates the page
where you can find their complete
interpretation. If the hexagram
you have thrown contains
changing lines, these direct you
to a 'follow-up' hexagram.

Like life itself, the *I Ching* is
a hermetic labyrinth of wonders
from which you can only escape
by closing the book.

The Follow-Up Hexagram
Once you have changed the strong
and weak lines into their
opposites, a new 'follow-up' hexagram is created which provides
information about a future phase
of life. The information on the
left-hand page is the most useful
for studying this hexagram, since
follow-up hexagrams contain
no changing lines.
The information on the right-
hand page can, of course,
be useful for clarifying your study
of the follow-up hexagram.

} These hexagrams are components
of the starting hexagram and offer
directions for successfully dealing
with your present situation.

The lines of the hexagram correspond to
various parts of the body. The instructions
you find there provide insight into your
current physical and spiritual state.

▬o▬ : Strong Changing Line
▬x▬ : Weak Changing Line

旅  **56**

two seals

A table

Two hands

On a table lie two official seals, which are presented to selected officials as a sign of their office.

SUN (Weighing Your Words)

The character Sun represents the selection of administrators who communicate their ruler's commands as literally as possible so that the ideas and ideals of the superior authority are translated into practice. Similarly, you are advised to keep your thoughts pure and to confirm your words in deeds. If you say no matter what just to get rid of others, or base your words on illusory concepts, you will lose the confidence of those around you.

In the hexagram, the upper trigram of the wind symbolizes your realm of thought, where you develop a vision that is translated into words and deeds by the lower trigram of the wind, or your breathing. If your mind is modeled on the fire/sun, you have the inner certainty that your words contain truth. However, if you sell your heart to the outward display of the marsh/moon, you speak a lot of hot air, and your thoughts never become anything more than castles in the air that fool yourself and others. Words determine the future. If your words reflect ideas and ideals that do not tally with the laws of nature or the norms and values of a civilized society, you would be better off saying nothing.

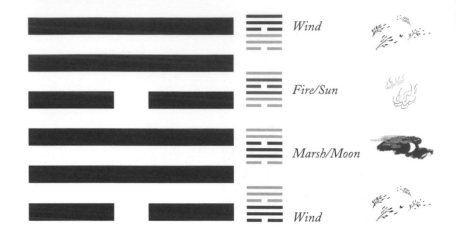

Wind	
Fire/Sun	
Marsh/Moon	
Wind	

Weighing Your Words
A sign of wisdom is that you do not speak before you know for certain that you can keep your word. By saying what you do and doing what you say, you not only build self-confidence but also win the confidence of others so that you can move through life with inner peace. The following directions may lead you to breathe in such a way that you generate trust. (57)

The Management of the Inner Being
Attune your realm of thought to the intense calm of the sun, which oversees everything and illuminates all sides of an issue. 37

Sincerity
If you are sincere, you will perceive that the secret of life cannot be captured in words. This does not give you the right to deliberately distort your idea of Truth. 61

Duality
Self-knowledge protects you from outward display based on insecurity so that your words are sincere. 38

Dissolving (Dissolution)
Use your inner surety to test the impressions other people make on you. If you breathe calmly and regularly, you will be able to sense what sort of person you are dealing with. 50

Vigorous Mind
Do not speak out any thoughts that make your breathing irregular. It is better to say that you do not know something than to go to ridiculous lengths to maintain a facade, for this will diminish your zest for life. 28

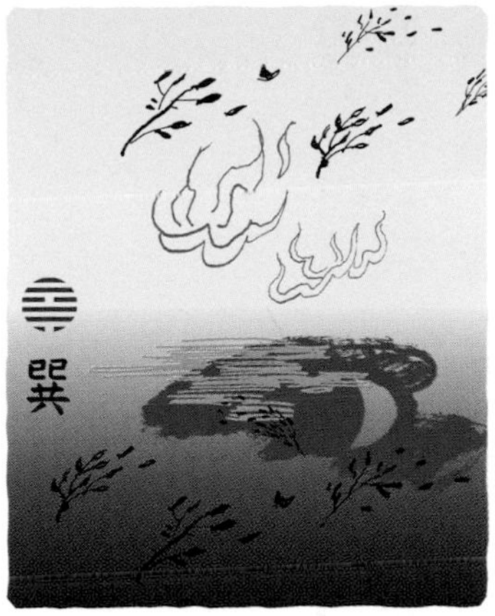

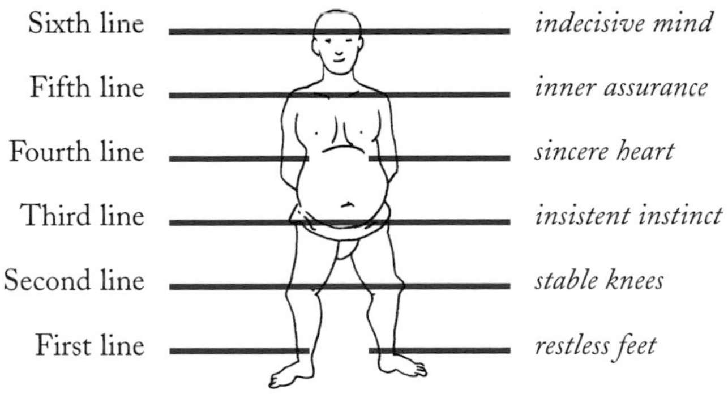

The Individual Lines

Sixth line
The beginning of the wind symbolizes an awakening conciousness which does not yet have any notion of the effect words may have. As soon as you wake, your mind starts racing and you are not able to stop yourself from talking. In your case, a ban on speaking would be a good idea.

Fifth line
The middle of the wind, or your consciousness, is based on your inner surety, which burns like a pure flame. Everything you say is carefully considered, and even though at first you may not be believed, trust will inevitably come your way because you always match your words with deeds. Do not change your approach in the slightest.

Fourth line
The full moon which inevitably wanes, and the end of the wind, or the words you speak out with all the sincerity and impartiality of the sun, are signs that you abhor illusions and that you speak from the heart so that you can touch the hearts of others.

Third line
The waxing moon outshines your slumbering, inner fire because the start of the wind, or your breathing, is powerless. Out of insecurity, you use all available means — in a rather underhanded way — to try to translate your words into actions. You are still hoping to realize your castle in the air.

Second line
The new moon and the middle of the wind, or your breathing in and breathing out, represent your mouth, which is not dumbfounded by the question of how you will put your vague ideas into action. You do not neglect to consult others in order to find out what you are taking on. This sincere attitude to life is well received by all.

First line
The end of the wind suggests that you are pausing for breath. You cannot match you words with deeds and stand anxiously shuffling your feet. In this situation, where you do not know what to say or do, the best attitude to adopt would be that of a soldier waiting calmly for his orders.

Introduction
The Sun hexagram is determined by *Vigorous Mind (28)*. Do not fix your thoughts, or the upper wind ☴, to the illusion of the marsh/moon ☱, or you will make promises you cannot keep. Concentrate on your inner surety ☲ so that you can match every word you speak (☴, lower wind) with a deed.

Strong and Weak Changing Lines
Extra attention should be paid to strong and weak lines in the hexagram you have thrown. A strong line signifies that you are addressing the situation with too much force, whereas a weak line calls for a bolder attitude.

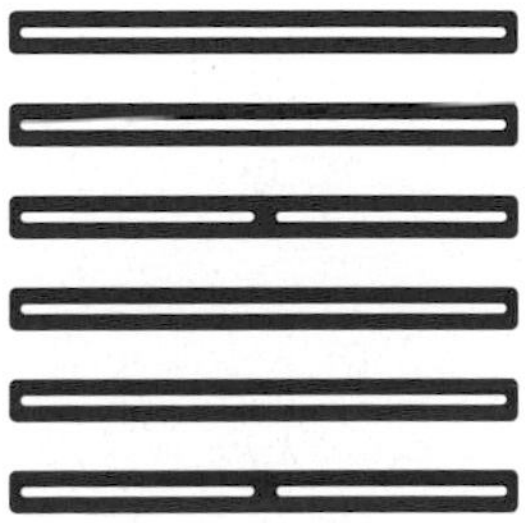

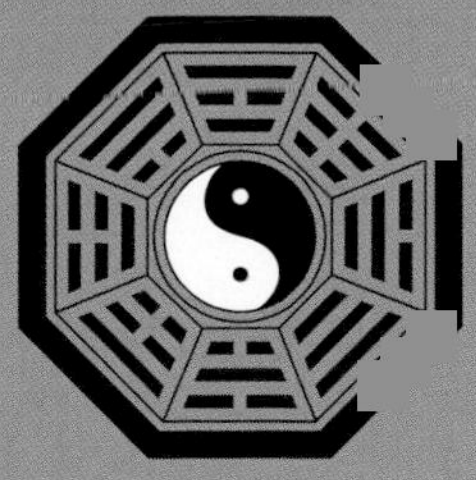

The Hermetic *I Ching*
The answer to your specific question is not found only in the starting hexagram. For a deeper insight, you can also study the various separate hexagrams that make up the starting hexagram. The number next to these hexagrams indicates the page where you can find their complete interpretation. If the hexagram you have thrown contains changing lines, these direct you to a 'follow-up' hexagram.

Like life itself, the *I Ching* is a hermetic labyrinth of wonders from which you can only escape by closing the book.

The Follow-Up Hexagram
Once you have changed the strong and weak lines into their opposites, a new 'follow-up' hexagram is created which provides information about a future phase of life. The information on the left-hand page is the most useful for studying this hexagram, since follow-up hexagrams contain no changing lines.
The information on the right-hand page can, of course, be useful for clarifying your study of the follow-up hexagram.

} These hexagrams are components of the starting hexagram and offer directions for successfully dealing with your present situation.

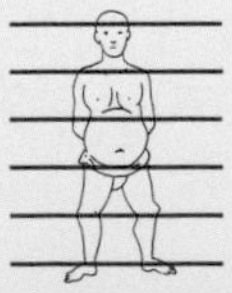

The lines of the hexagram correspond to various parts of the body. The instructions you find there provide insight into your current physical and spiritual state.

—o— : Strong Changing Line
—x— : Weak Changing Line

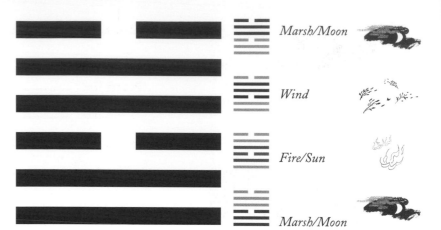

兌

兌

A person speaks friendly words which dissipate grief
and promote joy and well-being.

TUI (Encouragement)

The character Tui represents moments of spontaneous and artless giving and receiving. Human beings are social animals who have learned from the day they were born to mirror their surroundings. This grants them the gift of being able to hearten others.

In the hexagram, this quality is symbolized by the repetition of trigrams representing the marsh/moon. This indicates that you are, from head to toe, a being that absorbs and radiates energy. Your radiation reflects your inner fire which is fanned by your breathing. For this reason, the wind and the fire/sun form the core of the hexagram. Your cultural and social prejudices are generally based on antagonism and the idea that everything has its price. If you can push these thoughts into the background, a feeling of intense, human warmth will come to the fore. By attuning your breathing to your survival instinct, which warns you in times of danger or discomfort, you can let your heart speak freely. You will know intuitively when the time for this is over.

Marsh/Moon

Wind

Fire/Sun

Marsh/Moon

Encouragement
We all remember an occasion when a friendly word or gesture restored our zest for life, and we know how important that was to us. Therefore, do not repress the gift of being able to give such joy by chasing material possessions or by thinking you are too sophisticated and intellectual for such behavior. The following directions serve as a reminder of how you can allow this source of encouragement to well up spontaneously.

(58)

Vigorous Mind
Do not immerse yourself in the concepts of others if you notice that they make your breathing agitated.

28

Inner Change (Distillation)
Realize that you do not need to, and indeed cannot, improve on creation. Only through inner change can you achieve the insight that everything is as it should be.

49

The Management of the Inner Being
Attune your breathing to the deep peace radiated by the sun so that fear of rejection does not make your heart shrink like the waning moon.

37

Sincerity
If you are sincere, you know that the secret of life cannot be captured in words, and you speak encouraging words to others from the depth of your heart.

61

Duality
Self-knowledge protects you from outward display born of insecurity and so ensures that your words are sincere.

38

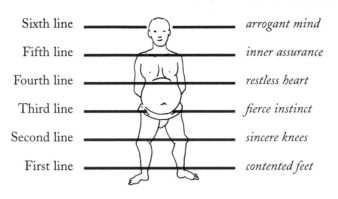

Sixth line		*arrogant mind*
Fifth line		*inner assurance*
Fourth line		*restless heart*
Third line		*fierce instinct*
Second line		*sincere knees*
First line		*contented feet*

The Individual Lines

Sixth line
The full moon, which is about to wane, indicates that you are intent on giving pleasure to others and do not take into account that you cannot sustain another's happiness for long. Speak words that express a zest for life, and do not hang on to the idea that other people's happiness is dependent on you.

Fifth line
The beginning of the wind, or your breathing, which becomes irregular under the influence of the waxing moon, suggests that you are trying to encourage others even though you see they are imprisoned by illusions. Do not enter into debate about these concepts; just speak the sort of friendly words that make life more pleasant.

Fourth line
The new moon and the inner fire blazing in the middle of the wind, or your breathing in and breathing out, symbolize an endless stream of encouraging words with a didactic undertone. Despite your agitation, you stimulate others because you show them genuine warmth.

Third line
The end of the wind, or your breathing out, is not fueling your inner fire, so the full moon controls your instinct. You are only interested in the fleeting satisfaction of your own needs. This transient incentive will bring neither yourself nor others comfort or encouragement.

Second line
The waxing moon and the beginning of your inner fire determine your attitude towards life. You radiate sincerity and zest for life, so even your presence is enough to give others a temporary boost.

First line
The new moon indicates that you are reflecting the light that you receive from others. By calling to mind a moment when your zest for life was restored by encouraging words, you can radiate an energy that encourages others.

Introduction
The Tui hexagram is determined by *Vigorous Mind (28)*. If you model your breathing ☴ on the peace radiated by the fire/sun ☲, you will have a benign attitude to life ☱ (below) which is not colored by self-interest. Therefore, you can spontaneously offer others moments of encouragement ☱ (above).

Strong and Weak Changing Lines
Extra attention should be paid to strong and weak lines in the hexagram you have thrown. A strong line signifies that you are addressing the situation with too much force, whereas a weak line calls for a bolder attitude.

The Hermetic *I Ching*
The answer to your specific question is not found only in the starting hexagram. For a deeper insight, you can also study the various separate hexagrams that make up the starting hexagram. The number next to these hexagrams indicates the page where you can find their complete interpretation. If the hexagram you have thrown contains changing lines, these direct you to a 'follow-up' hexagram.

Like life itself, the *I Ching* is a hermetic labyrinth of wonders from which you can only escape by closing the book.

The Follow-Up Hexagram
Once you have changed the strong and weak lines into their opposites, a new 'follow-up' hexagram is created which provides information about a future phase of life. The information on the left-hand page is the most useful for studying this hexagram, since follow-up hexagrams contain no changing lines.
The information on the right-hand page can, of course, be useful for clarifying your study of the follow-up hexagram.

} These hexagrams are components of the starting hexagram and offer directions for successfully dealing with your present situation.

 The lines of the hexagram correspond to various parts of the body. The instructions you find there provide insight into your current physical and spiritual state.

━━o━━ : Strong Changing Line
━━x━━ : Weak Changing Line

兑 58

*Examine something meticulously by passing it
from one of your hands to the other* — A person

Running water (the stream of life) —

A person outside an empty space he has created —
Two hands —

HWÂN (Redemption)

The character Hwân means to remove, to disperse, to open, and to develop. The construction of the character suggests that you are opening yourself by disposing of the ego formed during your life and returning to the innocence you had at birth when your view of life was untarnished.

    In the hexagram, the wind on the mountain and the thunder rising up from the river symbolize that you have freed yourself from the stream of life through deep meditation and that you have your past in perspective. At birth, you are like a blank page that has been thrown into the river of life. If you turn your thoughts back to that moment and then allow yourself to drift towards the here and now, you will come across every situation that has made an impression on you. You can digest and let go of these moments if you realize that you would never have arrived in the present without them. In this way, you heal yourself and ultimately arrive at your original virgin state. Now that your breathing is no longer disturbed by your bruised ego, your heart beats steadily and only quickens with physical exertion. You sense the miracle of your physical being and you face your surroundings without the slightest prejudice, as if you were born anew.

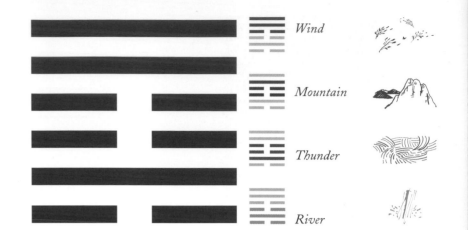

Wind

Mountain

Thunder

River

Redemption
Once you have liberated your mind from prejudices, your mastery over yourself will reflect the intense peace of heaven, which keeps the earth in her orbit and so maintains a natural balance. As soon as thought, word, and action are inextricably linked, you are consciously one with your innate being. The following directions show how you can free yourself of your ego. (59)

The Blessed Marriage
The earth is like a wise old woman with an eternally youthful appearance. If you want to enjoy life as she does, do not hang on to situations that conflict with her nature. 53

Increase
Genuine growth is based on the awareness that your spiritual growth must not be hindered by the quest for material possessions. 42

Nourishment
The waste products of your physical nourishment are excreted. The impressions left by your experiences linger on in your body. Undertake a thorough investigation of yourself. 27

Youthful Innocence
Do not think that letting go of your ego will restore your childhood, when you were like water plunging down a mountain without attachment to anything. 4

Cutting the Knot
Proceed calmly, like a leaf on the stream of life. When curiosity lures you to the bank, do not cling on to it. Look at the situation, offer your opinion of it when asked, and move on. 40

Sixth line ——————— *clear mind*

Fifth line ——————— *inner assurance*

Fourth line ——————— *vital heart*

Third line ——————— *determined instinct*

Second line ——————— *stable knees*

First line ——————— *reserved feet*

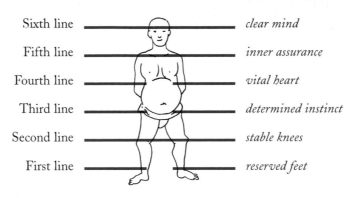

The Individual Lines

Sixth line
The beginning of the wind, or your consciousness waking from deep meditation, indicate that you are free from thoughts of the past. The bloody spiritual wounds you have suffered in the past have healed. Their scars will alert your instinct when you make the wrong decisions.

Fifth line
The position of the middle of the wind, or your breathing in and breathing out, on the top of the mountain suggests that you are weighing your past during deep meditation. Fear is driven out of you in the form of sweat; as it drips from your body, room is created for inner surety.

Fourth line
Below the top of the mountain the thunder loses its force, and the end of the wind suggests calm breathing which is not influenced by your past. Your heart only beats more quickly with physical effort and when your instinct alerts you to danger. This indicates that you are able to assess the true worth of others, with complete impartiality.

Third line
In the core of the thunder which rumbles at the foot of the mountain where the river begins, you are weighing up how you can move along on the stream of life without prejudice or suspicion. Be guided by your survival instinct, which bears the scars of past experiences and warns you of danger.

Second line
The thunder awakens in the core of life's stream. The process of digesting your past during deep meditation allows you to adopt a new attitude when you once again take part fully in life. As a result, you do not end up in the same situations as before when you learned the tricks of the trade through bitter experience.

First line
The running water threatens to throw you off your feet. This indicates that in order to hold your own in life, your feet must be controlled by a strong will. Step into the stream of life only when your breathing is calm, and you are not — as your were in childhood — like water rushing headlong down a mountain.

Introduction
The Hwân hexagram is determined by *Nourishment (27)*. By calling to mind the path you have traveled (second line) ⚎ and chewing over this experience until you have the inner surety (fifth line) that your breathing ⚏ is no longer being hindered by bitter thoughts (sixth line), you enable your heart (fourth line) to beat calmly and focus on your survival instinct (third line). As a result, you are completely revived and have both feet (first line) firmly on the ground.

Strong and Weak Changing Lines
Extra attention should be paid to strong and weak lines in the hexagram you have thrown. A strong line signifies that you are addressing the situation with too much force, whereas a weak line calls for a bolder attitude.

The Hermetic *I Ching*
The answer to your specific question is not found only in the starting hexagram. For a deeper insight, you can also study the various separate hexagrams that make up the starting hexagram. The number next to these hexagrams indicates the page where you can find their complete interpretation. If the hexagram you have thrown contains changing lines, these direct you to a 'follow-up' hexagram.

Like life itself, the *I Ching* is a hermetic labyrinth of wonders from which you can only escape by closing the book.

The Follow-Up Hexagram
Once you have changed the strong and weak lines into their opposites, a new 'follow-up' hexagram is created which provides information about a future phase of life. The information on the left-hand page is the most useful for studying this hexagram, since follow-up hexagrams contain no changing lines. The information on the right-hand page can, of course, be useful for clarifying your study of the follow-up hexagram.

} These hexagrams are components of the starting hexagram and offer directions for successfully dealing with your present situation.

 The lines of the hexagram correspond to various parts of the body. The instructions you find there provide insight into your current physical and spiritual state.

▬o▬ : Strong Changing Line
▬x▬ : Weak Changing Line

渙  **59**

Bamboo — 竹

The daily portion of soup —

The right half of an official seal or the sceptre of a high-ranking official.
Therefore: authority, the right standard or measure

An official seal

KIEH (Regular and Orderly)

The character Kieh portrays part of a bamboo shoot (between two knots) and means a time limit, a law, a prerequisite, or moderation. From the construction of the character, one can deduce that a regular way of life based on natural order diminishes the chance of exhaustion and stress.

In the hexagram, the rain falls with heavenly regularity and fills the lake on the top of the mountain, which overflows when it becomes too full. This symbolizes a stable person who does not take in more spiritual and physical nourishment than he or she can contain and digest in a given period. If you have this attitude, you are also aware of the marsh/moon and know, by observing how full it is, when it is time to exert yourself and when you can slacken the reins. As a result, you are also able to stimulate others — with the right regularity and dosage of energy — to become active or to relax.

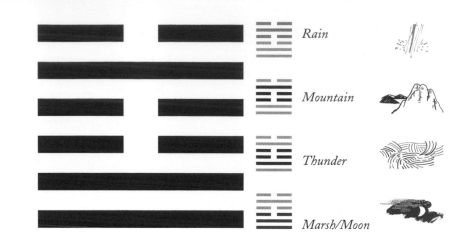

Rain

Mountain

Thunder

Marsh/Moon

Regular and Orderly
If you live according to rules that are too rigid, zest for life disappears; lack of any regularity leads to indifference. The moon waxes and wanes again. If you have a belly full of something, it is time to calmly digest your efforts and experiences. The following directions show how you can achieve this regularity.

(60)

Initial Difficulty
Give at the right time, and withdraw again in time. You are on the wrong track if you wait until you are exhausted before retiring because then you will feel daunted by the prospect of throwing yourself back into life again.

39

Confusion
Growth and confusion go hand in hand. If you alternate growth phases with periods of contemplation, you are on the right track.

3

Nourishment
Too much or too little physical or spiritual nourishment is bad for you.

27

Relaxation
You have struggled to attain physical and spiritual nourishment. Now take the time to enjoy what you have so that material things do not become a millstone around your neck.

41

Fertility
A period of growth lasts as long as you feel you are becoming 'fuller' and is over once you feel your energy is waning.

54

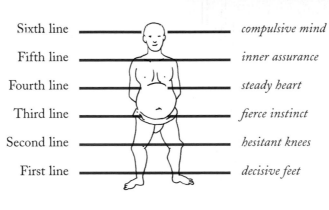

Sixth line ———————— compulsive mind

Fifth line ———————— inner assurance

Fourth line ———————— steady heart

Third line ———————— fierce instinct

Second line ———————— hesitant knees

First line ———————— decisive feet

The Individual Lines

Sixth line
No one can predict exactly when the rain will fall. Even when you feel rain is in the air, you only feel relief when the shower comes. In the same way, you can be puzzling over a problem when a satisfying solution suddenly springs to mind. Experience teaches you when it is time to brood and when it is time to rest.

Fifth line
The rainwater that forms a lake on the top of the mountain is a sign that you are relaxed as long as you have inner surety and an overview. You have found the right attitude to life, and you can use your wisdom and love to help others because you are regular and orderly.

Fourth line
The rainwater flowing away below the top of the mountain and the end of the thunder or the waning moon indicate that you are overlooking the situation with a calmly beating heart. You are on the verge of gathering new experiences by sharing your acquired knowledge with others.

Third line
The full moon at the foot of the mountain, which is shaking in the middle of the thunder, indicates that you know nothing about order. Ignoring all reason, you blindly follow your instinct which is inflamed by illusions. Do not try to shift the blame onto your circumstances. Think about your own behavior and look at home for the cause.

Second line
The beginning of the thunder and the waxing moon symbolize a period when you can withdraw to enjoy what you have. Do not allow yourself to be lured into external affairs. The perfect order maintained by nature will call you to action soon enough — all too soon, you will feel.

First line
The new moon represents rest and contemplation. Naturally, your feet are made to carry you along — but if they are in charge, there is no question of order and regularity.

Introduction
The Kieh hexagram is determined by *Nourishment (27)*. Your inner surety (fifth line), or your upper jaw, indicates when your mind (sixth line), or the lake ☱ on the top of the mountain ☶, is overflowing so that you can relax your lower jaw (second line). Your instinct (third line) and your heart (fourth line), which are influenced by the thunder ☳ and the moon ☵, warn you in the event of physical exhaustion.

Strong and Weak Changing Lines
Extra attention should be paid to strong and weak lines in the hexagram you have thrown. A strong line signifies that you are addressing the situation with too much force, whereas a weak line calls for a bolder attitude.

The Hermetic *I Ching*
The answer to your specific question is not found only in the starting hexagram. For a deeper insight, you can also study the various separate hexagrams that make up the starting hexagram. The number next to these hexagrams indicates the page where you can find their complete interpretation. If the hexagram you have thrown contains changing lines, these direct you to a 'follow-up' hexagram.

Like life itself, the *I Ching* is a hermetic labyrinth of wonders from which you can only escape by closing the book.

The Follow-Up Hexagram
Once you have changed the strong and weak lines into their opposites, a new 'follow-up' hexagram is created which provides information about a future phase of life. The information on the left-hand page is the most useful for studying this hexagram, since follow-up hexagrams contain no changing lines.
The information on the right-hand page can, of course, be useful for clarifying your study of the follow-up hexagram.

} These hexagrams are components of the starting hexagram and offer directions for successfully dealing with your present situation.

 The lines of the hexagram correspond to various parts of the body. The instructions you find there provide insight into your current physical and spiritual state.

▬▬◦▬▬ : Strong Changing Line
▬▬×▬▬ : Weak Changing Line

節  **60**

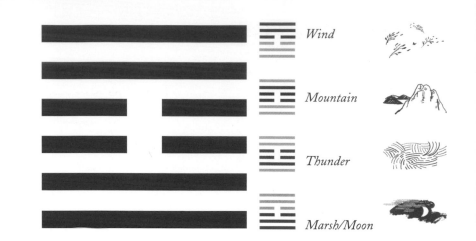

An arrow penetrates the bull's-eye of a target.

A female bird protects her brood with her claws.

中孚

KUNG FÛ (Sincerity)

The characters Kung and Fû indicate a natural sincerity. The symbolism implies a kind of instinctive behavior aimed at preserving spiritual freedom — at the risk of your life, if necessary.

In the hexagram, the wind, or your breath, which arises in the heavens and blows from the top of the mountain, suggests that you are surveying your surroundings objectively and with inner surety. Your heart beats with the peace that the universe radiates, slowing down or speeding up only when alerted by your survival instinct. Your bodily instincts are allied with the changes of the moon which regulates the ebb and flood of the earth's waters, so your attitude to life is attuned to a natural rhythm independent of personal preference. With these achievements, you see through any artificial or forced behavior and prepare a timely response. Because you have got your heart in the right place, people who blunder about like pigs in the earthly mire or those who have submerged themselves like fish in material pleasures will not bother you with their ideas and will treat you with respect.

Wind

Mountain

Thunder

Marsh/Moon

Sincerity
As long as the secret of life evades description, every person has the right to develop according to his or her natural tendencies and insights, as long as they do not deny others that same right by behaving like a bully. The information that follows may clarify for you how you can preserve this inner sincerity. (61)

The Blessed Marriage
A marriage with earthly existence is only truly blessed if you realize — with regards to yourself and others — when it is time to plough, sow, reap, and rest. 53

Increase
True growth is based on the realization that your own, or others', drive for material possessions must not stand in the way of your spiritual development. 42

Nourishment
Do not allow yourself to be force-fed with ideas that you find unappetizing, and make sure that others are not compelled against their will to eat from your manger. 27

Relaxation
Once you have an overview, you can genuinely enjoy the modest insights your environment offers, which have enabled you to achieve this level of development. 41

Fertility
Whenever fruitful diversity is threatened by the illusion of uniformity, it is time for you to resist. 54

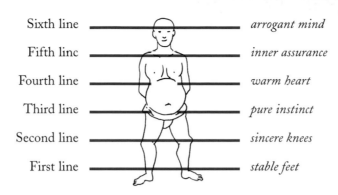

Sixth line — *arrogant mind*

Fifth line — *inner assurance*

Fourth line — *warm heart*

Third line — *pure instinct*

Second line — *sincere knees*

First line — *stable feet*

The Individual Lines

Sixth line
The beginning of the wind, or your breathing, indicates an awakening consciousness. Do not feel superior to others because of your overview of life, for you are no more able to formulate the secret of life than they are. Do not be a rooster, which cries victory at dawn and creates the impression that it is he who wakes the heavens.

Fifth line
The middle of the wind, or your breathing in and breathing out, on the top of the mountain signifies that you possess an overview and inner surety. You speak sincerely and you are always an inspiration to others because you know when it is time to plough, to sow, to harvest, and to rest.

Fourth line
The end of both the wind and the thunder below the top of the mountain indicate that you maintain your overview and that you instinctively free yourself from a situation in which you are burdened — like a horse drawing a cart — with someone else's illusions. You cut loose from this 'moon-cart' before it is overfilled with illusions, and so can breathe freely once again.

Third line
At the foot of the mountain, which is shaking in the middle of the thunder, the full moon hangs over your head like a giant illusion. Your survival instinct warns you of the danger of embracing ideas that fill you with lyricism one minute and reduce you to tears the next.

Second line
The beginning of the thunder and the waxing moon stand for a sincere attitude to life. You offer others the opportunity to mirror you, handing out what intuitive knowledge you possess without being pushy or claiming that this is Truth.

First line
The new moon shows that you are every bit as sincere as your feet, which are always obedient. Take care not to allow concepts you find unattractive to be forced upon you, otherwise you will make yourself a slave to others.

Introduction
The Kung Fù hexagram is determined by *Nourishment (27)*. Your inner surety (fifth line) radiates from your attitude to life (second line) and is based on natural, unforced breathing ☱ which makes your heart (fourth line) beat calmly. Your instinct (third line) will warn your heart if other people's concepts ☳ represent a danger for your spiritual development.

Strong and Weak Changing Lines
Extra attention should be paid to strong and weak lines in the hexagram you have thrown. A strong line signifies that you are addressing the situation with too much force, whereas a weak line calls for a bolder attitude.

The Hermetic *I Ching*
The answer to your specific question is not found only in the starting hexagram. For a deeper insight, you can also study the various separate hexagrams that make up the starting hexagram. The number next to these hexagrams indicates the page where you can find their complete interpretation. If the hexagram you have thrown contains changing lines, these direct you to a 'follow-up' hexagram.

Like life itself, the *I Ching* is a hermetic labyrinth of wonders from which you can only escape by closing the book.

The Follow-Up Hexagram
Once you have changed the strong and weak lines into their opposites, a new 'follow-up' hexagram is created which provides information about a future phase of life. The information on the left-hand page is the most useful for studying this hexagram, since follow-up hexagrams contain no changing lines.
The information on the right-hand page can, of course, be useful for clarifying your study of the follow-up hexagram.

} These hexagrams are components of the starting hexagram and offer directions for successfully dealing with your present situation.

The lines of the hexagram correspond to various parts of the body. The instructions you find there provide insight into your current physical and spiritual state.

▬o▬ : Strong Changing Line
▬x▬ : Weak Changing Line

中孚

61

To divide something that is already small. A flash or a moment

Walking along, step by step

A skeleton. The character also indicates a deformed mouth caused by a cleft palate.

小過

HSIÂO KWO (Repression)

The characters Hsiâo and Kwo represent a sin that will be forgiven or a white lie. In a situation where your freedom is restricted and you cannot stand up for what you believe because of the threat of harsh punishment, it is wise to use your mouth to twist the truth — which you feel in your very bones — until the tide turns.

In the hexagram, the stable mountain is concealed by the radiance of the marsh/moon which is constantly subject to change. This indicates that you are hiding your indomitable attitude to life behind the facade of seeming resignation. Since an intolerant regime is based on the same sort of deceptive certainties, you can move in tune with your environment like a reed waving in the breeze. The wind, or your breathing, which begins at the fourth line, is fully concentrated on ensuring that your heart beats calmly so that your fierce survival instinct and rebellious thoughts remain hidden from the outside world. You can, with inner surety, concentrate on adopting an attitude to life attuned to blowing with the prevailing wind because you know from experience that every wind sooner or later dies down.

 Thunder

 Marsh/Moon

 Wind

 Mountain

 Repression
If your environment is tyrannized by an intolerant regime, remain inconspicuous through apparent subservience, be cautious in word and deed, show appropriate sympathy when the regime is in mourning, and strike as soon as the opportunity arises. By living according to the following directions, you can rise above repression. (62)

 Fertility
Change your outward appearance like the moon, and follow the movements of the regime as if you subscribe to them. 54

 Continuity, Balanced Movement
Take care not to allow your rebellious thoughts to disturb your heartbeat, and attune your breathing to your survival instinct so that you are not betrayed by impulsive reactions. 32

 Vigorous Mind
When you need to twist the truth, which you feel to the marrow of your bones, do so, and forgive yourself this harmless insincerity. 28

 The Game of Love
Earthly life is characterized by highs and lows. As long as you can maintain your inner peace and keep your eyes open, you will find that even repression is a learning experience that passes. 31

 The Blessed Marriage
This marriage is only truly blessed if you — in relation to yourself and others — know when it is time to plough, to sow, to harvest, and to rest. 53

 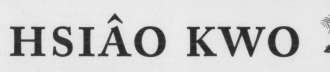

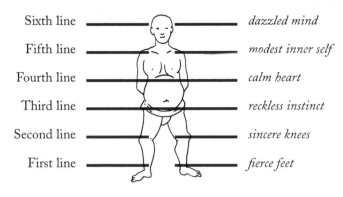

Sixth line ——————— *dazzled mind*

Fifth line ——————— *modest inner self*

Fourth line ——————— *calm heart*

Third line ——————— *reckless instinct*

Second line ——————— *sincere knees*

First line ——————— *fierce feet*

The Individual Lines

Sixth line
The approaching thunder indicates that you cannot control yourself and you foolishly allow your mouth to express your feelings of uneasiness. That little voice which keeps flying away like a quacking duck has to be kept under control — otherwise you will soon be sentenced to eternal silence.

Fifth line
At the core of the thunder the full moon hangs above the earth like an evil eye, and there is no question of the tyranny weakening. For the time being, move along with it calmly. If you do sense that you are about to say something when the time is not yet ripe, swallow your words before they can escape.

Fourth line
The waxing moon and the beginning of both the thunder and the wind indicate a calmly beating heart, which is not influenced by disturbing thoughts. You are hiding quietly behind your smokescreen and moving along with the crowd until the air clears.

Third line
The new moon hangs in the middle of the wind at the top of the mountain. This suggests that you are behaving arrogantly.
You cannot keep your mouth shut, and you hide behind a smokescreen that is as transparent as glass. This is asking for trouble.

Second line
The end of the wind, or the end of breathing out, below the top of the mountain indicates that you would be wise to adopt an attitude that makes you appear weak and needy. Hiding behind this facade is an unbroken self with unshakeable inner assurance.

First line
At the foot of the mountain, you have nowhere to hide.
Similarly, you cannot climb the mountain without being noticed.
Behave like your feet, which are as innocent as a newborn babe and cannot speak even when spoken to.

Introduction
The Hsiâo Kwo hexagram is determined by *Vigorous Mind (28)*.
If you pretend to know nothing (sixth line) and hide your inner surety (fifth line) behind the illusion of the full moon ☶, others will take you for a simpleton. If you use calm breathing to translate this superficiality into your physical attitude, your disguise is complete.

Strong and Weak Changing Lines
Extra attention should be paid to strong and weak lines in the hexagram you have thrown. A strong line signifies that you are addressing the situation with too much force, whereas a weak line calls for a bolder attitude.

The Hermetic *I Ching*
The answer to your specific question is not found only in the starting hexagram. For a deeper insight, you can also study the various separate hexagrams that make up the starting hexagram. The number next to these hexagrams indicates the page where you can find their complete interpretation. If the hexagram you have thrown contains changing lines, these direct you to a 'follow-up' hexagram.

Like life itself, the *I Ching* is a hermetic labyrinth of wonders from which you can only escape by closing the book.

The Follow-Up Hexagram
Once you have changed the strong and weak lines into their opposites, a new 'follow-up' hexagram is created which provides information about a future phase of life. The information on the left-hand page is the most useful for studying this hexagram, since follow-up hexagrams contain no changing lines.
The information on the right-hand page can, of course, be useful for clarifying your study of the follow-up hexagram.

} These hexagrams are components of the starting hexagram and offer directions for successfully dealing with your present situation.

The lines of the hexagram correspond to various parts of the body. The instructions you find there provide insight into your current physical and spiritual state.

▬⊖▬ : Strong Changing Line
▬✕▬ : Weak Changing Line

62

The daily bowl of Chinese soup —
Breathing in and gulping —
Running water —
A corn field. Perfect harmony, a whole, order —

既濟

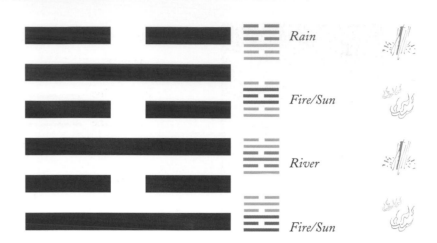

Rain

Fire/Sun

River

Fire/Sun

KÎ CHI (Successful Movement)

The character Kî stands for breathing and daily nourishment, and the character Chi represents the successful crossing of a stream. From this symbolism and the construction of the characters, one can deduce that your life proceeds harmoniously if you breathe calmly and process your daily experiences in a balanced way, thereby generating inner surety. Then your spirit is as perfectly ordered as the corn field, which is a sign of nutrition.

In the hexagram, the upper fire/sun which is partly concealed by the raincloud indicates that your inner surety is subdued by preoccupying thoughts. These thoughts are a source of fertile knowledge leading to new insights. The lower fire/sun and the river represent your physical appearance, which will last longest if you do not anticipate events or run after things. Then your heart beats calmly and you can maintain an attitude towards life based on inner peace. What is lurking at the end of your journey through life is seldom pleasant. The sun rises again even when you are dead. The question of whether the inner light you have gathered so carefully will continue to shine hangs in your mind like a dark cloud that cannot easily be dissipated.

Successful Movement
The sun eventually breaks through any bank of clouds. In the same way, you can see through every earthly appearance if you allow your light to illuminate it from all sides. On your journey through life, you get whatever chance serves up to you. If you investigate each and every one of these puzzles, you are ultimately left with just one question — which will only be answered once you have dissolved. The following directions solve a number of problems. (63)

Water, the Giver of Life
The ideal way to move through life is like a calmly flowing river which conquers all the obstacles earthly matter throws up in its path and — without attachment to anything — flows to the sea. 29

Restricted Movement
Do not be like a young fox, which does not look before it leaps. Before you begin something new, first get to the bottom of the situation in which you find yourself. You will see that everything you do not solve now will be served up to you again, in one form or another. 64

Fire, the Transforming Element
Once you are aware of your inner fire as clear insight, you understand the value of your body as fuel, and you do not let yourself be tempted to behave recklessly. 30

Successful Movement
Move like an old fox, which first sniffs out all sides of a situation and only starts to act once he begins to grasp what it is all about. (63)

 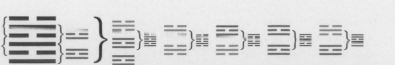

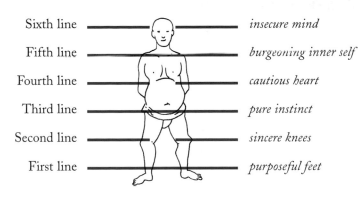

Sixth line — *insecure mind*

Fifth line — *burgeoning inner self*

Fourth line — *cautious heart*

Third line — *pure instinct*

Second line — *sincere knees*

First line — *purposeful feet*

The Individual Lines

Sixth line
The mystery of death hangs over your head like a dark cloud. Do not waste your life on a question you cannot answer. Enjoy the here and now. If you see every day as a new adventure with an unknown outcome, you will be able to take the last step with the same attitude.

Fifth line
The sun is hidden behind the core of the raincloud, but it keeps on shining. Therefore, you should not think that there is no light just because you cannot see it for the moment. Do not throw away your future. If you slay your ox in a fit of depression, you will never be able to plough again. As long as you trust in your inner surety, hope glimmers.

Fourth line
The core of your inner fire dissipates the last wisps of the cloud layer so that you get to the bottom of your current situation and are ready to turn your gaze to something new. You are so cautious that you leave nothing to chance and take every possible precaution before you continue life's journey.

Third line
The rising sun and the flames of the lower fire try to get control of the river of life. This attempt is as futile as trying in advance to drive away all the somber thoughts that lie in wait for you. Your survival instinct warns you when the time is right. Do not run ahead of events.

Second line
The core of the fire, which tries to evaporate the running water, indicates that you lose your harmonious attitude to life by fiercely attacking a problem you cannot really grasp. Take distance, and meticulously study the situation from all angles so that you can discover the way in.

First line
The beginning of the fire represents a fiery start to your journey through life. You are like a young fox that has wet its tail and does not look before it leaps. Take your time to let the tail dry, and work through your experiences so that you learn from them. Then you can behave like a smart, old fox.

Introduction
The Khî Chi hexagram is determined by the fire/sun ☲. You step, full of fire, into the stream of life. Adopt an attitude to life (second line) that is consistent with your inner surety (fifth line). Do not allow yourself to be led into actions your instinct (third line) warns you are dangerous, and control your thoughts (sixth line) in such a way that your heart (fourth line) beats calmly.

Strong and Weak Changing Lines
Extra attention should be paid to strong and weak lines in the hexagram you have thrown. A strong line signifies that you are addressing the situation with too much force, whereas a weak line calls for a bolder attitude.

The Hermetic *I Ching*
The answer to your specific question is not found only in the starting hexagram. For a deeper insight, you can also study the various separate hexagrams that make up the starting hexagram. The number next to these hexagrams indicates the page where you can find their complete interpretation. If the hexagram you have thrown contains changing lines, these direct you to a 'follow-up' hexagram.

Like life itself, the *I Ching* is a hermetic labyrinth of wonders from which you can only escape by closing the book.

The Follow-Up Hexagram
Once you have changed the strong and weak lines into their opposites, a new 'follow-up' hexagram is created which provides information about a future phase of life. The information on the left-hand page is the most useful for studying this hexagram, since follow-up hexagrams contain no changing lines. The information on the right-hand page can, of course, be useful for clarifying your study of the follow-up hexagram.

These hexagrams are components of the starting hexagram and offer directions for successfully dealing with your present situation.

The lines of the hexagram correspond to various parts of the body. The instructions you find there provide insight into your current physical and spiritual state.

☰—○ : Strong Changing Line
☰—× : Weak Changing Line

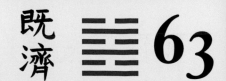

63

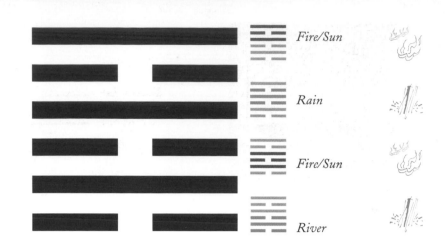

Fire/Sun

Rain

Fire/Sun

River

A tall tree. Also a cycle or a denial ——

Running water ——

A corn field. Perfect harmony, a whole, order ——

WEI CHI (Restricted Movement)

The play of the characters Wei and Chi indicates that you overlook your surroundings like a tall tree and collect impressions without testing them in practice. Nevertheless, you are under the impression that you possess inner surety that is every bit as nutritious as the corn field. You would be wise to descend from your ivory tower and test the value of your ideas in the stream of life before you raise them to the status of clear insights.

    In the hexagram, the upper fire/sun indicates that you have a perspective on a learning situation that hangs below you like a thick layer of clouds. You observe the developments from a distance, so you cannot know from experience what it feels like to be caught in the shower. Once you translate this supposed inner surety into your attitude to life, you will see that you can come quite a long way, but through your lack of experience you will regularly be tripped up by the unexpected twists and turns that are typical in life.

Restricted Movement

Do not behave like the sun, which passively observes the earthly life unfolding beneath it. If you do, you may well be theoretically well-informed, but in practice you move like a young fox that has wet its tail and lost its ability to maneuver, which makes it an easy prey for its enemies. The following directions can turn you into a smart, old fox.

(64)

Fire, the Transforming Element

Once you are aware that your inner fire only leads to clear insight if you test it in practice, you are also aware of the value of your body as fuel.

30

Successful Movement

Move like an old fox, which first sniffs out all sides of a problem and does not run away at the first glimmer of understanding. It follows its instinct to get to the bottom of the situation.

63

Water, the Giver of Life

The ideal way to move through life is like a calmly flowing river which conquers all the obstacles earthly matter throws up in its path and — without attachment to anything — flows to the sea.

29

Restricted Movement

Do not be like a young fox, which does not look before it leaps. Before you begin something new, first get to the bottom of the situation in which you find yourself. You will see that everything you do not solve now will be served up to you again, in one form or another.

64

WEI CHI

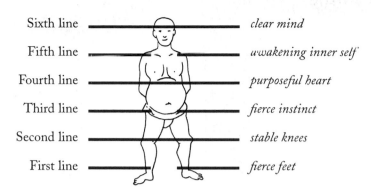

未
濟

The Individual Lines

Sixth line ———————— *clear mind*

Fifth line ———————— *awakening inner self*

Fourth line ———————— *purposeful heart*

Third line ———————— *fierce instinct*

Second line ———————— *stable knees*

First line ———————— *fierce feet*

Sixth line
You imagine you radiate the wisdom of the sun, and you are so delighted by your so-called insights that you are drunk on them. If you want to stay in the running, carefully test the viability of your ideas — even though you may find out you are like a young fox that has wet its tail.

Fifth line
The core of the sun is veiled in the last wisps of the layer of clouds. The sincere person tests his findings in practice in order to find out what they are really worth before elevating this theoretical knowledge to the level of inner surety and offering it to others.

Fourth line
The first rays of the sun and the flames of the lower fire break through the core of the cloud bank. You are burning to stay alive, and therefore fired with determination to test the practical value of your supposedly clear insights so that the very depths of your heart can be freed from all delusion.

Third line
The core of the fire tries to exert influence over the running water, symbolizing that you are attempting to get to the bottom of a situation without immersing yourself in it physically. Do not be afraid of taking this step. Widen your perspective and rely on your survival instinct, which warns you in times of danger.

Second line
The middle of life's stream and the beginning of the fire indicate that you are still too inexperienced to throw yourself directly into a problem. Move like an old fox, which first sniffs out all sides of an unfamiliar situation and only tries to get to the bottom of it once he has begun to grasp it.

First line
The flowing water has no idea where it is headed. Do not be like a young fox, which does not look before it leaps. First study the situation carefully and stay where you are. Like a tree, you will gain more of an overview as you grow.

Introduction
The Wei Chi hexagram is determined by the fire/sun ☲. Through passive observation (first line), you get some idea of how you should behave in life. Only elevate these thoughts (sixth line) to the level of inner sureties (fifth line) once you have translated them into your attitude towards life (second line). Then you can use your heart (fourth line) and your survival instinct (third line) to decide whether these impressions are also viable in practice.

Strong and Weak Changing Lines
Extra attention should be paid to strong and weak lines in the hexagram you have thrown. A strong line signifies that you are addressing the situation with too much force, whereas a weak line calls for a bolder attitude.

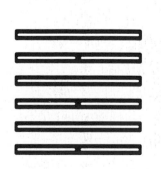

The Hermetic *I Ching*

The answer to your specific question is not found only in the starting hexagram. For a deeper insight, you can also study the various separate hexagrams that make up the starting hexagram. The number next to these hexagrams indicates the page where you can find their complete interpretation. If the hexagram you have thrown contains changing lines, these direct you to a 'follow-up' hexagram.

Like life itself, the *I Ching* is a hermetic labyrinth of wonders from which you can only escape by closing the book.

The Follow-Up Hexagram
Once you have changed the strong and weak lines into their opposites, a new 'follow-up' hexagram is created which provides information about a future phase of life. The information on the left-hand page is the most useful for studying this hexagram, since follow-up hexagrams contain no changing lines.
The information on the right-hand page can, of course, be useful for clarifying your study of the follow-up hexagram.

} These hexagrams are components of the starting hexagram and offer directions for successfully dealing with your present situation.

The lines of the hexagram correspond to various parts of the body. The instructions you find there provide insight into your current physical and spiritual state.

━━o━━ : Strong Changing Line
━━x━━ : Weak Changing Line